The Art of Conducting

Da Capo Press Music Reprint Series

The Art of Conducting

Michael Bowles

With an Introduction by **Sir Adrian Boult**

DA CAPO PRESS • NEW YORK • 1975

Library of Congress Cataloging in Publication Data

Bowles, Michael, 1909-
   The art of conducting.

   (Da Capo Press music reprint series)
   Reprint of the 1959 ed. published by Doubleday,
Garden City, N. Y.
     1. Conducting. I. Boult, Sir Adrian Cedric,
1889- II. Title.
MT85.B73 1975   781.6'35   74-23419
ISBN 0-306-70718-7

This Da Capo Press edition of *The Art of Conducting* is an unabridged republication of the first edition published in Garden City in 1959. It is reprinted with the permission of Doubleday & Company, Inc.

Published by Da Capo Press, Inc.
A Subsidiary of Plenum Publishing Corporation
227 West 17th Street, New York, N.Y. 10011

THE ART OF CONDUCTING

The Art

of

Conducting

DOUBLEDAY & COMPANY, INC., GARDEN CITY, NEW YORK

Michael Bowles

1959

Library of Congress Catalog Card Number 59–8258
Copyright © 1959 by Michael Bowles
All Rights Reserved
Printed in the United States of America
Designed by Diana Klemin
First Edition

To my dear wife

ACKNOWLEDGMENTS

To Sir Adrian Boult for his friendship and encouragement through many years, and now for his reading the manuscript of this book and contributing an introduction.

To John Henry Mueller, Chairman of the Department of Sociology, and Bernard Heiden, Professor of Composition, both of Indiana University, for reading the manuscript and making many valuable suggestions.

To Messrs. Boosey and Hawkes, Ltd., for permission to use the quotation from *Cockaigne* by Elgar on page 96.

To Macmillan and Company, for permission to use the quotations from *The Letters of Mozart and his Family*, edited by Emily Anderson, on pages 42 and 43.

To Miss Enid Stearn for literary assistance.

INTRODUCTION

It may be said that conducting is the newest separate branch
to emerge in the whole field of artistic expression. Music is by
far the youngest of the arts, and conducting the youngest part
of musical interpretation. There has so far been no time for
someone's "method" to be evolved and opposed to someone
else's, as we have seen with all other forms of interpretation,
vocal and instrumental. This will no doubt come in time, and
we can look forward perhaps to a school of those who use a
very light stick actuated mostly by the fingers, and those who
think that the elbow (or perhaps the wrist) should take control:
in other words, those who believe in economy and those who
know that at any rate part of every audience likes to see a conductor behaving with elegant irrelevancy. Or there might be a
school of rehearsers who insist on absolute perfection in the first
measure before they wish to hear a note of the second measure and
who will insist on full concert pressure, emotional white heat, and
complete perfection through every minute of a three-hour
rehearsal; while others will amble easily through a whole move-

9

ment before they enter on any criticism, will aim at a gradual increase of artistic power and pressure as rehearsals proceed, and will, like the athlete, try to secure a steady improvement culminating in a maximum result at the actual performance. Perhaps it will be many years before such things crystallize into textbook form—indeed they may be superseded before anyone bothers to write about them; but in the meantime there is ample room for a book which will lay out the problems in a way which can be understood not only by the aspiring conductor but by most of his audience, and suggest solutions which are obviously satisfactory and sometimes offer alternatives for the student's choice.

Our author brings to these solutions the wisdom and experience of a practiced conductor. After many years in Dublin he held the post of Musical Director to the New Zealand Government for some time and has since been occupied mostly with university work in the United States. I feel sure that his book will be welcomed as an important addition to the growing library of books on conducting and will be of immense value to those who aspire to practice the art as well as to those whose interest in the music they hear encourages them to explore further the how and why of its problems.

Adrian C. Boult

London, England

CONTENTS

Contents

INSTRUMENTS
99

PROGRAMS
141

REHEARSAL
160

CODA
196

THE ART OF CONDUCTING

Prelude

It is alleged on occasion that a conductor's attributes are made up of ninety per cent effrontery and ten per cent knowledge. In the calm atmosphere of the schoolroom and away from the dust of the marketplace it will be agreed that this is something of an exaggeration and, of course, misleading in the case of so many conductors deservedly prominent in the national and international scene. There is, however, a germ of truth in the canard in so far as it reminds us that much of a conductor's effectiveness depends on his personal characteristics and on his capacity to persuade others to his will, whatever his individual method may be. Attributes of character are so very important that I feel it possible a beginner conductor would assimilate more from a master-and-apprentice relationship than from that of teacher-and-student.

At the same time, there are things to be taught and learned about the bases of a conductor's work, about the *application* of a knowledge of music to the work of training an ensemble. During the past 150 years, certain routine procedures have emerged which are useful whether dealing with a grade-school choir or a community orchestra in a center of fifty thousand inhabitants or so—to say nothing of larger institutions.

Very few singers and instrumentalists may prudently hope to earn their living exclusively as virtuoso concert artists and very few may hope to be conductors in that special sense. But very many do useful and vitally important work in the training of ensembles, in the presentation of choral and orchestral concerts, and in the general spread of a love for music in their communities. That what they do may not always be very prominent does not lessen the responsibility—and possibility too—of producing really first-class work in whatever circumstances they may find themselves. The possession of genius in a conductor is admirable but rare. The development of the love of music and the art of performing it do not, fortunately, have to wait entirely on the emergence of genius. Excellent artistic results in performance are possible with lesser mortals, given a conscientious attention to discernible if sometimes overlooked detail.

The essays in this book are derived from courses of lectures given while teaching at a university. The courses were "required" for graduate music students, the requirement being based on the sensible notion that most such students may expect to be involved in some kind of ensemble-training sooner or later.

Owing to temporary administrative exigencies, it was not possible to arrange to have the use of the college orchestra for illustration and demonstration, and in these circumstances it seemed better to examine the fundamental bases of a conductor's work and of his attitudes to it than to attempt direct teaching. My intention, therefore, was to leave the student with some thoughts to guide him past the elementary pitfalls when he came to deal with an ensemble and to put him on the road toward developing his own techniques.

I am conscious of many shortcomings in these essays, all the more when I think of my limitations in comparison with the enormous scope of the subject. I venture to offer the essays, however, not with the hope of telling anyone how to be a conductor, but with the hope of stimulating him to look clearly and freshly at the problems which confront him and, above all, to develop his own thinking on the subject as a conductor should.

It may be well here to point to those amateur and semi-amateur groups which are now happily so much in evidence in this country. The love for music exists strongly, and there is much scope for the exercise of a guidance that is calmly competent, a guidance that will canalize effectively those emotional forces that are obviously available. It may be well, too, to remember that amateur and semi-amateur activities are the backbone of the art of music and of its development in any country, no less now than during the past three hundred years. We live in an age of great technical advancement, and in art work there is danger from the emergence of perfectionism for its own sake. Certainly professional commentators who express very high technical standards do much for the art of music, but a standard of excellence of performance valid in one situation may easily degenerate into being mere intellectual snobbery in another. George Bernard Shaw, in *Man and Superman*, set forth the thought that "Hell is full of musical amateurs," but it is likely he would have been the first to laugh had it been pointed out to him that he was not a professional musician either.

Besides those interested in the elements of conducting, I hope that some of what I say may be useful to those who are otherwise involved in the presentation of music, such as members of orchestra committees and those very important people who buy tickets for concerts. I hope I may stimulate their general thinking on those musical matters with which they concern themselves and that I may at least help them to a greater understanding of the special problems of a conductor. After all, it is not only desirable that the performers should know what they are doing, it is equally desirable that the listeners should know what is being done.

The pieces of music cited in illustration of points raised in these essays are selected simply because they are likely to be already familiar to the reader and therefore more immediately effective for their purpose here. I do not cover a wide repertory because I assume that any student of conducting will already have reached the point of recognizing his own particular tastes and preferences in music and will be capable of proceeding to the development of his own repertory. The books mentioned in the note on "Supplementary Reading" are all readily available in the average institutional library and, with the exception of two of the Charles Burney commentaries, can easily be bought anywhere.

Orchestra

Apart from its charm as an intellectual pursuit, the study of history has its uses. One of these is to help us to evaluate the manifestations of the contemporary scene in the light of previous experiences: if we know something of where we have come from, we may faintly hope to have a better idea of where we are going. To that end, a knowledge of the history of the orchestra and of the evolution of the conductor's function is desirable.

But the musician who has graduated to the point of proposing to teach ensemble work to others will already have acquired some historical information in the course of his general musical education. It is not therefore intended to go into much detail here. Rather is it hoped that by the selection and consideraton of a few leading points we may attempt a review of our present concepts and, perhaps, some sort of perspective of the orchestra and the conductor, of their present place in the community.

At one time the conductor held his place by virtue of being a composer, and there was no division of function. As he was appointed and supported by a single patron or by a small group of patrons, the opinions and desires of the public in general were scarcely relevant. The emphasis in music-making was then on the composition of music—on the innate qualities of compositions and less on the quality of the performances, which, as we may infer from various items of information, were pretty bad by modern standards. Because of the universal changes in political and social organization, the support and patronage of music have now come to rest on the public at large. The instincts of the general public may be accepted as reliable in the long run, but the average level of immediate information and discrimination is not so high now as it was among the smaller groups of music patrons in former times. Among other things, this has led to a policy, perhaps not consciously formulated, of building up acceptance for performers, with the inevitable emphasis on the technical quality of the performance as distinct from the quality of the music itself.

Orchestra activities in general have expanded enormously, especially in the last thirty years or so, and the names of virtuoso conductors and virtuoso orchestras have become household words, even among those who never go near a concert. Supremely effective publicity methods have produced, even among serious music students (to say nothing of the humble amateur and ordinary member of the public), a situation where there is sometimes a tendency to be overimpressed with the glamor, with the coruscating facets of impeccable technical skill, and with what an irrepressible cynic might describe as "the sound and the fury" of music. Some, if they think of it at all, may have difficulty deciding whether, in their admiration for a performance, they are charmed by the music itself or are simply possessed of an excitement such as may be experienced in watching a trapeze act.

This point is brought up'here because the art and profession of the conductor have become hedged about with glamor—natural in some cases but synthetic in many—and because the success of a conductor in a community depends too often on circumstances which have nothing to do with music or with an assessment of his purely professional abilities. During the last sixty years or so conducting has come to be a specialized musical activity requiring the same order of technical facility as we expect in a trained violinist or pianist or singer. Glamor certainly has its uses in the easement of public relations, especially among the more unthinking sort of people, but the conductor who depends principally on a glamorous personality for his hold over an orchestra and its audience is in very much the same case as the medical practitioner who depends on a reputation for faith-healing instead of on the rational skills acquired by formal training. We do not regard a doctor or a lawyer as an unreliable second-rater simply because he is not nationally notable. Any trained professional, as his experience develops, can look forward normally to reasonable progress and usefulness in his community. The same attitude toward conductors is indicated, especially in this country, where there has been such a wide and healthy enlargement of the number of community and college orchestras during the last thirty years. In a conductor, symptoms of megalomania or paranoia or related neuroses may be exciting and publicity-worthy, but they are not essential attributes. Their incidence in a conductor might better be regarded as part of his occupational hazards, similar to the incidence of silicosis among stonemasons.

Of course virtuoso performances are of first-class importance to us all and, when possible, no opportunity to hear them should be missed. They present a technical perfection that is a valuable corrective to our hearing; and when, as frequently but not always happens, technical virtuosity is combined with true respect for the essence of the music the result may well be an unforgettable experience. But an experience, if it is to be for the good of the community as a whole, should stimulate the general well-being. As we know, there are many experiences which, although good in themselves, may do us harm if they come upon us before we are sufficiently matured to be able to hear them. On the same basis the effect of an expensive series of concerts at virtuoso level may be sterile in a musically immature community and may tempt it to neglect its own efforts, to withhold support from its own less perfect but most important music-making. In this sense the conductor of a community effort may count himself among those with a very important part to play in the development of the art of music. At worst he can help to intensify the appreciation of a virtuoso performance. At best he can widen and deepen the public's listening repertory and can lead the community toward being able to distinguish securely between what is essential and what is accidental in music.

Naturally in our regard for the less-than-perfect performance we would not intend to ignore the technical advances of the last hundred years, nor would we intend to soften our own efforts in the direction of perfection. We would not wish to treat good examples of the art of music with less than the faithful and loving respect they deserve. But there can be too much awe and fearfulness. Good music is not material for a sort of museum mentality, for the Lilliputian examination of pedants. It exists not solely in the composer's writings but also in the *act of communication* between composer and listener. The success of the communication depends on the composer's ability to give and the listener's capacity to receive; perfection in the medium (the performance) should always be aimed at, but basically such perfection is not absolutely essential. Music is a living art and, as such, is not only sensitive but also robust, able to stand up to familiarity of approach and even to a little well-intentioned abuse on occasion.

Whether for good or ill, the support and sustenance for the

art of music are now irrevocably a matter for the public concern, and the need to develop public taste on a good and healthy basis is vitally important. But taste is merely a refinement of appetite, and appetite grows *with* indulgence. If the general appetite is weak owing to infrequent—if eclectic—indulgence, the development of taste may become preciously cerebral and in the end degenerate. It is interesting to find Mozart writing from Prague in 1787 to express his great pleasure because, at a ball given by a Baron Bretfeld, "the people flew about in great delight to the music of my *Figaro,* arranged for quadrilles and waltzes." There is no doubt that Mozart's taste in music was delicately sensitive, but we may think it was robust also, and we may speculate on his possible attitude to those of us who cannot bear our Mozart unless it is flawlessly performed, who would prefer to listen to a recording than to participate in a live performance either as a player or as a listener. (Obviously we refer here to unavoidable technical defects in an honest performance and not to misconceptions of the essence and spirit of the music.)

Throughout the eighteenth century, when for the first time in any of the world's civilizations the art of music became an adequately organized and developed medium of artistic expression, the great composers who then appeared regarded themselves simply as trying to please their patrons, using whatever performer material was available. It is well for us that they, together with hundreds of lesser composers, were not discouraged from producing their music by the fact that they could only expect second-rate performances in a technical sense. It is well for us that they enjoyed the support and admiration of those whose taste, fortified by a healthy appetite, was sufficiently sensitive to perceive the qualities of the music in spite of the same second-rate performances. We may wonder whether the modern emphasis on technical perfection may be a trifle inordinate and whether it tends to defeat its purpose. Certainly throughout the whole world the number of significant composers who earn their living exclusively as composers is too easily counted. The composer with talent and promise has little hope of recognition and the encouragement that come from it unless he is played by a "major" orchestra, and generally he finds that the cost of producing an impeccable set of parts for the busy conductor is much greater than he can hope to recoup through performance fees. It is not surprising that some tend to retire into ivory towers, to lose real contact with real patrons, and to produce sounds that fall more than a little strangely on even the most receptive and sympathetic ears.

TWO

The orchestra might be regarded as a sort of organic growth drawing and continuing to draw its sustenance at various levels. Its evolution from an aggregation of itinerant musicians for festive occasions in the fifteenth century to the homogeneous instrument we expect to hear today is the result of a cross-pollination and fertilization of musical concepts in various countries and in successive generations.

By the end of the sixteenth century there had been many important discoveries in the technique of combining different strands of melody in a single pattern, and composers in fact had begun to be overimpressed with their own technical facility. There was a tendency to produce music in which preconceived theoretical concepts were predominant, music that was interesting intellectually but, owing to immoderate emphasis on complexity of detail, tended to lose sight of its main purpose: to delight the ear and to intensify appreciation of the verbal texts with which it was then almost invariably associated. A reaction set in expressed, in general terms, by such recommendations on musical matters as came out of the Council of Trent and, in some detail, in the conclusions of the Florentine School of 1600. But, like most reactions as yet unfortified by the actual doing, the change in attitude was carried a little too far. In the work of such as Peri and Caccini there was a tendency to eliminate the musical interest altogether in favor of pointing up the verbal interest. Monteverdi, however, although he accepted the reasonable idea that the words ought not to be obscured by musical complexities, did not allow this to inhibit the development of musical values. And so, for example, we have in *Orfeo* a collection of instruments whose variety and number was large at that time and whose introduction into the score was aimed at increasing the musical interest.

Many sources cite Monteverdi's score of *Orfeo* as marking the beginning of the modern orchestra, but some will be found to disagree with that view. Cecil Sharp, in his *History of Music*, puts the point very well when he says that the orchestra of *Orfeo* "represents the last of the old order, the consummation of the sixteenth century tradition of instrumentation, rather than the beginning of the new." It is true that, while Monteverdi used many different instruments for variety and "color," the idea of using them in ensemble as the matter is understood nowadays was not yet firmly established. The core of his orchestra comprised the plucked string instruments: lutes, theorbos, and so on. Owing to physical defects in the instruments and technical limitations of the players, bowed string instruments and wind instruments had but a subsidiary place. There was, too, a difficulty in the matter of uniform tuning (something not utterly unknown even still), and a Florentine theory laid down the principle that "the smaller the number of the instruments employed, the less defective will be the harmonies."

Whatever view may be taken of the Monteverdi orchestra, whether it should be regarded as the beginning or the end of a period in musical history, it seems clear that it coincided with a turning point and that the orchestra, as a formally conceived group of players for whom a score was prepared beforehand, dates from about that time.

Especially after the Thirty Years' War (1618–48), the courts of kings, princes, and electors in the middle of Europe maintained some sort of permanent military establishment. Part of the permanent establishment was a corps of drummers and trumpeters, useful for making audible signals in time of battle and useful for the decoration of court and military ceremonial during the peaceful intervals. To embellish lighter moments—banquets, wedding festivities, and so on—these musicians played other instruments, and with the notion of having a composer on hand to supply a steady variety of musical diet the generalized concept of a permanent orchestra came into being. After the Treaty of Westphalia the middle of Europe was broken up into many small and more or less autonomous states whose prosperity came to be represented partially by the size of the prince's musical establishment and the reputation of his resident composer. It is probably due to these political circumstances that there came into being eventually so many orchestras in the German area and such a widespread interest in orchestra music for its own sake as distinct from its being an appendage of the theater. This widespread interest continued, as we know, to our time.

In Germany, too, the many military establishments prompted the use of music to enliven the troops on the march. Trumpets, confined to their open tones, were too restricted in melodic scope. Violins, just then emerging as really fluent and expressive instruments, were too weak in tone for the out-of-doors, and so there was a steady demand for flute players and, in time, for clarinet players. From Bohemia, where the Thirty Years' War began, the hunting horn found its way into Germany and began to be used as a musical instrument both indoors and out. As a result of all this there was a steady supply of a variety of wind instrumentalists which, combined with the increasing influence in northern Europe of Italian makers and teachers of stringed instruments, became the foundation of the orchestra as an institution in Germany.

Although it saw its most considerable expansion in Germany, it is interesting to notice that the first formal military-band establishment was set up in France, designed by Lulli at the direction of Louis XIV. In France, however, the melody was not carried principally by flutes as in Germany. The major tendency was toward the double-reed instruments: bagpipes, shawms, and oboes. Lulli's establishment required mostly oboes of various lengths, from soprano to bass. Flutes were also used, but these were held vertically, just as recorders are; and the transverse flute, which came later to France, was first known as the *German* flute. These instruments, with horns imported from the German area and the *Vingt-quatre violons du roi*, were the beginning of formally organized orchestral activities in France.

As the principal interest of the French court, however, lay in the theater, the principal regard for orchestra music therefore derived from its usefulness in the accompaniment of operas, masques, tableaux, and ballets. Interest in orchestra music for its own sake did not begin until the *Concerts Italiens* and the *Concerts Spirituels* in 1725. During the early part of the eighteenth century there were also a few other orchestral establishments, such as those of the Duc d'Orléans, the Duc de Noailles, and La Pouplinière, a wealthy tax-farmer, but from the middle of the seventeenth century to the end of the eighteenth the greatest part of French musical activities was centered on Paris.

In England there had always been a widespread interest in music and in playing on instruments but little in the organization of ensembles on any kind of formal basis. In the middle of the sixteenth century Henry VIII maintained a large "band" at his court, as did Queen Elizabeth in her time. This was mostly of brass instruments for ceremonial occasions and solo instruments for the accompaniment of singing. It was not until the Restoration, in 1660, that a formal orchestra establishment ap-

27

peared for the first time. Impressed with what he had seen in France and elsewhere during his exile, Charles II set up "The King's Band" on the model of the *Vingt-quatre violons* of Louis XIV. It was composed mostly of imported musicians, and the general intention was to introduce into England "music in the manner of the French." Although the effect of his influence—through his courtiers and through the Royal Chapel and The King's Band—was to discredit in some degree the indigenous English musical culture, he did not succeed in establishing "music in the manner of the French" either. What he did succeed in establishing, however, was the fashion of looking abroad for music and for the musicians to play it. This fashion was confirmed later when the Hanovers came to the throne of England, bringing their own music in their train. This characteristic of looking abroad for music has been prominent in the English-speaking world since those times, but happily less so in times nearer to our own; "happily," because the change is evidence of the revival of an indigenous contribution to the universal art of music, firmly based on the activities of "the natives."

The most important development of the orchestra as we now understand it came from Italy, and it may be traced to the perfection of the principles of violinmaking during the period which began about 1550 with the first of the Amati family. (The great French, German, and English makers did not begin to appear until about a hundred years afterward.) Indeed the violin family of instruments had scarcely been accepted outside Italy as a musical medium in its own right until after the beginning of the eighteenth century. Even then, as may be deduced from contemporary scores, the tone was felt to be weak, needing frequent reinforcement with flutes and oboes in the treble parts and with bassoons in the bass. From available records of contemporary French and German orchestra establishments it would seem that as many wind as string instruments were employed, if not more occasionally. That the tone of string instruments was much weaker then than nowadays may also be deduced from the circumstance that until nearly the middle of the eighteenth century violins were held with the right side under the chin instead of the left as nowadays and were played with the old Tourte bow, which was later superseded by the Tartini improvements. It is significant too, that many "pedigree" violins have since been fitted with a longer finger board to take the higher tones and have had the bass-bar strengthened to support a string stress of some ninety pounds as compared with about sixty pounds in former times.

THREE

The developments of the orchestra can also be related to those of the formal organization of music in extended forms—from music "apt for voices and viols" and simple dance tunes in the seventeenth century, through the early-eighteenth-century dance suites and *concerti grossi*, to the sonata-symphony form as extended by Beethoven and confirmed by Brahms. One of these developments was the use of the *basso continuo* as a formative device in extended compositions which emerged in the early seventeenth century. An effect of this, as we know, was to confirm a tendency toward the use of chord sequences as a constructional basis for music, a change from the older plan of preserving interest by imitative and other devices in leading the voice parts. Elaborations over a figured bass were commonly left to the ingenuity of the keyboard player, and a melodic style began to emerge which was instrumental and not altogether vocal in character.

In polyphony, music was conceived as an interweaving of the interdependent melodic strands, and when the piece was finished no part could be left out without detriment to the over-all effect.

At the same time, an examination of the resultant chord sequences, considered by themselves, shows that, the result was dull and uninteresting. The subtle rhythmic impulses were derived from the melodic texture, which often presented moments of great beauty.

As a result of the use of the *basso continuo* there was a development of music into extended forms and at the same time a simplification of the contrapuntal texture. The principal interest of most pieces was carried by a treble line and a bass line, the bass line implying chord sequences embodying the rhythmic impulses. Even much of Bach's music, except when he writes fugally after the manner of the earlier polyphony, consists simply of a treble and bass line, with the occasional obbligato part; and while we derive much pleasure from his wonderful facility in part-weaving we also derive much from the close integration of finely conceived chord sequences and rhythmic impulses. At any rate, the concept of an orchestra up to at least the middle of the eighteenth century followed this pattern in that it was a collection of violins, oboes, flutes, clarinets, trumpets, and horns playing the treble part; violas, violoncellos, basses, and bassoons playing the bass part, and all seated around a keyboard instrumentalist who filled in the indicated harmonies and gave such other assistance as might be necessary. The early-eighteenth-century composers would vary the combination of these instruments throughout a composition, but the variations in instrumentation would be such as were indicated simply for the sake of contrast between loudness and softness and not for the sake of instrumental "color" as we understand it nowadays.

Of course this is merely a broad outline, and many examples can be found in music of the time of the use of various instruments for special effects, of the emergence of some idea of instrumentation for its own sake. "And the Trumpet Shall Sound" from the Handel *Messiah* is a very obvious case in point.

Another example is seen in the Bach *Passion According to St. Matthew*, where the lonely tones of the *oboe di caccia* are reserved for those parts of the text describing the Agony in the Garden, the Condemnation by Pilate, and the Crucifixion.

As the principal developments in the manufacture of the violin family of instruments came from Italy, so also did the principal developments in playing techniques. Perhaps there may be defects in the records, but it would seem that the Italians were much less interested in wind instruments than were their northern contemporaries until even the first half of the eighteenth century. At any rate, we owe the establishment of the string orchestra as a flexible musical instrument to the very great number of Italian violinist-composers who appeared about that time, including such forerunners as Giovanni Gabrieli, in whose concerto for violoncello occurs the first example of a free-style cadenza for solo instrument, and Tartini, who perfected the bow and many bowing techniques.

As a broad generalization it may be said that the principal development in the use of wind instruments took place in the northerly parts of Europe, and the development of the string orchestra and its techniques was a leading characteristic of the more southerly parts. By that time the strings had come to take their place as the core of the orchestra, and by the time the orchestra was beginning to take on a stabilized form of organization, we may notice that Vienna had become the capital of the musical world. This was no blind coincidence and came about because Vienna, the capital of a political unit with holdings both north and south of the Alps, was therefore a general clearinghouse for the musical ideas of northern and southern Europe.

FOUR

The direct relationship between political and social history and musical history is one not too frequently examined in musical commentaries. In the sense that the human race is one, the art of music is one and indivisible but, as with people, subject to local variations. As we have seen, the establishment of orchestral activities on a formal basis in England can be dated from the Restoration of Charles II and his court, who brought home ideas they had received during their exile. The developments in France, under the regime of Lulli and subsequently, owe much to Italian influence. That orchestra music in England and France was principally centered on Paris and London, with very little outside, can be associated with the fact that these countries were always homogeneous political units. That it became so widespread throughout Germany and Italy might be ascribed to a similar cause: both these areas were a conglomeration of petty states, each of which maintained a court which patronized the arts according to the means and tastes and pretensions of the reigning prince. A by-product of the fall of the Ottoman Empire in 1700 was the eventual introduction of the "Turkish Band" (cymbals, triangles, gongs, and so on) into Europe and into the orchestra. The Napoleonic Wars brought to Frenchmen a deeper appreciation of the orchestral works of Beethoven and his predecessors, and an intensification of French interest in purely orchestral music seems to date from that time. It is something more than chance that a French interest in Russian music arose after the middle of the nineteenth century, when there were political developments against the newly founded hegemony of Bismarck. There has been a special English interest in German music and musicians from the accession of George I right up to the Entente Cordiale with France in 1904: thereafter there was a special English interest in French music. Debussy was not unaffected by the popular interest of his day in *chinoiserie* and in the sensuous beauty of sounds and impressions existing without reference to the normal logic of musical progression; France had a developing political interest in Indo-China about that time.

As a coda to observations of this nature, it cannot be asserted that artistic developments always come about for non-artistic reasons, but it might be asserted that artistic developments can be related to all kinds of human activities, even political ones.

The foundation of the Halle orchestra in 1857 was the first important orchestral development in England, outside London, during the nineteenth century. German-born Sir Charles Halle came to London in 1848, where he immediately established himself as a reputable musician. In 1849 he was invited to go to Manchester to conduct the "Gentlemen's Concerts," of which the players and the financial supporters were almost all German businessmen then permanent residents in the Manchester area. For the Art Treasures Exhibition in 1856 he was invited to organize a first-class orchestra for special concerts. Owing to the unexpectedly favorable attention they received from the ordinary English public, he decided to underwrite some thirty concerts himself when the exhibition was over. After a dangerously shaky beginning the thirty concerts showed a total profit of two shillings and sixpence—a penny a concert. Very much encouraged, he organized a new series for the 1858–59 season. Since then the orchestra has had a flourishing existence and has developed loyal audiences for orchestra music in some forty towns and cities of the English Midlands.

Although from the 1840's* onward there have been many series

*The London Philharmonic Society was founded in 1812, and of course there was the Salomon series before that. The reference here is to orchestras on a continuing, professional basis.

of concerts given in London with different types of program policy and different results, the next event of *institutional* importance in English orchestral affairs was the association of the late Sir Henry Wood with the Queen's Hall Concerts in 1895. This was an annual series of six concerts a week for seven weeks during the late summer. Known as "The Proms," they have existed for seventy years, but the annual season is now eight weeks. Their enormous and continued success established among Londoners (and English people generally), in all walks of life, the idea that first-class orchestra music was a normal enjoyment, an idea that had been prevalent enough in Italy and Germany at that time but which had not yet taken hold in England to any appreciable extent.

The next major event of institutional significance in England was the beginning of wireless broadcasting, to be financed from an annual tax (originally about $1.50 but now $3.00) on each receiving set. Among its many activities, the British Broadcasting Corporation directly supports the BBC Symphony Orchestra (110 players) and seven regional orchestras of sizes varying from 45 to 75 players; all employed continuously for twelve months in each year. It also produces partial support for other orchestras through fees for special programs. The general music policies of the BBC were under the guidance of Sir Adrian Boult, who was appointed Director of Music in 1930 and who was also principal conductor of the main orchestra for twenty years. Instead of reducing the ticket-buying potential for orchestra concerts, the BBC programs made a major contribution to their increase.

This rather long sketch of English orchestral activities is intended to point out that English orchestras have always been closely integrated with the public patronage of buyers of concert tickets, and there has been developed a healthy musical life with a good crop of composers, who have felt encouraged to devote themselves exclusively to their risky and arduous occupation. There are, it is true, some subsidies from public funds of one kind or another which have been allotted in comparatively recent years, but these are not large enough to alter the basic dependence of the orchestras on their real patrons, the small ticket buyers.

FIVE

It is difficult to be objective and extremely difficult to be comprehensive in discussing the contemporary scene in this or any other country. It is also much too easy, even with the very best intentions, to produce controversial remarks that tend to generate more heat than light. At the same time it seems necessary to take the risk of offering some comment in an attempt to assess the place of the orchestra in the community.

Organized music of one kind or another is indigenous to most European countries. It comprises audiences, composers, orchestral establishments, choral societies, repertory opera houses, and other continuing efforts. In this country all this is exotic, a transplantation. It takes some time for any transplantation to settle down, and here the oldest musical establishment of any significance is little more than a hundred years old. A hundred years is not a very long time in any important human activity and certainly not long enough to determine what, *if anything,* is wrong with the state of music here or what, *if anything,* is to be done about it in any special way. Nevertheless, there are some characteristics related to music-making which might usefully be observed, even if there is no immediate intention of drawing definite conclusions.

In matters of legislation all the states of the Union guard their autonomous rights and watch carefully any trends toward the extension of federal control over them. There is no question here of commenting whether this is good or bad; the feature is being observed as might be the Great Lakes, the Appalachian Mountains, the choice of a national anthem, or any other similar phenomenon. We may observe that congruent with this regard for autonomy there is a tendency toward large, monolithic organizations on a national (federal) scale for business and other activities. The generally declared principle is that they make for increased convenience and efficiency of operation and for the presentation to the public of a more highly processed commodity in larger quantities. (The possibility of lower prices is adduced, too, although there are cynics to be found who will insist that prices are sometimes regulated less by the cost of production than by an assessment of what the market will bear.)

In the comparatively short period of a hundred years the country has built the highest buildings in the world, the greatest mileage of first-class roads, the largest business organizations, and the greatest *per capita* wealth. In music it has established four or five large and superb orchestras, besides others of lesser caliber. It has established one repertory opera that is among the three or four best in the world and two that can stand the most severe comparisons. There are some music-publishing companies among the largest and most prosperous in the world and some broadcasting and recording companies whose technical experts and sales and promotion departments are among the most successful in the world. These mammoth institutions are serviced by a few artists' agencies that have a power and influence more extensive than most agencies elsewhere.

Owing to the national aversion to using public funds (with the inevitable contingent controls) for regional cultural purposes, orchestras are supported principally by donations from wealthy private sources. Broadcasting services are organized on a commercial basis, with income derived from the sale of advertising space, and exploit the uses of music rather than support it as an art. Publishing houses are, very understandably, in business for profit, and the discovery and encouragement of obscure talent is not their primary interest.

Private patronage is excellent as a concept. It worked well for the development of music in Europe up to at least the beginning of the nineteenth century, but there are differences now. With very few exceptions most private patrons who contribute heavy subsidies to orchestras do so simply from a very praiseworthy sense of civic duty and not from a real, personal knowledge of music and a love of it for its own sake. More by default than intent, therefore, the real patronage of music devolves on the agencies, and an artist who in former times sought a patron now tries to get his name on an agency roster.

Music is big business and, however good the intentions of individuals may be, the unavoidable tendency is to condition the consumer, audiences at concerts, and buyers of recordings to a "brand name" psychology. Mme. Anaesthesia, the famous soprano (formerly of the Met), or Wilhelm Schnorkel, the pianist (of European fame), may make intensive tours of concerts before large audiences, but it is their personalities and not their music that is being sold.* The result is that music so very often receives a series of what we may call "shots in the arm," stimulation but not sustenance. The result, too, is a confused public attitude toward music and its presentation, and in many states occasions for the enlargement of minor talent are neglected, talent that might have very great importance on the *local* scene.

As we have agreed already, the organization and management of highly priced and much-admired virtuoso institutions are valuable public services, but it might be remembered that in Europe the great orchestral and operatic establishments and the careers of great composers were the fruits of a tree of which the very many lesser activities in composition and performance were the roots and branches. Owing to historical circumstances,

---

*Some representatives of a well-known agency are described on their office stationery as "Sales Representative." Interesting.

this country began with experience of the fruits and is now expected to develop the rest afterward, a reverse of the natural process. But the corporate intelligence which has gone so far toward forming a homogeneous people out of so many diverse ethnic elements may also be expected to establish a system of musical institutions which will result in a close relationship between the composer and his patron and which will, in time, produce music that expresses the genius of the American people completely and correctly.

Conductor

The history of conducting, as we understand the function nowadays, does not go back further than about a hundred and fifty years. It is true that for almost as long as music has existed, and certainly since the end of the fifteenth century, there has been some notion of the usefulness of having someone assist a group of performers by means of hand signals. Information of a circumstantial kind may be culled from memoirs and works of reference on whether, for example, a roll of paper or of parchment was held in the hand while directing a choir or whether a stick was used audibly to beat out the time. Little is said of the actual relationship between the director and the performer or of the effect of this relationship on the actual performance. This may very well be due to the circumstance that, apart from giving some indications of the tempo, the "conductor's" influence was negligible.

Until late in the development of polyphony the singers would have had their music by heart, anyway. The tempo would have been a matter of custom, and the dynamic variations would come directly from the singers' understanding of the verbal texts. Any gestures would have been rudimentary and no more than a sort of mnemonic. In fact, to compare conducting in the sixteenth century with conducting in our time would be analogous to comparing the use of fourteenth century neumes with our modern system of notation.

By observing the control of a modern group in plainchant, we may form a concept of the function of a conductor in the sixteenth century and before. The music is the same, and the style of singing and its direction would not be too dissimilar. In religious communities that sing the Office every day it may be possible to expect an almost perfect unanimity of tempo, of phrasing, and of nuance, without any direction at all. Because of the daily repetition, the tempo of the various chants would be set in a traditional and communal concept, and the music might proceed upon its way with an easy but inexorable certainty—an ideal attribute of the choice of tempo for any piece of music. With less well practiced groups some form of direction would be necessary, now as well as formerly. What might be needed in a passage such as the following would be a gesture to prepare the singers, followed by one to lead them into a clean beginning. Thereafter the direction would consist of little more than small gestures to remind the singers of previously rehearsed syllable stresses.

EXAMPLE

To sing plainchant well is not, of course, quite so simple as this. With a thorough knowledge of the music and an agile sense of anticipation, a good director can do much to bring up those reticent but subtly effective gradations in tempo and dynamic which make good plainchant so deeply satisfying to the listener.

The main point here, however, is that his gestures would have no recognizable or stylized pattern of outline any more than the music would have a regularly recurring pulse.

Even in the more complicated music of the late-polyphonic period, both in church music and in madrigals on secular themes, the style of the conductor's gestures would still be about the same. With the *real* independence of parts and the occurrence of important and significant stresses at "irregular" intervals, beats in any sort of preconceived pattern would be useless. Although after about the middle of the sixteenth century choir books were pretty commonly used, composed music was not then so widely distributed that any group would have a very large repertory and the emphasis was still on memory work rather than on reading. Groups were small in size, and the singers' knowledge of any work would cover not only their own parts but those of the others. (To have the participants able to perform for the most part without absolute dependence on direction is the ideal result of adequate and well-managed rehearsal at any time.)

As the development of the orchestra can be related to developments in the formal organization of musical material into extended pieces, so also can the history of conducting be related to the same source. The idea of silent gestures made by one not actually performing fell into disuse in the early part of the seventeenth century. This was coincident with the emergence of the *basso continuo* as a musical procedure, together with the rhythmic implications of chord sequences, the admission of a regularly recurring pulse and the corresponding bar line in written music, and the use of the keyboard as the core of the ensemble. After the acceptance of the measured pulse and the evenly spaced bar-lines in written music, all the participants in a performance were subject to a unified metric pattern. Beyond some sort of understanding to ensure a clean-cut beginning to the performance, further gestures became almost unnecessary.

41

From the early part of the seventeenth century until almost the time of Beethoven at the end of the eighteenth, such direction as an ensemble needed depended upon one who was taking an actual part in the performance. Every musician of the time was an executant, and the conductor, who was usually the composer also, controlled the performance from his seat at the keyboard both by playing and making such gestures as might be needed from time to time.

Because of improvements in the quality of playing on bowed string instruments and its increasing significance in the orchestra, a variation began to appear at the beginning of the eighteenth century. There was then a period of transition during which the direction came to be divided between the keyboard player and the first violinist. In his *Reminiscences*, Michael Kelly describes most of the performances he attended in various European centers as having the orchestra directed by the keyboard player and the band directed by the first violinist. (There was at that time a distinction in English between the word "orchestra," used to describe the entire ensemble including singers, and the word "band," used to describe the group of instrumentalists only.) The situation was never completely clarified and came in the end to depend on whether the composer (and therefore the director) was primarily a string player or a keyboard player.

It is possible, however, to discern the emergence at this time of the practice of having operatic performances directed from the keyboard and concerts of purely orchestral music directed by the first violinist. Gluck appeared at a concert in Vienna in 1752 "violin in hand at the head of the orchestra," but he directed an opera performance in Bologna in 1763 from the clavier. There is a letter from Mozart in Paris in July 1778 in which he is complaining about the rehearsals for his symphony (K 297): "The next morning, I decided not to go to the concert at all; but, in the evening, the weather being fine, I at last made up my mind to go, determined that if my symphony went as badly as it did at the rehearsals, I would certainly make my way into the orchestra, snatch the fiddle out of the hand of Lahoussaye, the first violin, and conduct myself." Writing from Vienna in October 1782, he says, "The Russian royalties left Vienna today. My opera was performed for them the other day, and on this occasion, I thought it advisable to resume my place at the clavier and conduct it. I did so partly to rouse the orchestra who had gone to sleep a little." Haydn was a violinist, as we know, and directed his orchestra at Esterhazy in that capacity. But when he went to London it was laid down in his contract that he should "preside at the piano" and that Salomon, as violinist, would "direct the band." The two areas of influence might be compared with that of director and producer in the film world nowadays.

Throughout most of the eighteenth century there was little difference in size between an "orchestra" and what we now call a "chamber orchestra." Most of the music was, comparatively speaking, straightforward in texture and general impulse. The average number of players was small enough for each one to be within easy hearing distance of what the keyboard player was doing, and concert rooms and theaters were also small. The direction was very much as we see it in a small theater or hotel ensemble nowadays, in which the pianist keeps the players together and the first violinist (or other leading instrumentalist) gives such additional indications of nuance, and so on, as may be necessary. This was the general pattern throughout Europe.

In Paris, however, besides the influence of the keyboard player or the first violinist, or both, it was decided to be necessary to have a maestro seated on the stage with the score in one hand and in the other a stick which he banged on a table placed in front of him. This noisy method began with Lulli and was continued in the theater until about the middle of the eighteenth century. It was also used for a time in concerts of purely orchestral music; the early performances at the *Concerts Spirituels* (1725–91) were so directed. The practice may have been begun because the orchestra pit at the Paris Opéra was too deep for good visual contact between the players and the singers. (Rousseau, in 1768, was still complaining about this, but by that time the "conductor" stood facing the stage with his players seated around and *behind* him.) The basic intention was to ensure absolute unanimity between the players and the singers. This may have been effective, but something of a nuisance if there was any desire to realize adequately the other qualities of the music. It would certainly not do nowadays even in the most elementary of school productions, although it is possible to imagine occasions when the conductor in even a professional theater might wish he could do something of the kind to retain control over a singer with a gorgeous high note and strongly personal "artistic feelings."

It is stated that the first conductor to use a baton only was one Anselm Weber, who appeared one night at the Berlin Opera in 1780 with a baton "made of leather stuffed with hair." Whether this is so or not is immaterial. Real changes in musical practice have always come about gradually and it is unprofitable to try to pin any change down to a single incident or a single date. We may observe, however, that the transition from direction by a keyboard player to that of a first violinist was completed in, roughly, the period 1750–1800, when Haydn and Mozart and others were developing and extending the formal lines of orchestra music and introducing an increasing delicacy in the variation of tempo and dynamic. J. S. Bach and his contemporaries were content to play loud chords on the harpsichord during the first few measures of a piece "until the correct tempo was understood by the players." We can imagine such a method still being usable in, say, the *Brandenburg* Concerto No. 3, but if it were used at the beginning of the Mozart Symphony No. 40 in G minor, our pleasure might conceivably be the less for it.

The real beginnings of the use of the baton in the direction of a performance might more reliably be placed in the period 1800–50, when composers, including Beethoven, were beginning to extend a subjective and openly romantic element into music. With the slight increase in the size of orchestras and the increasing use of sudden, nervous switches in tempo and dynamic for the sake of surprise and dramatic effect, it was becoming necessary to have someone who would not only set the tempo at the beginning of a section but also control the players throughout a performance. Even with a conductor, the opening of Beethoven's Symphony No. 1 can be something of a mess. Without a conductor, it is impossible to imagine an acceptable performance of his opera *Fidelio*. However, at that time, both players and audience were more interested in the general "feeling" of the music than in the meticulous realization of the details of the score. The idea of conducting as a musical specialty, of an awareness of the technical processes in preparing a good orchestral performance, did not appear much before the middle of the century.

From about 1850 onward, there was an increased awareness of the orchestra as a homogeneous musical instrument and of the possibilities of developing orchestration as a musical specialty. The works that appeared with Berlioz and Wagner and with the French and Russian composers of the 1870's and the 1880's require attention to the orchestration effects as well as to the material of the music itself. In Vienna they were still conservative in this matter, and in the music of Brahms, for example, our attention is still not drawn to the orchestration so much as to the basic musical material and the way in which it is handled.

Although it is something of a digression, we might suggest here that the principal reservation of Hanslick in regard to Wagner was based on a notion that Wagner was too much drawn to orchestration for its own sake and to other extramusical concepts in the working out of his art. Hanslick distinguished between the music itself and such adventitious aids as orchestration. In one article he listed a number of earlier composers and said that their music contained a vital principle and the seeds of further development; that there would never be a Wagner "school" of composition; and that the future development of music would not grow out of Wagner's work. The ground of the old Hanslick–Brahms–Wagner controversy has been trampled by hundreds of antagonists and protagonists, and there is no intention here of reviewing the intrinsic musical value of Wagner's work; that has been settled long ago. The digression merely offers an occasion to point out that good orchestration and good music are separate concepts and, by corollary, that it is possible to be a skilled conductor and defective as a musician, and vice versa. We might point out here, too, that the final separation in the function of a conductor and of a composer dates from about 1850.

TWO

Of the great number of commentaries on conducting and its techniques that have been published since the middle of the last century, the most significant are the book *On Conducting* by Wagner and the article on conducting in Berlioz's *Treatise on Instrumentation*. These two musicians did more than any others of their day to develop the art of orchestration, to enlarge the orchestra, and to extend its potentialities as an expressive musical medium. Berlioz, with his large sweeping concepts covered with busy little figurations using many instruments in sharply contrasted textures, and Wagner, with his short phrases shimmering in and out of the orchestral mass and needing subtly significant changes of pace and dynamic—both produced scores that were impossible to realize without a thoroughly competent conductor. Such orchestration as theirs was too complex to be securely comprehended at all times by all the players. It was essential to have someone who, after the composer, would create the piece in the minds of the players and of the audience, someone who would not only guide and control the tempi with their subtle sea changes but who would also feel and imagine the music as a whole.

Neither Wagner nor Berlioz was the most tactful personage of their era, but it is reasonable to accept the savage nature of their remarks on the shortcomings of conductors as evidence of a deep and real sense of frustration, at least. Beethoven had firm ideas on how his music should be played but does not seem to have commented upon conducting as a specialty. He was not shy or backward, and we might think that his failure to comment on conductors and conducting was because of the deafness which covered the greatest part of his composing life. We might also think it was because he had not come to the point of giving special attention to orchestration as such. As Rimsky-Korsakov says, "[Beethoven's] music abounds in leonine leaps of orchestral imagination, but his technique [of orchestration], viewed in detail, remains much inferior to his titanic conception."

Wagner and Berlioz were not deaf, and with their special interest in orchestral tone quality as they conceived it in their orchestrations they would be particularly aggravated by inadequate conductors. In fact, the only conductor in Europe who enjoyed the good opinion of both seems to have been one Habeneck, a Frenchman. His conducting technique was limited. He directed in the old style with bow and violin in hand and was apparently unable to work from a full score, but he seems to have won their good opinion simply because he was honest and persistent in his efforts to have the music cleanly and competently played.

Curiously enough, in spite of his special interest in orchestral "color," in the tone of an orchestra, and in the *melos* of the music,

Wagner's chief complaint in his book is about conductors' choice of tempi. He regards the correct choice of tempo as the most important single matter for a conductor's attention. He also discusses the need for passing, minor modifications of the over-all tempo in their relation to variations in the melodic stress and in general context. There are remarks on his *Mastersingers* Overture, on the Beethoven Fifth and Ninth symphonies, on Weber's *Der Freischütz* Overture, but although he discusses some details minutely he is never pedantic. It is clear that he has the true working artist's view that a worth-while piece of music should be regarded as a sort of vital principle whose component phrases have *character* and *personality*, whose rhythmic impulses are logical and compelling, and whose "shape," or area of influence, truly expresses the essence of the composer's creation.

But whatever he discusses, Wagner always comes back to the matter of tempo and, indeed, is conscious of being somewhat repetitious on this point: "I am persistently returning to the question of tempo because . . . this is the point at which it becomes evident whether the conductor understands his business or not."

He is particularly severe on Mendelssohn, especially in his association with the Leipzig Gewandhaus concerts. He mentions a conversation in which Mendelssohn said that "most harm was done by taking a tempo too slow; that, on the contrary, he recommended quick tempi as being less detrimental. Really good execution, he thought, was at all times a rare thing, but shortcomings may be disguised if care were taken that they should not appear very prominent; and the best way to do this is to get over the ground quickly." Whether Wagner's quotation is fair or unfair to Mendelssohn we cannot now say, but we may accept it with other indications as evidence of the current attitude to orchestra performance in Europe at that time. Mendelssohn was certainly very highly regarded in Germany and England not only as a composer but as a conductor.

When Wagner was engaged by the Philharmonic Society in London to direct a series of concerts in 1855, the season was subsequently described by commentators as "the most disastrous on record," and "he was not asked again." Wagner mentions his London visit in his memoirs, and even if we discount his own very high opinion of himself, we may accept the view that the difficulties were not entirely his fault. It would seem that the main trouble was that he attempted to take some works at a correct tempo, slower than that to which the Londoners had become accustomed since Mendelssohn's time, and he inconveniently laid bare some serious and basic defects in passage-playing.

The allotment of rehearsal time seems to have been generally inadequate in England in the early part of the nineteenth century. Meyerbeer went to London in 1832 for the first English performance of *Robert le Diable*. When asked for a comment after the first rehearsal, he said, "It is very good. With seven or eight rehearsals to get the dynamics right it will go wonderfully." He then discovered that the rehearsal he had just attended was to be the only one. To this day there is in England a tendency not to give too much time to rehearsal, confirmed partly by the continuous need of orchestras to "live off the land." At the same time this inadequacy of rehearsal time might be regarded as having produced one excellent quality. Orchestra players in England are, on average, superb sight readers, with a lively sense of anticipation and great quickness of wit in emergencies. Granted a strong poetic sense and a complete command of his own techniques, a conductor who is prepared to take those risks (and there are risks) involved in slightly inadequate rehearsal time can hope to produce in his performances a charming, improvisatory quality, an impression of spontaneity and freshness which may be lost at times with too many exhaustive rehearsals.

The contemporary defects in conducting which impressed

Wagner give some indication of how much advance there has been since his day. A short list would include the following: incorrect choice of tempo; a too rigid adherence to a tempo once chosen; beating a solid four-in-the-bar where *alla breve* was indicated, regardless of the character of the piece; failure to establish "where the melody lies" in a given context; no *true piano* and no *true forte*; lack of control, resulting in involuntary accentuation in passages not so marked; treating music as "an amalgam of grammar, arithmetic and digital gymnastics and failing to put life and soul into the music," and so on.

Near the beginning of his essay on conducting, Berlioz unburdens himself most feelingly. He says: "The composer must indeed count himself fortunate when the conductor into whose hands he has fallen is not both incompetent *and* malicious, for against the destructive influences of such a man, nothing can avail. The most excellent orchestra is crippled by him; the finest singers are perplexed and exhausted; there is no longer any ardor or precision in the rendering. Under conducting of this kind, the composer's finest audacities become mere oddities, enthusiasm is killed, inspiration is brought to the ground, a genius is made to look like a madman. The worst of it is that the public is not in a position at the first performance of a new work to detect the mutilations, stupidities, errors and sins against art which such a conductor has on his conscience."

Berlioz expresses his views somewhat intemperately and may induce a feeling of reserve in the cautious reader. A generalized statement aimed at one particular "enemy" was and is now an occurrence not utterly unknown in the exciting field of music, and Berlioz had many enemies. We might wonder whether all the conductors he encountered were both incompetent and malicious. As for the malice, it may be observed that all his major works were performed during his lifetime, and to organize the sort of musical forces indicated by some of his scores required considerable good will before a rehearsal could even begin. But regarding the general level of competency, what he says may at least tend to confirm our view that conductors were not up to the demands of new music then being written or to an emerging demand for clarity of outline in orchestral work. At any rate, the precepts in his essay may still be read with profit, although—as with Wagner—some of his remarks are rather obsolete because they refer to defects which are unthinkable in any present circumstances. We can be grateful for his intemperate attitude toward conductors, however, because he did much to raise the standard of orchestra playing in the Paris of his day, a circumstance that was not without its effect in London later on.

From all indications it seems evident that we might place in the 1860's the establishment of the idea that conducting was a musical specialty requiring command of a special order of technical ability and that a conductor was expected to be not only an artist but a competent craftsman. The idea bore fruit later in the careers of such as Richter, Nikisch, von Bülow, Weingartner, and others who did so much to establish the detail as well as the spirit of what we now regard as "standard" orchestral repertory.

THREE

"Familiarity breeds contempt" is an old saw and, like so many old saws, it is slightly misleading. In Germany, as in every other country, conducting as a specialized branch of music scarcely existed at the middle of the century, yet within thirty years almost all the great exponents of orchestra music throughout Europe were German. In this country, from the time when formally organized orchestral institutions began with the New York Philharmonic in 1841 and the Boston Symphony in 1881, the principal conductors for a long time were German or of German origin. The same can be said of England up to about 1890. Italy and France were principally interested in opera and the theater generally, and their activities had comparatively little influence in the area of purely orchestral music. "The German Tradition" is a phrase that occurs in musical conversation, and it is asserted that if any recognizable tradition in orchestra music has been established here it might be described as a "German" one. (There have been different influences, of course, in more recent times.)

But if we consider this "tradition" and its true basis, we may come to a conclusion that it does not rest on a fact that, owing to some biological characteristic peculiar to them, the Germans have a special insight into the qualities of orchestra music which is denied to other people. It rather rests on a fact that Germans, for historical and related reasons, were very familiar with performances of orchestra music—good, bad, and indifferent—during an important and significant period in the development of the profession of conductor. Simply, they knew music. They had a familiarity with music that bred a high and wide regard for it.

Conducting an orchestra and acquiring that real understanding of orchestra music which is essential to being a conductor may usefully be compared to riding a bicycle: an application to the study of written material is good; watching the performance of first-class exponents is good; receiving instruction from those who have practical experience is good; but there can be no knowledge in a real sense until the actual doing. In the German and Austrian areas of the 1870's, there was no clearly established tradition of conducting as such, but there were regularly functioning ensembles for purely orchestra music by the hundreds. Every beer garden had a reasonably good ensemble. Hundreds of military bands gave out-of-door concerts with a high proportion of transcriptions from the best of the orchestra repertory. The German appetite for music was large, and opportunities for conductors of all sorts were numerous. The refinement of public taste, with the skills of those who catered to it, was not the result of eclecticism of any kind but was derived securely from the successive satisfactions of a healthy appetite.

Making due acknowledgment to the fine trail-breaking work of Theodore Thomas, it may be said that the orchestra was suddenly established in this country with the organization, within a short period, of two or three large and excellent orchestras in the East and the excellent Chicago Symphony in the Midwest. The art of the orchestra was born here somewhat after the fashion of Amaryllis in Bernard Shaw's *Back to Methusaleh*—"out of the egg and fully grown." Because of this not-quite-natural birth, there have been financial and other strains of more or less severity. It was necessary from the beginning to attract a public so naïve as to be unable to distinguish between what was due to a personality and what was due to the music he performed. It was also, quite understandably, necessary to continue to import musicians who had not only an already acquired experience of the repertory but who had the glamor and *réclame* of coming from foreign parts. In more recent times the emergence of music has meant, as we have seen, a continuance of the "brand name" psychology, good in many ways but unreliable in so far as it premises the development of musical appetite through discrimination instead of the development of discrimination through appetite.

The support of professional orchestras is no longer, of course, confined to Boston, New York, Philadelphia, and Chicago, but the pattern of financial pressures with that of technical perfectionism combined with the need for importing conductors from other countries is still much as ever it was. Orchestras are most expensive to maintain and, as a matter of business common sense, it is felt to be safer to employ a leader whose technical facility is already developed and whose glamorous possibilities are ready-made than to experiment with a potential native talent in a milieu that is still largely immature musically.

If the situation is not exactly perfect, it is not static either, and there are encouraging signs. One of these is the dramatic increase in the number of teaching institutions during the last forty years, but even here there is need for some caution. It is of the nature of academic institutions to be academic and, unless their activities are grounded in much community music-making of any and every kind, it is possible to develop a false eclecticism —expressed in the young man who, armed with little more than detailed analyses of the most modern trends, regards himself as a musician superior to the humble, simple-minded fellow who is merely fond of music and who, with that true love that asks no questions, will support any reasonably good performance he can find.

Also, as we have mentioned already, there has been a notable increase in the number of amateur-cum-professional and college orchestras during the last thirty years. Their activities might be regarded as both a support and a corrective for those of the major institutions, and they present a most important and fruitful possibility for the serious musician, both composer and conductor. It is only by hearing his works frequently, whatever the quality of the performance, that the composer can know exactly the effect of what he may be trying to do. It is only by conducting at any and every opportunity that the beginner conductor can hope to develop his complicated skills in any real sense. Granted there is a good community appetite for music and that there is also the communal wisdom to recognize and support progressive if not altogether major-quality work, any conductor can hope to make a really effective contribution to the establishment of the whole art of music in this country. There is always room for a Toscanini or two. There is still more room for a Theodore Thomas or two.

Interpretation

In musical company, and especially in non-professional company, we may frequently hear references to artistic feeling, to personal musicality, and to subjective attitudes generally, and we may receive an impression that interpretation is mostly a matter of personal inclination on the part of the performer. There are so many radically different readings of music presented on the grounds of "This is *my* interpretation" that it may seem right to conclude that excellence in music is just a subjective phenomenon.

Such a conclusion would be unsound, of course, because a piece of music, like any other work of art, has an objective excellence that is independent of the capacities of either the performer or the listener to appreciate it. The reputation of a work may be enlarged or diminished as the result of repeated performances, but this will not mean that its intrinsic worth will have been in any way changed. It simply means that the knowledge of the interpreters and the listeners has been extended, that their perceptions have been sharpened and their appreciation has become more precise. It is toward the objective understanding and exposition of the true qualities of a composer's work that the honest efforts of an artist-interpreter are rightly directed.

It is true that the faculty of intuition, of direct artistic insight into the composer's mind, plays an important part in the work of an interpreter, especially in the more advanced stages, where the integration of the interpreter's musical qualities with those of the composer may be involved. Some, owing to exceptional talents and very great experience, may hope to proceed directly to a correct conclusion about how a given piece of music should be read and played, but for most persons of good but lesser talent a premature reliance on intuition, on direct artistic insight, may lead into error, into what Shakespeare's *Desdemona* describes as "a lame and impotent conclusion." This possibility is especially important in relation to the training of students and in the guidance of amateurs, and a serious musician with a constructive purpose in his work will always prefer to take a small step in the right direction rather than a large and glamorous one in a misleading direction. For any normal procedure, therefore, it is much safer to bring the intuitive faculty into use when all the other available sources of information have been explored, and not before.

For the sources of definitive information are many, and to interpret a score correctly—that is, to formulate a reliable opinion of what the composer intended to communicate to the listener —it is well to have something of the attitude of a detective, the firm intention of sifting thoroughly all the discoverable evidence before adopting final conclusions. Much more can be done with an attitude of this kind than is sometimes understood to be possible. There may still be an incompleteness in the concept of the composer's thought after the details of the score have been mastered and the historical and other relevant factors have

56

been evaluated, but it is only at this point that the exercise of intuition is either desirable or necessary.

The principal source of definitive information is, naturally, the score itself. Here the composer presents those symbols, notation, indications of tempo, dynamics, and kindred matters which will best express the essentials and accidentals of his music. It is a mere truism to say that, for whoever proposes to interpret a composer to his listeners, a first essential is a mastery of the detail of the score, but it may be advisable to draw attention to this very elementary consideration. So many beginner conductors are concerned too soon with the over-all artistic effect and its aesthetics. They come to rehearsal under the impression that they have made adequate preparation by means of formal analysis studies and by listening to the performances of others, only to find that they have no more than a rough idea of what is to be said and done to make the music a reality to the players. A characteristic of the inexperienced conductor that is frequently observed is that he has too much to say on the beauties of the music and too little on those small technical points to which an experienced professional will give his main attention and through which the artistic qualities are brought to reality almost automatically.

A thorough mastery of all the details of the score is the best means whereby a conductor may establish his very own convictions of what is to be said and done. To have heard and understood the performances of others is important and necessary, without any doubt, but only as *one* of the means of establishing his own convictions. One's own convictions are the true basis of hoping to convince others and having an easy and effective control over any orchestra. An ersatz interpretation might impress an audience for a time but, however polished and faithful to the best models, it is unlikely to stand up for long to the test of being imposed on a group of players over a number of intense rehearsals.

TWO

That a conductor is able to imagine exactly the relative pitch of the notes as he reads them is a primary assumption, and so we will begin by saying that in studying a score the first care is to establish clearly in mind the correct tempo for the various sections of the piece. That was Wagner's advice, and it is very sound advice. As rhythmic impulse is the basis of all music, whether of a motet by Orlandus Lassus or a Russian dance by Moussorgsky, so also is the choice of tempo a fundamental consideration in the formation of any interpretation.

At the time of composing, a composer will have in his mind a certain tempo, and no other, for a given passage, and the problem is to come as closely as possible to an understanding of what this "correct" tempo is. There are usually indications such as *adagio* and *allegro*, and so on, but these words have no meaning in an absolute sense. *Adagio*, for example, is taken to mean "very slowly," but how much exactly is "very"? Metronome markings, in which the number of beats per minute may be set out exactly, are more reliable if the composer has been careful and precise in reading his metronome, which is not always the case. But any composer would be uneasy if he thought the metronome mark would be followed with arithmetical precision right through a performance; he would know that his music was being presented in an inflexible, dehumanized, and therefore inartistic manner. Written tempo indications, therefore, are not absolutes. They are merely important, to be kept in mind as we look to what we may deduce from other sources.

As we know, there are two parts in the act of hearing. The first is the physical part, in which the eardrums vibrate in

Interpretation

sympathy with the source of the sounds. The second is the
mental part, in which the implications of what is heard are
absorbed by the intellect and the spirit. Obviously the general
intention of any composer is that the detail of his music should
be not only heard but understood and appreciated. The mental
hearing, with its analytical function, is always slower than the
physical hearing, and so it follows that the choice of tempo
will not depend on, for example, the facility of the players but
will have reference to the musical texture. A piece with a
multiplicity of ornamentation and detail is likely to have been
conceived at a slower pace than one with a less complex texture,
although both may have been marked *allegro molto*. From this
we realize that our rough ideas of the tempo gleaned from the
words *adagio, allegro*, and so on, will become clearer through
a consideration of the texture.

Another consideration is the chord structure. As we know,
the rhythmic impulse of the music is implied in the chord
progressions, and the frequency of chord changes will be some
indication of the tempo. In fact, it would seem that the complex
of chords might be allowed greater influence than the complex
of melodies in an assessment of the tempo. A complex of melodic
patterns over a simple chord structure can be more easily
absorbed by the listener than can simple melodic patterns over
a complicated chord structure. In any case the co-ordination
of our understanding of the chord structure with that of the
melodic patterns will bring us still nearer to a correct choice
of tempo.

Our thoughts on the texture of the music, on its melodic
and harmonic threads, may now, perhaps, be related to the
general import of the piece. Our attitude toward a quickly
moving Bach fugue, where the intention is to have us enjoy
the multiplicity of precise detail so characteristic of baroque
art, will differ from our attitude toward the closing measures
of *Götterdämmerung*; an extreme case of the need of forcing

59

the tempo right through the complexity of detail in order to re-create an impression of the chaotic, confusing, exciting effects of an enormous catastrophe. It is possible, too, to find a complicated musical structure used to express a simple psychological concept. The opening measures of Richard Strauss's *Don Juan* provide a case in point. As we know, the work as a whole presents something of the characteristics of a very tangled personality, but in the opening measures we are obviously presented with the simple concept of bounding vitality without, at the moment, other implications. The choice of tempo is little more than balancing what is fast enough to bring out the crackling brilliance of the triple figures as they appear in the wind instruments against what is slow enough to allow the strings to articulate with security and clarity. In fact, the determination of the tempo for a passage of this kind, conditioned as it may be by the multiplicity of the details, is almost easy. It is not so easy when we are faced with a piece in which there is little detail but in which we are presented with other implications that are important and serious. For example, the slow movement of the Beethoven Violin Concerto makes little demand on our capacity to observe technical detail, but it is a direct and searching challenge to the artistic insight and to the maturity and experience of the musical intellect.

When we have allowed our mind to dwell on such points as the foregoing we might be tempted to add a complication or two, such as speculation arising out of the period in which the piece was written.* However, we might consider ourselves as now having a good working idea of the tempo, sufficiently defined to bring to rehearsal.

In view of the concept of a conductor as one who knows

*Did Dvořák mean the same thing in writing the word *andante* as did, say, Mozart? In the symphony "From the New World" the slow movement was originally marked *andante*. Seidl, who directed the first performance, suggested a slower tempo to which Dvořák agreed, and so it was marked *largo*. Nowadays the tempo in the average performance is nearer to the original mark, *andante*.

everything and whose mind is definitely and dramatically and dynamically clarified at all points, it may seem to be a dangerous procedure to come to rehearsal while still having some reservations on the correct choice of tempo. But there are two kinds of uncertainty: the first, of one who has already passed the point of decision; the second, of one who is striving toward that point but has not yet reached it. Of these, only the first is harmful to personal control. Players normally are helpful and will respond to the conductor who is unsatisfied and is still seeking a perfection. His real control of them does not require rigidity, and there is certainly a technical gain by, for example, varying the tempo slightly between one rehearsal and another.

It is always best to delay as much as possible a final decision in the vitally important matter of tempo, especially in new and unfamiliar works. There is always a possibility that the piece will reveal in rehearsal some small but vital characteristic that could not have been observed from reading the score. In the final analysis, the perfect choice of tempo is a poetic matter for the conductor, as it was for the composer. It is subject to the action of true artistic insight fortified, of course, by adequate preparation at a lower level. If through variations in tempo at rehearsal the players are trained to follow the conductor exactly, whatever he does, they will be ready for that critical instant in performance when, with a sudden flash of insight, he may lead them beyond the threshold, into those realms of the pure art of music where the tempo is perfectly integrated with the texture.

THREE

The resources of notation are much more refined, and the publication of music is much more accurate nowadays than in former times. Composers have come to set out in considerable detail their wishes in regard to such matters as bowing marks for strings and tongue-phrasing for wind instruments. Dynamic marks may be used to indicate not only the general level of tone but also the balance between different instruments and different sections in an orchestration. Because of this wealth of detail, the interpreter who reads a modern score closely may hope thereby to attain an authentic, precise, and comprehensive knowledge of the composer's intentions. Besides this, he will have his contemporary knowledge of current styles in the playing of various passages and of the quality and weight of tone produced respectively on contemporary instruments. He will also have his contemporary knowledge of the milieu in which music of the times exists and from which it draws its sustenance, and he will know something of the social and philosophical factors which conditioned the composer's mind at the time of writing.

This kind of information is most valuable when approaching the interpretation of any music, old or new. It is therefore unfortunate for the conductor of the amateur or student ensemble that so much contemporary music requires, even for a fair representation, an almost impeccably high standard of technical proficiency in the players; there is so much emphasis on the quality of orchestration. Partly because of this and partly because there is, on the average, a higher dividend of artistic satisfaction over technical resources in older music, much of the repertory of student and amateur ensembles must be drawn from music composed before, say, the 1880's.

Between 1700 and 1800, when so much of our musical repertory was being written, the orchestra and its music were in a stage of rapid and extensive evolution. Composers were seldom explicit in their directions on tempo and kindred matters. The players, their contemporaries, were expected to "know" and, besides, most performances of orchestra music were directed by the composer themselves. Most of the indications of tempo and dynamic which appear on modern publications of these scores were added by nineteenth-century editors and are not, therefore, authentic in the strict sense of the word. There are so many interesting openings for the investigation of relevant factors that an interpreter might easily get himself into a morass of scholarship and forget that music is still a living art. Just the same, there are thoughts which might usefully pass through his mind when considering music of that period.

One of these thoughts arises out of the matter of pitch. Ideas of pitch varied from locality to locality and ranged between about A–430 and A–450, but it would seem that the over-all tendency was for a pitch lower in the first part of the eighteenth century than toward the end. A lower pitch is naturally less strident than a higher one, especially with wind instruments, and this thought may affect our reading of dynamic marks in Bach scores, for example. It may also be relevant to think that, although trumpet tone appears to have been reasonably close to what we hear nowadays, horn tone was much coarser. Brass instruments were mostly used melodically in the early part of the century, but by the time of Mozart and Haydn their principal use was in *support* of the harmony. This might affect our reading of the indication *forte* in works written near the beginning of the century as compared with those written toward the end. String tone was weaker then than nowadays and, the technical limitations of the players being what they were, no eighteenth-century composer could have expected the slick, facile speed at which some of his music may be performed now.

Eighteenth-century composers had in mind for each section a smaller number of strings than has been the custom since the middle of the nineteenth century. They also had in their ear a lighter quality of tone. The facility in passage-playing was much less than nowadays, and for this as well as for other reasons what they considered to be a quick tempo would have been slower than ours. This is not a recommendation to return to inferior technical methods, to seating the orchestra exactly as in Handel's time, to playing the violin by holding the right side under the chin instead of the left, and so on. It is simply that we ought to have these things in mind as we decide on the precise emphasis to be allotted to a sforzato or the true understanding of the words *allegro* or *presto* or *andantino*. It is elementary to expect at least some difference in tone quality and general style in the performance of a Haydn work as compared with those of a Brahms work.

The use of a continuous vibrato by string players is a comparatively modern innovation. When first discovered, it was used as a special effect, desirable on occasion. It was hardly yet accepted as a routine even as late as Beethoven's time, at least in the period before he became deaf. String players may nowadays feel uneasy if they are asked to eliminate their accustomed continuous vibrato. They may feel that their tone becomes thereby dull and uninteresting, "white" and lacking in expressiveness. At the same time, it is worth while to speculate on the degree to which eighteenth-century composers had a pure, almost thin, tone in mind, especially for their slow movements. The alteration in character of the slow movement of the Beethoven Symphony No. 4 when played strictly without string vibrato, is worth investigation by an inquisitive interpreter.

Then there is the matter of the harpsichord. As we have seen, most scores up to the 1760's were laid out for one or two parts over a figured bass, the middle parts to be sustained by a keyboard player. In modern editions most of the middle parts have been added by later editors, and in some cases they need checking to ensure that the essential harmonies have been adequately covered. A score set out in the old style is nowadays frequently heard with the full complement of the strings of a large orchestra, and the harpsichord, if present, has an effect that is more visible than audible. C. P. E. Bach, writing about 1780, expressed the contemporary opinion, "No piece can be performed satisfactorily without the accompaniment of a keyboard instrument. Even in music on the largest scale . . . when one would feel confident of not hearing the harpsichord in the least, one misses it if it is left out." (In his time "music on the largest scale" implied an opera with an orchestra of about twenty pieces.)

There are those who, in a *sinfonia* by Boyce or a *concerto grosso* by Vivaldi, would prefer the rich sonority and the velvet tone quality of a large body of strings. There are those who might prefer a number of strings small enough for the harpsichord tone to be effective, as originally intended. While the modern custom may lead to much beauty of tone, and to a pleasuring of the sense of hearing, the music itself takes on a somewhat different character thereby. Nobody wants to be either archaic or modern in a doctrinaire sense, but it is obvious that the diligent interpreter of eighteenth-century music has much to think about.

The relative emphases on detail in baroque art, on proportion in classical art, and on emotional elements in romantic art are all factors relevant to a view on the tempo of a work. Even in our day, many Viennese will be astonished but not necessarily impressed with the faster tempo commonly adopted in this country for such works as the Mozart "Haffner" Symphony. What Mozart himself may have thought we cannot know, but it is useful to remember that he was Austrian, that the pace of living was more leisurely before the Napoleonic era than afterward, that his music was intended for the pleasure of an experienced audience, accustomed to the leisurely savoring of minor detail. In fairly recent recordings of the Handel *Concerti Grossi* it is interesting to observe the differences in tempo as adopted by, say, the Adolph Busch Ensemble and the Boyd Neel Orchestra. The first is somewhat on the slow side with a broad, expansive quality. The second is somewhat on the quick side and gives an impression of brisk lightness. It can be argued that Handel was German and that therefore a "German" interpretation is likely to be the more reliable. It can also be argued that Handel wrote for English audiences and that therefore the English concept would be the more reliable. It is interesting, too, to compare recordings of the Bach *Brandenburg* Concertos under Furtwängler with the more recent ones under Casals. However, these comparisons are not introduced here with the intention of deciding who is right and who is wrong. They serve as a reminder that we must keep our minds as open as possible and for as long as possible as we drift toward our determination of what is the "true" interpretation of any piece of music.

Whenever it can be derived from reliable biographical material, some thought on the composer's personality can be useful. We find Mozart, in one of his many letters, expressing his view that "an artist should be reticent." This referred to an idea, commonly held in his day, that emotion and tension in a work of art should be such as would be developed organically from the actual material and its treatment. It should not be conditioned by the variable and unreliable subjective emotional states which disturb the artist from time to time. In a reading of the Symphony No. 40 in G minor it is possible to allow too much thought to the effect of the external circumstances of his life at the time, the grinding anxiety of providing for his little family, his anxiety about Constance's behavior, his failing health, the depressing consciousness of the disproportion between the support he was receiving and the greatness of qualities which, with all due modesty, he knew himself to possess. It is possible, as a result, to look for an overripe and luscious tone quality, for an overly dramatic display of theatrical emotion which misses the beautifully delicate charm of the work. By remembering his remark about the reticence of the artist, we might decide on a relaxed tempo with a gentle, lilting style, giving light but meticulous attention to the dancing rhythmic patterns which appear so frequently. We might thereby produce an impression of a gentle but tragic pathos existing almost in spite of the composer's intentions, an impression which will continue to grow on the listener even after the performance is over.

Both Haydn and Mozart lived in an ordered, hierarchical society, as yet little affected by the turbulence of the coming revolution in France. Unlike Mozart, Haydn had an orderly existence personally, with financial and other security. Haydn "knew his place," a comparatively lowly one socially. He kept it with an altogether admirable and persistent discretion, fulfilling his life and work with real greatness and genius. He was a tidy man. It was said that he usually washed, shaved, and dressed himself in his best clothes before settling down to a session of composition. The young Beethoven's attitude toward him was not due to any disrespect for his musicianly ability but rather to a complete incompatibility of temperament, to the contrast between Haydn's orderliness and his own turbulent effervescence. Considerations of this kind may lead us to condition our reading of *forte* and *fortissimo* in those passages which occur in so many of the middle sections of Haydn's slow movements, for example. Our forcefulness would be contained, and we would aim at reproducing the undoubted intensity of his dramatic moments without resorting to the free application of violence acceptable in a work by Berlioz or Tchaikovsky. If we remember Haydn's sense of humor, too, we might reasonably allow ourselves to indulge in a little exaggeration of accent or nuance where he provides us with the material for comic effect; the pauses, the use of woodwinds, the sudden switches in tonality which we find in, say, the Symphony No. 97 in C are a case in point. As we know, a strong sense of humor was a leading characteristic of Haydn's and we may have no doubt it brought him safely through the many galling situations likely to afflict a man of his quality and standing. But a sense of humor is nothing more or less than a true sense of the proportion of things, whether serious, dramatic, or comic; and with such thoughts on Haydn's personality we might produce interpretations that were lighthearted and truly dignified at the same time.

"Thus Fate Knocks at the Door" is alleged to have been Beethoven's reply to an inquiry about the meaning of the opening phrase in the famous symphony. Artists are sometimes plagued by earnest but dull persons who want a verbal explanation of the "meaning" of a piece of art work, and the replies are sometimes offhand and unthinking. This may or may not have been the case here. Even if Beethoven meant to be taken seriously, it is unwise to allow too much weight to phrases of this kind, especially in their relation to music. They are, at best, mere "tags," labels which identify but can never completely express the contents. Certainly the famous opening phrase of this symphony carries very serious and dramatic musical implications, but a too great reliance on the verbal description may lead to something of a misinterpretation. The idea "Thus Fate Knocks at the Door," combined with the prospect of a very large and powerful modern orchestra and a modern tendency toward "bigness" of tone, has led to interpretations that could be described as overstrained if not actually megalomaniac in impression. After all, the essentials of a fateful moment lie in finality and inevitability and not necessarily in explosive violence. Perhaps Beethoven may have had something of this idea in his mind when he scored the opening for strings only, with two clarinets at the weak point of their register. He marked it *fortissimo*, but we might ask ourselves why he did not use the full orchestration which appears in the vociferous opening to the last movement. We might think we ought to try simply for a clean and straightforward firmness instead of for a "terrific," explosive effect.

FOUR

It is not possible, of course, to touch on every aspect of the work and thought of an interpreter, and those points which have been so briefly touched upon are intended merely to suggest other lines of thought. Before leaving the subject there is one final point which might be mentioned. It is a very little point, but it is frequently overlooked and, when overlooked, leads to stodgy performances of a great deal of eighteenth-century music that is intended to be robust and invigorating.

This is simply the dot used to indicate the lengthening of the time value of a note. Nowadays the understanding is to allow a dotted note an additional one half of its time value, but until nearly the end of the eighteenth century the dot had an indeterminate value and the reading was guided solely by the context. The routine understanding was that a dotted note should be held as long as it was felt to be desirable, with the value of the complementary note shortened accordingly. If we think about it, we can easily see that a strict application of the modern understanding can produce a stodgy effect in spite of excellences otherwise.

An illustration may be found in a passage such as the following:

EXAMPLE 1

Handel: Concerto Grosso No. 2

The general context of this passage indicates a vigorous, springing style, in contrast with the succeeding *larghetto* section, which although having a quicker time beat is more gentle in quality. Although the passage was written as set out above, it is obvious that Handel expected to convey the impression that might, for example, be conveyed by the following:

EXAMPLE 2

Handel: Concerto Grosso No. 2

But the time value of the dot depended on the general context only. Because of the tempo, the following would not be altered.

EXAMPLE 3

Handel: Concerto Grosso No. 1

If we look at the beginning of his Concerto Grosso No. 3 we find a somewhat more complicated situation. Here the music is intended to produce an impression of much less vigor than in the *largo* passage already quoted. The quarter notes coming after the dotted half notes should be somewhat shorter than, for instance, the quarter notes in measure 6, but not yet short enough to introduce an element of vigor. These remarks may appear to be very complicated, but if they are read with the score for immediate comparison it will be seen they are really very simple.

In this, as in all cases to do with music, the final decision is not a matter of arithmetic but of the good taste and sense of musical proportion of the performer.

We might regard the interpreter as a creator of music, but by a process the reverse of the composer's, the piece of music itself being the focus. The composer begins with a force which, although recognizable by him, is as yet undefined. By the composer's work the basic rhythmic, melodic, and harmonic elements and the form of the piece of music are reduced to order and set down in the score. The interpreter begins with the score and, as it were, works backward. His final success will be measured by the degree to which, by realizing the technical details and their implications, he succeeds in re-creating the musical force that originally moved the composer.

An
Interpretation

It may be helpful to examine a work in some detail at this stage. We might select the Beethoven Symphony No. 1, first movement, because it is the first such work by the greatest of the symphony composers, a part of whose greatness lies in that he combined in his music the best characteristics of the "classical" period which preceded him and of the "romantic" period which came after him. Even in this young work we see something of both characteristics. It follows exactly that formal pattern for organizing musical material which had been established through the work of his great predecessors. At the same time, because of the irrepressible vigor of his own personality, we are introduced to something of a personal quality in the music, to the influence of those subjective states which colored so much of the music of Schumann, Berlioz, Wagner, Tchaikovsky, and many since their time. In addition this particular work is well within the scope of the reasonably proficient college or amateur orchestra and offers some routine problems common to most of the symphonies written between the middle of the eighteenth century and the middle of the nineteenth.

The earliest available material is the set of parts published by Hofmeister (C. F. Peters) after the first performance, which took place in Vienna in April 1800. This material, as well as the full score published twenty years afterward by Simrock of Bonn under Beethoven's supervision, is the principal source of the editions commonly available to us nowadays. The original manuscript is lost, but some material later used in the last movement appears in work sketches done while he was studying with Albrechtsberger.

Previously Mozart, Haydn, and others had been using woodwind instruments in pairs, but from this symphony dates the practice of having a full choir of two flutes, two oboes, two clarinets, and two bassoons at the same time as a routine of orchestration. At the time of its first performance the number of first violins in an orchestra was usually between seven and ten, with the others in proportion.

Beethoven had been in Vienna for eight years when the symphony appeared and had established himself as a pianist and as an improviser of great power and fecundity. As a composer he had already to his credit some sonatas for piano, including the "Pathétique" sonata, the first two piano concertos, some string trios, quartets, and so on; but in order to establish himself finally with the experienced Vienna audience he would need a symphony. The production of this work was therefore of critical importance in his career.

In many biographies there is much attention drawn to Beethoven's waywardness in domestic and social affairs, to his sudden rages and his generally highly developed individuality, and we receive an impression of an unpredictable temperament, even a disorderly one. Waywardness and irregularity of behavior are commonly accepted as characteristic of an artist. With lesser people this may be a fundamental characteristic, but with really great men it is much more likely to be superficial, accidental rather than essential. Although Beethoven's social relationships may have been explosive at times and although we find in his music wide and deep emotion expressed completely and without inhibition, we also find good order, economy of means, steadiness of musical purpose, and a faithful regard for tradition, for those discoveries of his predecessors in the use of musical resource had been admitted to universal usage. It is therefore probable that our best approach to interpreting him is with the thought that, even in his most emotional and lyrical moments, he was robust, firm, and clearheaded in all that he did.

This is especially true of his first symphony. He was writing for an audience that had enjoyed for many years the symphonies of composers such as Haydn and Mozart. It was a conservative and very experienced audience, unlikely to accept mere innovation as a substitute for originality or to accept a *rubato* style for its own sake as a substitute for well-judged and delicately balanced expressiveness. It may be well if we too are conservative and avoid any tendency toward a "personal" interpretation but aim at a close attention to every detail in an effort to allow Beethoven to speak for himself. Obviously no sort of passiveness in the interpreter is indicated by an attitude of "allowing the composer to speak for himself." Some sort of lack of co-operation is implied in the idea of being *passive*, but it is scarcely necessary to point to the need for the utmost mental activity and co-operation in the work of interpreting any composer, in allowing him to "speak for himself."

In this piece, as in all music, the choice of tempo is a matter of critical importance, and so we begin with this. We have some indication from the words *adagio molto* and from the metronome setting ($\flat$=88) which appear at the head of the preamble to the movement. We have Beethoven's authority for these indications but, as we know, *adagio molto* is only a relative term and the metronome setting may have been produced on an instrument that does not correspond exactly with our modern one. (Mälzel's improvement on existing "chrono-meters" had only just appeared.) However, both these indications will give us a rough idea as we come to examine the music itself.

The texture in the first three measures is the sort that can be played at almost any tempo, and so for our purposes we must begin by looking at the fourth measure, where the first melody appears. This melody is simple in character, and with Beethoven's directions in mind we shall imagine it at a tempo slow enough to answer the description *adagio molto* but not so slow as to cause the phrases to lose shape—for the music to "lose way," as a yachtsman might put it. On the other hand, it should not be so quick as to give the slightest impression of haste or agitation in the sixteenth-note passages of the succeeding measures. The general impression received from the preamble section as a whole is one of easy, relaxed, but wary confidence, such as, in a pardonable flight of fancy, we might imagine to have been Beethoven's attitude toward his public at the time the First Symphony was produced. With this in mind we will realize that whatever tempo we decide upon must move the section quietly but inexorably, without variation of any kind, from the first note to the last.

Having come to a rather definite conclusion about the correct tempo, we return to the beginning. As we are preparing the work for performance we shall naturally try to combine our recognition of the various features with our imagination of how best they are to be presented through the players. We observe that each of the first three measures begins with a *forte-piano*, and we ask ourselves, "What sort of a *forte-piano?*" In view of the tempo and the absence of brass in the orchestration, it seems it should not be a violent one and that the main part of our attention should go to the following *diminuendo* mark, to the falling away of tone into the resolution of the harmony. In fact, we might think it adequate to Beethoven's purpose if the woodwinds concentrate simply on a very clearly defined beginning to their tones and leave the effect of *forte-piano* to be realized through the pizzicato string chords.

Some theorists of the last century have commented on the V—I cadence in F major in the opening measure and, because the work as a whole is in the tonality of C, they have gone so far as to describe it as a startling innovation. In Haydn and his predecessors it is usual to find the tonic chord in the opening measures of an introduction—the idea being to establish the tonality of the piece in the listener's ear as quickly as possible. If we accept the idea that here Beethoven was an innovator, we might fall into the trap of regarding the first measure as establishing the tonality of F major and, logically, the second as establishing the tonality of A minor, a notion which will have a halting effect on the over-all rhythmic impulse. It is better to regard Beethoven as being a traditionalist who simply gave a new twist to the traditional intention of establishing the tonality as quickly and as firmly as possible. We might then feel the measures to be part of a single phrase, a sort of oversized anacrusis to the chord of G major which bursts upon us in the fourth measure and which, being the dominant, establishes our tonality all the more firmly and quickly.

The opening measures, too, present a little problem in intonation. The interval between the first and second flutes and between the first and second oboes is one which very rightly is not recommended in the old-fashioned textbooks of elementary harmony. It is an insecure combination and always needs careful handling. We may remember, too, that the device of equal temperament is a compromise for the use of keyboard instruments and that in actual practice all semitones are not exactly equal. In the first measure the E—being a sort of leading note in the context—is closer to the F than is the B♭ to the A. A common defect is that the F turns out to be too high. In the second measure there is not quite the same difficulty, because the progression is from the second to the third and from the sixth to the

fifth degrees of the scale of A minor, involving semitones that
are naturally more nearly equal. The intonation difficulty is aggravated by the fact that the tones allotted to the clarinets occur
on that part of the instrument where for physical reasons the
intonation is a bit shaky.

Intonation problems are only temporarily settled by exhortations to "play in tune," and it is always best to seek some radical
method of effecting a permanent improvement. In this case
it might seem best to have the bassoon play its bass line a little
above the mark *piano* so that the others may hear him and be
able to adjust their tones accordingly while they play.

The metronome mark (♪=88) would seem to indicate a beat
of eighths, but in view of the texture it is wiser to conceive these
three measures as a slow four-in-the-bar. Whatever the tempo,
it is always best to relate the gesture as closely as possible to
the texture. Eighth note gestures here, while they may not
actually confuse the players, may leave room for misunderstanding occasionally, and to plan against any possible misunderstanding is always a good thing, especially when dealing with comparatively inexperienced players.

Unless checked there is a normal tendency to emphasize the
highest note in any given phrase. It frequently but not always
happens that the highest point in the curve of a phrase will be a
climacteric and can bear a little accentuation, but normally the
rhythmic impulse is the surest guide to finding the tones which require the greatest emphasis. In the case of the melody beginning
at the fourth measure in this work, the rhythmic impulse points to
allowing the principal emphasis to occur on the first note of each
measure. We ought to guard, therefore, against any accentuation
on the A in the fourth measure, and we ought to seek a little
accentuation on the F in the fifth measure and the A in the sixth.
Otherwise the phrase will have a bad shape and will give an
impression of musical immaturity.

In the fifth and sixth measures there is a phrase for the flute which does not seem to be very important, but we notice that Beethoven has thought fit to support it at the octave with the first bassoon and to bring in the French horn later. If we look further we might relate it to the phrase used to introduce the scale with which the section concludes and also to the brass phrase used to introduce the concluding material at the end of the whole movement (measures 290 seqq.). It is not necessary to do much about this flute phrase. Its presentation to the listener will be adequate if the strings can hear it as they play their own parts. In the fifth and following measures there is an important little phrase on the oboe and clarinet, but because of the long note with which it begins and the penetrating quality of oboe tone it will be prominent enough without any difficulty. It is, of course, not always necessary or even desirable to explain every minor detail to the players, but it is always necessary that the details should be passing through the conductor's mind during a performance. When all these considerations, large or very small, are correctly balanced in the conductor's mind it is astonishing to what degree the balance is reflected in the players' performance without a word being said.

The chords in the eighth and ninth measures present a problem common to all orchestra music of this time and earlier. In the absence of valves, brass instruments could use only such of their open tones as fitted in with a given chord and, except for passages in the nature of a fanfare such as we see at the beginning of measure 279, it is frequently necessary to revise the dynamic marks, writing *mezzo piano* for *mezzo forte*, and so on. Rimsky-Korsakov, whose works are models of orchestration, reckons that one trumpet is equivalent to four bassoons in weight of tone in a *forte* passage. Actually a loudly played trumpet can be expected to dominate any moderately sized orchestra, and here the bassoons (2) carrying the essential bass line with the lower strings could easily be obscured by the trumpet tone. As the trumpets carry the root in the first chord and the minor seventh

78

in the second, the progression can easily have a lopsided effect unless the trumpet tone is carefully regulated. After all, *forte* really means "strongly," which is not altogether the same idea as "loudly," and the over-all strength of the music here is not lost if the trumpets produce something less than a stridently prominent *forte*.

The scale passage in the last measure is frequently played *rallentando*, but neither by direction nor by implication does the composer seem to require this. A rallentando here is likely to convey no better impression than one of anxiety about whether the coming transition to *allegro con brio* will be brought off successfully. In regard to the last group of thirty-second notes, there are two schools of thought. Some treat them as if they were sixteenth notes in the new tempo, and some treat them strictly in their relationship to the old. The first method has sanction in custom, but if he really wanted it that way it is possible Beethoven might have written the passage as follows:

EXAMPLE

Whatever he may decide on this point, the conductor must have his decision very clear in his mind, because sudden transitions of tempo are always very dangerous. The impression to be created at this point of the work under consideration is one of calm, straightforward confidence, so secure that it needs no emphasis of any kind, as we may deduce from the mark *piano* at the beginning of the movement proper. During rehearsals the players ought to be trained to manage the switch in tempo almost without the conductor's gestures; if they have to depend too closely and obviously on what he does, an undesirable impression of caution and anxiety is almost unavoidable.

TWO

The mark *allegro con brio* ($\downarrow = 112$) at the beginning of the movement proper indicates a pretty smart pace, which is kept in check by the dotted figuration. If the movement is driven on at a pace that is at once lively and consistent with the secure articulation of the dotted figuration, it will be found that the resultant tempo will be close to that indicated in the metronome setting. The principal intention is to convey an impression of springing force that is intensified, not weakened, by being kept somewhat in check.

As we are considering an impression of controlled force we might remember that *crescendi* must always be carefully managed to make sure that peaks of emphasis are correctly timed. For the correct placing of points of climax the timing of the effort is much more important than the degree of force used, and in measures 17 and 18 the woodwinds might very well delay their crescendo until the second half of measure 18; the general dynamic level, both here and in measures 23 and 24, is set by the weight of string tone.

From measure 30 onward we are free for the time being of the restraint of the dotted figuration, and because of this we must guard against a tendency to accelerate. The easy, inexorable strength of the movement as a whole will be spoiled by involuntary changes of pace; any kind of acceleration, however little, can convey an impression of weakness, of lack of balance. In fact, we might suggest at this point that the most important attribute of any conductor is an impeccable sense of pace and that .the success of any performance will depend on this more than on anything else.

Measures 31 and 32 are marked *fortissimo*, but we should

remember that the peak point of the whole passage is not reached until measure 45 and those following, when the tonality of the second subject group is established. Therefore, the fortissimo through measure 33 must be conditioned to allow for further expansion up to measure 52.

The *sforzato* marks in the passage beginning at measure 53 can easily be overplayed. The weight of any accent is always related to the context, and here the context is rather quiet and *piano*. It is possible here, perhaps, that we shall serve Beethoven better by almost ignoring the *sforzato* mark—by simply shaping the woodwind phrase as it should obviously be shaped and by bringing in the strings, when they come, with an especially clean but gentle attack. Besides, if the sforzati are overplayed, there will be a strong tendency to raise the general level of tone, and the fairly important bassoon phrase in measures 58 and 59 might be missed by the listener.

A common failing, especially among inexperienced or over-anxious players, is to anticipate a *forte* mark with an involuntary crescendo and a *piano* mark with an involuntary diminuendo. Until good habits are established it may be wise to mark measures 67 and 68 *diminuendo* and measure 76 *crescendo*. Beethoven was especially fond of the arresting effect of sudden changes in dynamic level. It is a device which occurs very frequently in his music and one which always needs special attention at rehearsal.

The quality of measure 69 and those following may offer a temptation to undue vigor. All that is required here, really, is a clean, clipped style of playing, keeping in mind that a larger climax has to be developed through measure 76.

The impression of the passage from measure 77 onward is one of relaxation and, as usual in such cases, we should guard against an involuntary change of pace—a deceleration in this instance. After all, in music of this period and earlier, the over-all shape of the piece is as important as the musical content, and it is most desirable, unless specifically directed otherwise by the composer, that all changes in tension and emotion are achieved without any alteration of pace. It is quite possible to do this provided the players—and the conductor—are sufficiently sensitive and agile in their control of dynamic variation. In this particular passage an easy but firm control is essential; easy, because we need to preserve a feeling of relaxation, and firm, because the tempo must be kept steady in order to take in stride the reappearance of the dotted figuration later on.

The coda of the section begins at measure 100, where the dynamic level is *piano*. Here, as in measures 57 and those following, the sforzati are "built in" in the orchestration and require the same sort of treatment. The *fortissimo* chords into measure 106 mark an important period in the movement. Their dramatic effect can be spoiled if a natural tendency to anticipate them by an involuntary crescendo is not firmly controlled.

Whether to go on to the development section and not make a repeat of the first section in works of this kind is a point that is debated from time to time. Originally the repeat was made, but in these impatient times the practice is not uniform. There are those who say that, unless the repeat is made, the balance between the sections and the formal proportions of the work as a whole, as conceived by the composer, are upset; besides, the audience should have an opportunity of being more familiar with the main themes before their development and elaboration are begun. There are those who admit the second part of this argument in the case of unfamiliar works but suggest that in works that are well known, as this one is, the repetition is unnecessary and there is a risk of being boring. On the other hand, it is possible to say that, if the performance—and the music—has real vitality, an exact repeat of the musical material will not mean an exact repeat of the impression created on the listener; and, moreover, whether the work is well known or not, the consideration of preserving its formal proportions is always valid. Of course there are cases—not this one—where a composer has misjudged his proportions or where the musical material might be deemed "too thin" to stand immediate repetition, and the conductor may then feel justified in omitting a repeat. But omitting a repeat is in essence a "cut" and, once the principle is admitted, we may wonder where the excising of parts thought to be boring or disproportionately long is to end. Perhaps we may be entitled to say that, for example, in the variations movement of his Divertimento No. 17 in D, Mozart would not have indicated all those repeats of sections if he were alive today in these excited, streamlined, and impatient times. Perhaps we might think that the danger of boring the audience exists less in the music itself than in defects of the performer's character and musicianship. Perhaps the induction of boredom is a legitimate artistic device for heightening the effect of what is to come afterward.

Perhaps there is no end to arguments of this kind and no conclusion. Perhaps whether to repeat or not is one of those cases where each conductor is entirely on his own and must make his own decision.

THREE

Throughout the development section the emphasis is on the intellectual side. There are hardly any emotional implications, and the principal enjoyment comes from an intellectual appreciation of Beethoven's skill in breaking up the material of the first subject group and flashing the pieces at us from different parts of the orchestra. Here it is wise to concentrate on the maintenance of a steady, unwavering tempo which will carry the players securely through their various entrances and exits and help them to an easy but strict observance, especially of the dotted-note figuration. An acceleration is possible, too, because of the thin orchestral texture. Any such acceleration will adversely affect the necessary feeling of strength and balance. The performance of measure 144 and those following will become difficult, and the bounding vigor of measure 160 and those following will be impaired either by having to take them too quickly or by having to slow down on approaching them.

In music, as in any medium of communication, repetition and insistence produce automatically a building up of tension. This would seem to be the implication of the woodwind passages from measure 155 through 159. Insistence and tension are none the less real for being quietly expressed, and certainly an excellent effect ran be obtained by playing these measures exactly as marked, without any crescendo whatever. This restraint will also help to heighten the effect of explosive release indicated by the sudden fortissimo at measure 160.

The long tones of the brass may tend to blot out the essential woodwind passages in measure 162 and the corresponding measures. The players should therefore differentiate between those parts when they are accompanying the woodwind and when they are accompanying the strings in measures 160 and 164. When paired instruments proceed in parallel thirds at the upper end of the register it is commonly found that the underneath part is penetrating and that the upper part—which, as here, carries the melodic line—is obscured. This might be kept in mind when dealing with the woodwinds at this point.

The recapitulation from measures 178 to 279 contains no new material for comment.

The coda to the whole movement begins at measure 271, and the sudden simplification of rhythm and texture again offers a temptation to acceleration. Corresponding passages in many works are played *accelerando*, with the intention, not altogether unreasonable, of producing an "applause" ending. Some composers write for this effect and so indicate their intentions if the context demands it, but in this particular work nothing of the kind seems to be indicated, either explicitly or implicitly. As we have said before, the over-all effect of the piece is one of impassive, unhurried strength, and a steady tempo from here to the end will only serve to confirm this impression. There is no need to worry about the climax. Beethoven has organized the necessary material effectively by the succession of fanfare-like passages which begin at measure 279. From here, through measures 288 and 289, the brass open tones correspond exactly with the chord structures, and they may be unleashed in their full glory, all the more effective for the slight restraints hitherto imposed upon them.

The very last measure is silent, but it must be "played" just the same. This is done simply by the conductor keeping his hands raised and having the players remain quite still while the measure of time is being counted through. When the conductor's arms are lowered to his sides, the piece finally comes to end.

Gesture

The concept of the interpretation of music may be divided into two parts. The first is complete when the interpreter becomes possessed of the composer's thought; the second, when he conveys that possession to the players and to the listeners. To convey his possession to the players the conductor may use verbal explanations in rehearsal, but of course he must depend solely on gesture during a performance.

Unspoken thought is more easily communicated than is commonly realized. If, for example, a conductor's concentration deteriorates for any reason during a performance, the players' concentration will begin to deteriorate almost immediately, no matter how little the conductor's outward appearance and attitudes may be unchanged and no matter how clearly he continues to preserve the outline of his gestures. If through the influence of the music his concentration becomes more intense, the players will respond precisely and automatically to that intensity, even if —as might easily be—the outline of his gestures are a little imprecise at the moment. From this somewhat elementary example we can begin to realize that, in conducting, the basic essential is clarity of mind about what is being heard and what is expected to be heard. Gestures in themselves are not of *primary* importance.

But if they are not of primary importance, gestures are certainly of very great importance. They not only illustrate the conductor's thought and feeling but also express his control over the players. They should therefore be kept at a minimum consistent with all necessary clarity and completeness in expression. A pitcher can go to the well too often, and a shepherd can cry "wolf" too often. So, too, can unnecessarily large and flamboyant gestures dissipate that reserve of power so often needed to press the players through a musical climax or that extra control needed to help them through an unusually tricky piece of musical texture. This does not mean that a conductor should be restricted or stiff in what he does at any time. It simply means that in conducting, as in all art work, economy in the use of means is a leading characteristic. The free, fluent expression of thought in good writing consists less in an outpouring of language than in, when possible, making one sentence do the work of two or three. A good painter will not wish to lay a brush to canvas unless the stroke is a direct contribution to the painting as a whole. It can happen that the more naïve sections of an audience may be impressed with a picturesque conductor, but although showmanship and spectacle as a part of concert-giving are not entirely to be neglected it must always be remembered that music is an art communicated through the sense of hearing and not through the sense of sight.

A conductor's style of gesture is very much an individual matter, just as his style of penmanship is. In penmanship all allowance may be made for personal variations, but there are certain basic patterns in the formation of letters which are fundamental to a communication. Our thought on the gesture of a conductor would be somewhat similar.

The hand and arm held with the palm facing outward always indicate "stop" in any language or in any context, and the manner in which the gesture is made may indicate any variation of this, such as "caution" or *rallentando*. On the same basis the palm held facing inward indicates an invitation—"come on" or *accelerando*. The palm held face downward indicates a restriction, a suppression, *diminuendo*; and upward, it indicates the reverse, of course. The variations in the application of this principle are infinite in practice, but generally it will be found extremely difficult to encourage performers into a crescendo or into an accelerando by holding the palms either outward or downward, no matter how vehement these gestures may be or how clear in outline. Most beginners are inclined to use the palms facing outward or downward, and this seems to be due to a fear, either conscious or unconscious, of letting their forces get out from under their insecurely felt control. With experience comes confidence, and with confidence comes a readiness to encourage the performers rather than suppress them; to turn the palms upward in order to draw out the music instead of trying to force it out.

Another difficulty for the beginner is the problem of what to do with the left hand. It is so often used as a mere shadow, as a mere reflection of what the right hand does. As we have observed already, all gestures should be minimum and relevant. From this it follows that the left hand should not be used at all until it is needed for a specific purpose. When not in use it should be allowed simply to hang by the side. To do this may seem awkward and restricting. At first the exercise of a little will power is necessary, but later on the extension of experience makes it possible to forget about this altogether. When he has reached the point of being able to forget all about his left hand a beginner may then hope to be able to use it effectively—that is, by bringing it into use consciously and for a definite purpose.

For all general purposes the greater part of a conductor's

communication with his players is through the right arm. The direction of the beat—up, down, or sideways—can be used by the player to verify where he is in any given measure; the rapidity of the movement indicates the tempo, and its intensity indicates the dynamic level. Until a beginner has acquired some considerable experience in directing the activities of an ensemble he ought to school himself to do everything with the right hand. It is on somewhat the same basis that students of composition write exercises in counterpoint restricted to the usage of sixteenth-century resources; such exercises sharpen the wits and enable them to avail of the greater fluency in free counterpoint with security and directness.

Even when a freedom of gesture that is both effective and fluent has been acquired, it is wise to continue to use the right hand for all normal purposes. The left hand is then in reserve for "abnormalities," for sudden accents, for extra intensity of tone at the end of a crescendo, for warning of coming changes in pace or in dynamic level, for marking a long note held in one section against a moving passage in another. It should be used only to draw the players' attention to some feature or other, and when the need for using it is over it should be allowed to drop back again to the side.

All gestures should be made at waist level or higher because, naturally, they are useless unless they are clearly visible to players as they sit behind music stands. In ordinary conversation unconscious gesture is usually made at waist level and below. Until it becomes a fixed habit, gesturing clearly above waist level will at first need constant self-reminders. In addition to allowing the conductor to be seen by the players, gesture above waist level sets up the diaphragm and leads to an easy but commanding posture, always an asset to any conductor.

The principal avenues of unspoken communication, with or without conscious gesture, are the eyes and the facial expression. Who seeks to receive an impression from another will normally look at his eyes and face. Therefore, gestures should be made not only above waist level but also in the line of sight between the conductor and the players. As anyone who has watched a conjuring trick will agree, a movement of the hand can be made in plain view, but the movement will not be observed if attention is at the same time drawn elsewhere. Because players normally look at a conductor's eyes and face, gestures made outside that general area can result in at least a division of attention, with a loss of concentration on what both they and the conductor are doing. It may be objected that a conductor is unable to see his score clearly if he makes his gestures in this area. This, however, is answered by the old and well-known adage, "A conductor should have the score in his head and not his head in the score"; if his preparation has been adequate, it should never be necessary to regard the score as anything else but a sort of mnemonic, useful for a quick glance from time to time. Besides, it is only by looking directly and continuously at the players, singly or in groups, that a conductor retains control over them during a performance and is able to detect and modify any inattention, overanxiety, or other hazard *before* it begins to damage a performance. Security of control therefore depends on the integration of the glance with the gesture.

In gesturing with either hand, the fingers should be always close together—but not rigidly or stiffly—but in order to present a picture of the hand as a single unit. Widespread fingers have an irresistible tendency to articulate independently, and this tends toward a diffusion of effect. The physical exhaustion of both players and conductor in music-making comes principally from the very great concentration required, and anything that tends to interfere with that concentration and make it more difficult should be eliminated. It is true that a little gesture with one or two fingers may be adequate to communicate with a few players but, over the area occupied by orchestra, a finger is not distinctly visible, and to be effective a gesture will always need the whole hand. Holding the fingers together may impress a beginner as being restrictive of his fluency of expression, but it is well to remember that a gesture with the whole hand can convey an impression as delicately and sensitively as is ever necessary. If the fingers are not kept together there is always a danger that what is intended to be a gesture may degenerate into being a mere gesticulation.

For the same reason, movements of the wrist independent of the forearm ought to be kept at a minimum. They are often too small to be effectively visible, and when—as it should be—a baton is used, additional wrist movements tend to produce a too swiftly made arc at the point, and may make it momentarily invisible. The baton is really no more than an extension of the arm. It is useful because it is more easily seen and, moving through a larger arc, it can present the tempo and other elements of the music with greater nicety. By using the wrist with too great independence, there is a danger that the impression conveyed by the point of the baton may be one of fussiness, of an effete sort of overrefinement. It is therefore wise, without being in any way rigid about it, to consider the line from the articulation of the elbow to the point of the baton as a single unit.

(A baton should be light in color so that it may be easily seen, light in weight so that it does not cause unnecessary fatigue, long enough to be an effective extension of the arm but not so long as to be "whippy" and present a blurred impression at the point. It should be held simply between the thumb and the forefinger, with the end resting comfortably in the palm of the hand. In time, holding it should become an unconscious act and gestures should be made almost as if it were not there.)

The elbows should be held close to the sides but not touching them—this, too, without any rigidity or restriction of legitimate movement. One concept of a conductor is that of a presence that irradiates the influence of the music and, if the elbows are held away from the sides, the physical expression of this concept—of radiation outward from a central point—is spoiled. A less tenuous and more immediately obvious effect is that elbows held away from the sides tend to take the gesture out of the line of sight or else to restrict the arc of movement of the forearm and the point of the baton. Besides all this, holding the elbows away from the sides can produce a pumping movement that looks ugly and is needlessly distracting to both players and audience. A certain tidiness and simplicity of movement are the hallmarks of the professional in most activities. A conductor always looks untidy and amateurish if he holds his elbows out.

Because any irrelevant movement is distracting, body movements other than those necessary to activate the arms and shoulders should be avoided. As in other recommendations, it is not intended by this that a conductor should stand stiffly, like a soldier on parade. A soldier standing stiffly on parade is really in a passive attitude, static rather than dynamic, and of course a conductor must always be dynamic. At the same time, whatever he does must be to the point, and to be effective a certain apparent restriction of movement, both of body and feet, would seem to be advisable. A characteristic of great spirits is that, while their effect on others may be subtle, complex, and strong, they themselves are not moved to any comparable extent. By analogy, it might be suggested that all necessary direction of an orchestra may be accomplished with complete effectiveness by little more than rotating the body at the waist, assisting with small movements of the feet. Dramatic disappearances under the score desk to indicate a sudden pianissimo and startling leaps into the air to emphasize a fortissimo may sometimes impress the more naïve sections of an audience, but they will hardly ever impress the hard-working orchestra player. If such movements indicate anything at all they indicate inadequate use of rehearsal time and a lack of confidence in the player response to normal gesture.

TWO

If gesture is correctly related to the music, it follows that the baton should be in continuous movement throughout a performance. This is more obvious in slow movements than in quick ones. With a slow beat, such as is required in the opening of the Beethoven *Leonora* Overture No. 3, the beat begins before the tone is expected to be produced by the players. At one part of the beat the conductor seems to make it an act of will that "Now!" the tone comes, and the players play accordingly. But the beat does not end immediately with the production of the tone. It must follow through to its logical conclusion before the next beat can be allowed to develop. In quick music this is not so obvious, but in principle it seems reasonable to think of any beat as being in three parts: the preliminary part, the effective part, and the "follow-through." This is a matter which perhaps cannot be completely understood, except as the result of practical experience; but it is obvious that a beat in which the follow-through is clipped is no help in a legato passage, just as a beat in which the follow-through is elongated is no help in a staccato passage. As in a golf stroke, the follow-through is just as important as the preliminary part in making the effective part successful.

It is not intended here to consider the elements of time-beating gestures. Information about how to beat two-, three-, four-in-the-bar, and variations—with the usual diagrams—is readily accessible in almost any book of reference. Besides, any musician who has come to the point of beginning as a conductor, as a teacher of others, is assumed to have enough previous musical experience to be quite familiar with the outlines of these beats.

Owing to personal idiosyncrasies or to the requirements of the context or for other reasons, many beats can be, and are, given in almost any direction, but there can be no relaxation in regard to the delivery of one beat in measured music. The downbeat must always be *down.* That the downbeat must always be down may seem to be so obvious as to be scarcely worth mentioning, but much of the difficulties of the beginner conductor comes from a neglect of this obvious and elementary idea.

The production of a downbeat that, without conscious thought, is invariably clear—and *down*—is the foundation of any system or style of gesture. Everything else depends on the correct delivery of this beat. For the conductor it is a useful check on any possible tendency to be vague either in mind or in gesture, and it helps him toward a clearly explicit and determined control of the orchestra. For the player it is important to him to be able to depend absolutely on its regular and clearly defined appearance. It marks the bar line and what is normally the principal pulse of the measure. For those not actually playing at the time it is a help in counting silent measures and an unfailing point of reference for the tempo. To say there is a lack of clarity in his downbeat is about the most serious complaint it is possible to make about a conductor in his external manifestations.

Another beat that is just as important as the downbeat is the preparatory beat. This is the gesture that precedes the action and prepares the players for the correct beginning of and entry into a piece, for the cutoff of a chord, for changes in pace and dynamic. It is the gesture which must invariably precede the executive beat on which the players act. The reactions of orchestra players may sometimes be very quick indeed, but of course they can never be instantaneous. No matter how well rehearsed an orchestra may be, a good quality in the ensemble depends absolutely on the preparation received through the preparatory beat.

Besides the small but very real gap between thought and action, there are physical factors to be taken into consideration. Wind instrumentalists need to inhale before they blow, and string players need to get the bow into position before they play. The manner in which they play subsequently will depend completely on the indications they receive beforehand. It is sometimes overlooked, too, that string players breathe as they play. Even with the bow in position, they all—either consciously or unconsciously—take a breath at the inception of a phrase, just as a singer or a wind player might, although not to the same extent. In fact, adequate allowance for breathing is at the root of all good phrasing in the instrumentalists as well as singers, and a conductor will do well to school himself to breathe with the players as he directs the inception and shaping of phrases. If he breathes correctly with them it is likely, too, that his management of preparatory beats will be logical and cogent.

If the preparatory beat is given in such a way as to indicate exactly what is expected when the tone is produced on the executive beat, the style of the executive beat becomes almost, but not altogether, immaterial. A piece such as the Mendelssohn *A Midsummer Night's Dream* Overture can never be securely begun with any sort of hasty preparatory movement, no matter how gentle and flowing the executive beat may be. The opening of the Wagner *Mastersingers* Overture obviously needs a large and firmly outlined preparatory beat. The opening of the *scherzo* of the Dvořák Second Symphony needs a quick, stabbing motion, given with an especially clear outline in order to help the players through the tricky, offbeat phrase. (In this particular case it might almost be said that if the upbeat is correctly delivered any further beat is scarcely necessary for the next few measures.)

The precise ending of a tone or a chord marked with a pause is just as important as the beginning, of course, and the ending must be prepared. There are various types of gestures used to end a pause which the beginner may work out for himself or may learn from watching others. The basis of any such movement would seem to be in a repetition of the preceding executive beat. For example, the following would be prepared by a repetition of the third beat of the measure, the tone ending on the fourth:

EXAMPLE 1

The following would be prepared by a repetition of the fourth beat:

EXAMPLE 2

When there is a pause immediately followed by a moving passage, the routine practice is the same, but care should be taken to indicate the continuing tempo correctly and clearly. In the following example the release is prepared by repeating the first beat of the measure:

EXAMPLE 3

Elgar: Cockaigne (In London Town) Boosey & Hawkes Ltd.

Where a pause is followed by a change in tempo or dynamic, the routine is the same as in the foregoing examples but the preparatory beat will indicate the new tempo or dynamic and will not be related to what went before.

THREE

The integration into a single gesture of the requirements of both tempo and dynamic is very much a matter for experience and practice. How to prepare, for example, the beginning of a passage that is quick, *staccato*, and *pianissimo* as compared with one that is quick, *legato*, and *fortissimo* is something that cannot be learned from a book. Everything depends on the context. A satisfactory technique can be developed by keeping in mind the need every player has of a clear indication of how he is to play *before* he plays. Indeed, assuming that rehearsals have been adequate, the responsibility for good ensemble in a performance is solely that of the conductor and his management of preparatory gestures.

As a performance continues, every beat is really a preparation for every succeeding one. In fact, the essence of gesture is preparatory at any time, and the conductor's musical thinking during a performance combines an appreciation of the actual moment with a strong anticipation of what is to come. This is how best he can help an orchestra, and when it is reflected in his gesture, his style will become fluent, cohesive, and commanding.

By way of review of what has been said already, we might consider the following points as a guidance in the development of a style: The conductor should adopt an easy but erect posture, with the heels close together but not touching. All gestures should be minimum and strictly relevant. All gestures should be made above the waistline and in the line of sight. The left arm should be used only when necessary. The elbows should be held near the sides. The fingers should be kept closed and the hand presented to view as a single unit. Movements of the feet should be kept to the minimum necessary to control the different sections. The knees should never bend noticeably.

It may seem that by following suggestions of this kind the conductor may develop a style that is stiff and restricted in expressive possibilities, but these suggestions should be taken as the framework rather than as the outline of a style. Any conductor must hope to develop his own style, expressive of his personality and of the music he directs. While that style is developing, however, it is wiser to concentrate on some underlying principles. Thinking too soon and too much of the style he hopes to develop in due time may tempt him to wonder too much what he looks like now and may induce a feeling of self-consciousness—a fatal characteristic. So long as he makes sure that every gesture is clear and to the point, that it is clearly understood by the players and produces *exactly* the effect he expects of it, the rest will come in time.

"The rest" is important because, besides the direct control of the orchestra and the severely practical considerations of time-beating and so on, the general pattern of a conductor's movements can help to interpret the music to the audience. The average audience is seldom as completely familiar with all the musical details of a piece as the performers are, and what the conductor does can help them to hear better in the analytical sense. Unexpected entries, especially in the middle parts, and other such obscurities can be clarified and revealed to the audience by the conductor's preparatory gestures. It has been very well said that every element of music except the sound of it can be translated into gesture, and we might sum up by saying that a conductor's gestures ought to be effective for the sake of the players, illustrative for the sake of the audience, and, although eloquent at all times, never so flamboyant as to obtrude themselves between the players, the audience, and the music.

Instruments

Although no conductor can be expected to be able to play all the instruments of an orchestra, he ought to know at least something of the characteristics of each one. He should know something of the inherent limitations of each instrument and of the difficulties and faults commonly found in performance. The conservation of rehearsal time is always an important consideration, and much time and trouble may be saved if the conductor is able to make precise suggestions on technical points as he comes to prescribe the particular musical effect he is looking for. To be able to do this is especially valuable when dealing with players whose proficiency is below professional level.

Any ensemble, composed as it is of human beings, must be regarded as a delicate instrument requiring delicate and considerate handling. This does not mean in any sense a timorous or tentative approach to rehearsal work. The approach should certainly be firm, but the firmness should be supported by a precise knowledge of what is being done or what should be done.

A sculptor faced with a cross-grained piece of limestone may sometimes develop what we might call "a considerable head of steam" when things are not going too well. But he is always obliged to remember his technical processes, however much he is pressed by the frustration of his artistic impulses. We might regard a conductor as being in somewhat the same case when facing an orchestra. In the old days, when orchestras were little more than *ad hoc* collections of individual players and when conductors, apart from a lively appreciation of the aesthetic possibilities of the music, were too seldom concerned with technical minutiae, the "blood and guts" method may have had its uses. It demanded considerable personal pressure to get large and exciting results in a short time from a collection of players with little training as a group.

Some degree of personal pressure will always be necessary because of the natural tendency to inertia which appears in the most willing and active groups of people from time to time, but the continuing attitude of the conductor should be that of *releasing* the musical energies rather then of *forcing* them out. Most orchestras, amateur as well as professional, meet regularly nowadays, with much the same personnel each time. Regular meetings, if they are to be carried on constructively, need a certain degree of equanimity on the part of everyone concerned. This equanimity is best preserved by the conductor who is able to offer a player technical advice instead of complaints (which may be well grounded) about his lack of musicianship. Everyone may then progress patiently and inexorably on the road to perfection, reserving the exercise of the naked force of personality to occasions of extreme emergency.

There may be problems in passages involving accurately balanced woodwinds, such as we find, for example, in the last movement of the Mendelssohn Violin Concerto. Earnest—and perhaps violent—exhortations to pay more attention and follow the beat more carefully or aesthetic generalizations on the fairylike quality required may easily lead to a frustrated impasse, especially with non-professionals. If the conductor has his mind on the technical problems of the players he might find that a little quiet drill in the observance of tonguing marks and in having the players listen to each other is about all that may be really necessary. The attack of brass instruments, especially in passages of a rhythmic nature, may be ragged. It may be a help to remember that the tones of brass instruments are produced with the syllables *Ta* and *Ka*. In a four-note grouping, the combination may be Ta-Ta-Ta-Ta or Ta-Ka-Ta-Ta. By having in mind the particular combination which will produce exactly the effect needed, it may be possible to eliminate much difficulty without much discomfort and without unnecessary repetition. A clarinet player may be playing flat in the upper register. Instead of developing high blood pressure—a reasonable reaction to faulty intonation—the conductor might be more usefully employed in asking whether the reed used is too soft.

The following remarks on the instruments of the orchestra are not, of necessity, fully comprehensive. The beginner conductor who has some training in, say, woodwinds may not find much about these instruments that is new to him, but he may find something of interest in the remarks on percussion. The general intention is to stimulate thoughts on the peculiarities of instruments and to suggest to the conductor that the basic procedure in orchestra rehearsal is similar to what he personally experienced during private lessons on his instrument: a patient persistence and much repetition guided by technical advice. In any case music is an aural matter, and reading about instruments is little help unless regarded as an aid to the development of a clinical ear for instrumental performances.

FLUTE (and PICCOLO) Although the history of the flute goes back as far as recorded history, our practical interest in the subject scarcely takes us beyond about the end of the seventeenth century. The universal acceptance of the present method of holding the flute horizontally dates from the early part of the eighteenth century. Sometimes we find the direction "flûte à bec" and sometimes "flauto traverso" in scores of that period. The flûte à bec was held vertically and would have had a tone similar to that of the modern recorder. These directions cease to appear in scores after the middle of the century, and the assumption thenceforward was that the transverse flute would be used.

Until almost the end of the nineteenth century flutes were made of wood. Those made of wood have a soft, almost reticent quality which is mostly absent in the bolder, brighter, and stronger tone of the modern flute—now made mostly of metal, usually silver. This is something to remember, for example, when dealing with the dynamic marks of a Haydn symphony—especially when the number of strings involved is more nearly commensurate with the number used in the orchestra of Haydn's day.

The flute was the first woodwind instrument to appear regularly in the orchestra. This may perhaps be ascribed to the fact that in Germany, where the orchestra as an independent medium of musical expression had its most extensive development in the eighteenth century, flute or fife bands were a regular part of the military establishment attached to every court, and flute players were therefore readily available. As we know, when the transverse flute first came into general use in France and England it was known as the *German* flute.

The tone is produced by blowing across the mouth hole. As it strikes against the farther edge the stream of air is divided, one part vibrating within the pipe to produce the tone and the other flowing away outside. As so much of the breath is not used in the actual production of tone, long slow passages may sometimes present some difficulty. It may be necessary for the player to give some thought to his breathing, to the insertion of breath marks in his score, just as a singer might do. A conductor is not primarily interested in the minor technical details of flute playing, but he is most definitely interested in the shape of a phrase, in whether the breathing does or does not accord with his intentions in regard to rhythmic patterns and impulses, and other related matters.

Because of the mechanics of tone production the flute has not, surprisingly, a dynamic range that is quite as wide as other instruments. The lowest tones are impossible to play *forte*, and the highest tones are almost impossible to play *piano*. Its wonderfully expressive qualities derive rather from the pure, ineffable nature of the tone itself and from the way in which a composer writes for it. Diminuendo and crescendo are possible, of course, but a conductor should not look for a too wide range. As against this limitation, the tone production is mechanically much simpler than in other instruments, and in the execution of rapid passages —whether tongued or slurred—there are superior possibilities. The comparative ease of tone production allows the player to come with greater confidence to passages requiring fluency, rapidity, and clarity of articulation. In fact, faults in the unanimity of woodwind ensemble passages may sometimes be traced to this very facility; a flute player may have a tendency to get ahead of the others.

The finger holes, opened one after the other, produce the diatonic scale of D major, and the range is from D immediately below the staff upward through three octaves. A few tones are possible both below and above these limits, but a composer seldom requires them except for the occasional special effect. The fundamental tone in all flutes is almost pure, and the overtones are few and weak in comparison with the other instruments. What upper partials there are disappear in the upper part of the register. For this reason the tone—although very attractive in quality—lacks something of the "lift," the lively qualities of some other instruments. In passages above the treble staff it may give an impression of being "flat," although if checked, even electronically, the tones may be found in fact to be correct in pitch. The late Sir Hamilton Harty, a very fine and sensitive musician, used to urge his flute players to play "sharp." He did not intend to be taken absolutely literally in this. What he meant was that they should lean toward the sharp side of the tone, especially in the acoustically dull upper register.

The idea of a *flauto piccolo* or *ottavino* had been known for a long time, but the piccolo as a regularly accepted instrument in the symphony orchestra was first introduced by Beethoven (Fifth, Sixth, and Ninth symphonies). Except for its smaller size and the corresponding effect on its compass and tone quality, it is the same as the flute. Its compass throughout lies an octave above the flute, but piccolo parts are written an octave lower than they are intended to sound, in order to avoid the use of too many leger lines. Because of its small size there is less margin for error in its manufacture and it seems to be more difficult to find a piccolo than it is to find a flute with really first-class pitch throughout. A player therefore needs to give close attention to his intonation at all times. Its principal usage is to put an "edge" on orchestral tuttis, and it is always prominent when it appears, with its very penetrating tone quality that can cut right through the largest of orchestras.

It is directed in many orchestra scores that the piccolo be played as a second instrument by the second or third flute player. When it is called for in the middle of a piece, it may therefore be colder than the other instruments which have been already in use and, as with cold instruments, its pitch may be flat for a few measures. This consideration applies to all instruments that are used only occasionally in the performance of a piece, and it is something which all orchestrators may usefully have in mind. Sir Edward Elgar, a superb calculator of orchestral effects, was once asked why he scored a certain passage for bass clarinet in a certain way; it was pointed out to him that the instrument would be inaudible as the music had been written. He replied by pointing to an exposed solo passage later on and said that he wanted to be sure that the bass clarinet would be warmed and in tune when the time came for it to be heard effectively. Players on the piccolo in similar circumstances have their own various methods of having the instrument warm and in tune when the time comes to use it: some blow through it silently, some keep it in the inside pocket of the jacket. In any case, the matter is something for the conductor to have in his mind.

O B O E (and C O R A N G L A I S) The earliest form of the modern oboe appears in instruments made in the late seventeenth century. Previously the player's lips did not come in contact with the double reed. It was covered by a mouthpiece, and there was control of little more than the duration of the tone. The shawm, a progenitor of the oboe that was common in France in the seventeenth century, was something like the modern practice chanter, an instrument used by players on the warpipes to develop their lung power and finger dexterity indoors, and without too much disturbance of neighbors. The reed on the shawm and on the old-style oboe was somewhat larger than the modern one. It was closer in size to that of the modern bassoon, and the tone was loud and coarse. The French still prefer a slightly wider reed than do the English or the Germans. It is not intended by this to convey an impression that French oboe tone is nowadays coarser than English or German tone. It is simply that there is an observable difference in quality, which is at least worth thinking about.

In its main aspects the fingering of the oboe is much the same as that of the flute, and indeed, when they first began to make a regular appearance in the orchestra score, oboes were doubled by flautists. The compass is smaller: from D immediately below the staff upward through two octaves. As with the flute, a few more tones are possible at either end, but they are not too often required. Comparatively inexperienced players may tend to relax the embouchure too much at the lower end of the compass and to produce a raw, coarse quality of tone, probably somewhat akin to what was common in the eighteenth century. There may be a tendency to "pinch" on the reed in the higher tones for the sake of security of control, with an effect of thinning the quality and sharpening the pitch. When we remember that without changing a fingering it is possible to vary the pitch of some oboe tones through almost a full semitone, we realize how much an oboe player needs to listen to himself closely at all times.

(This need of habitually listening to their own performance is a point sometimes overlooked by young players. They work hard at finger dexterity, reed or lip control, and many other technical difficulties; but, unless they listen to themselves clinically and critically at all times, the result—although it may be impressive— will not really be *music*.)

The tone of the modern oboe has a large number of partials which are stronger than the fundamentals in some parts of the compass. This gives the tone its penetrating quality, effective through a large number of other instruments at any dynamic level. Because both lips are in contact with the reed, the tone is also very sensitive in its response to the player's personality, and in this respect it comes closer to the violin than do the other wind instruments. On the other hand the oboe is less fluent than the flute in the execution of rapid passages, especially those requiring a separate tongue to each note.

Without renewed breath, single tones and long phrases can be supported longer by the oboe than by other wind instruments. The penetrating quality of the tone requires little effort to make itself felt through an ensemble, and the small reed is kept in vibration with very little breath. It is possible that the breath in a player's throat and lungs may become unusable before it has been altogether expended, and it may therefore be necessary to exhale as well as to inhale between the end of one phrase and the beginning of the next. This may mean a tiny delay as compared with other instruments and might well be kept in mind while directing a performance. As we saw in the chapter on "Gesture," a conductor ought to breathe with his players as he helps them to shape their phrases.

At the turn of the seventeenth century oboes were being used in "families" and were made with tubes of various lengths from soprano to bass. Besides the oboe as we now know it, the only other one of these instruments to survive into modern usage is the cor anglais, an alto oboe. The fingering, compass, and general characteristics are roughly the same as the oboe's, but the sound produced is an interval of a fifth lower than what is written for it in the score. (For example, when a passage in the scale of Bb is intended to be heard, it is written in the scale of F, a fifth higher.)

"Survival" is scarcely the best word to use in regard to the place of the cor anglais in orchestra scores because it had almost no orchestral use during the eighteenth century. Its regular appearance in the orchestra began in about the 1890's, and before that the only one to use it seems to have been Wagner, with a few examples from Berlioz and Meyerbeer. That it came back to the orchestra at all is due to an improvement effected in the 1830's, when it was discovered that if the lowest joint was made pear-shaped, instead of bell-shaped as in the oboe, the tone would be rounded and mellow instead of coarse and "wide open."

In many scores the specification is for the cor anglais to be played by the second oboe. This is quite possible, of course, but not so easy as it might appear. The reed is bigger and less easily managed and does not respond quite so readily. The player's ear may be disturbed for a measure or two at first by his producing tones a fifth lower than what he sees on the score. For the most part, the cor anglais is used in solo passages and for special effect. Its appearance in a piece is always prominent and frequently of critical importance. It is advisable, therefore, to have two players whenever possible: one for the oboe and one for the cor anglais.

CLARINET The history of the modern clarinet might be said to begin in 1730 when one Johann Christian Denner devised an instrument that was an extension of one previously known as the *chalumeau*. Denner's instrument seems to have had a very shrill tone quality which sounded in the distance somewhat like a trumpet. This accounts for the word "clarinet," derived from the word *clarino*, used to describe a sort of high, keyed trumpet now obsolete. In fact, the clarinet is a combination of two instruments, and the evidence of that combination is still observable in the difference between the warm, rounded quality of tone in the lower or *chalumeau* register and the more penetrating quality in the upper or *clarinet* register.

Although it appears variously under the name "chalumeau" or "clarinet" in some of the operas produced at Hamburg in the early part of the eighteenth century and in Paris up to about 1750, it did not find its way into regular use in the orchestra proper until about the 1780's. As the oboe was doubled by the flautist when it was first being introduced into the orchestra, so the clarinet was doubled by the oboist. Mozart used clarinets regularly in his later works but seldom at the same time as oboes. Haydn did not use clarinets at all, except for those symphonies he wrote for his appearances in England, where clarinet players were comparatively plentiful at the time. In fact, the regular use of both clarinets and oboes in the same score would appear to date from the First Symphony of Beethoven.

It is not necessary to discuss here in detail the acoustical characteristics of the clarinet, but we may observe that the bore is conical in the lower end and cylindrical in the upper. Some

of the partials are missing and, whereas the flute and oboe over-
blow into the octave, the clarinet overblows into the twelfth.
This brought certain difficulties in fingering which, before the
addition of the keys and the alternative fingerings of the modern
instrument, made it almost impossible to play in a tonality
remote from the fundamental tonality of the instrument. It was
therefore necessary to have instruments of different lengths and
different tonalities. They were all fingered in the same way, and
the different tonalities produced an effect of transposition. This
is why the clarinet is described as a "transposing" instrument.
Most of these clarinets have survived into modern usage: the D,
which sounds a tone higher than written; the Eb, a minor third
higher; the Bb, a tone lower; the A, a minor third lower; the
alto clarinet, a fifth lower; and the bass clarinet, a major ninth
lower. (The alto clarinet is not yet used much in orchestrations,
except in those for brass and reed bands, principally French
ones.) Some composers, including Beethoven, write parts for C
clarinet (sounding the same as written), but for some reason it is
generally felt that the characteristic clarinet tone comes best out
of the Bb and A clarinets. Most orchestra players keep a pair of
these—in Bb for tonalities on the flat side, in A for those on the
sharp side—and many orchestra parts are written with this in
view. The most modern tendency, however, is to play everything
on the Bb instrument and to transpose the parts at sight if
necessary.

Whatever the key of the instrument, the written range for a
clarinet is from E below the treble staff to G on the fourth leger
line above. The *chalumeau* register is from the lower tone to
Bb on the third line of the staff; the *clarinet* register is from B
on the third line of the staff upward. There is a part of the compass
called "the break." It lies between D below the staff and B on
the middle line. The smooth execution of a scale between F on
the first space and C on the third is one of the early difficulties
of a clarinet beginner. Even with fairly experienced players it is

important to be especially attentive to intonation in this area, and it may be found on occasion that these tones may lie at the root of intonation defects in woodwind chords.

As the mouthpiece is held between the upper teeth and the lower lip, which is in contact with the single beating reed, the basic mechanics of tone production are somewhat simpler than with the oboe. The tone is generally a little more secure, but what is gained in security is lost in responsiveness to a slight degree. It is nonetheless a very flexible instrument with a wide dynamic range, except in the highest part of the register. In rapid passages it is more fluent than the oboe. It is almost as fluent as the flute, but to a lesser degree in *staccato* than in *legato*.

In the upper part of the register the tone can be produced quite softly nowadays, at least as far as the C on the second leger line. It often happens in amateur and student orchestras that clarinet players are recruited from high-school and college bands where, although it should not be necessarily so, the notions of what is *forte* and what is *piano* seem to differ from those in a well-behaved orchestra. Clarinets in brass-and-reed bands are allotted principally the style of parts that are allotted to violins in an orchestra. Their general tendency is to play much too loudly, and the attention of these players to dynamic marks may need continuous coaching until good orchestral habits are established.

Parts for D and for Eb clarinet are found, but not too frequently, in scores written since the 1890's. In tone quality and compass they are intended to be an extension of the A or Bb clarinet, but because of their smaller size and a smaller margin for error in their manufacture they too often tend to be flat. They are seldom very reliable instruments, except in the hands of experienced players.

Parts for the bass clarinet are to be found more frequently than for these. Sometimes they are written in the bass clef but most often in the treble clef, in which the sound is an octave lower than for the Bb clarinet. The bass clarinet is similar to the others in its general characteristics; but for various reasons the tone may be somewhat unreliable in the lower part, and there may be a tendency to be flat in the upper part. With a good player it can have a beautifully nostalgic quality, most useful in the development of orchestral color, and it is most frequently used in solo passages that are not very rapid. It would seem to be a good instrument to put into the hands of a player whose ear and general musicality are superior to his manual dexterity.

BASSOON   In the basic principles of its construction, in fingering, and in its general response, the bassoon is very like the oboe but, of course, somewhat less flexible dynamically and less sensitive to the player's personality. Its fluency in passage-playing —both *legato* and *staccato*—makes it useful for solo work, and the firm, rounded tone blends excellently in ensemble passages.

The compass is the same as the oboe's but two octaves lower. The necessary length of tubing for the low range is bent back on itself, first descending from the mouthpiece and then ascending. References to the instrument appear from about the middle of the sixteenth century, at which time both channels were bored from a single piece of wood. For ease and accuracy in manufacture this was divided about the end of the seventeenth century into three parts: the *butt*, through which a U-shaped tube was bored; the *long-joint* and the *wing*, straight tubes which were inserted into the butt, just as in the modern bassoon. It is held upright, and a metal crook, the *bocal*, projects at right angles to hold the reed convenient to the player.

The word "bassoon" is derived from its place, the bass line, in the average chord sequence. The Italian word *fagotto* and the German *Fagott* derive from its appearance: not unlike a bundle of sticks. Its association with the orchestra goes as far back as the flute and oboe do. Until near the end of the eighteenth century, when in common with the other woodwinds it began to have a separate significance in orchestrations, it was used to fortify the lower string parts, just as the oboe was used to fortify the upper parts. Until about the middle of the eighteenth century it was usable only in the bass part of its register. The tenor part was defective and unreliable in regard to intonation. Even in the modern instrument there is a tendency to be unreliable in the tones between D on the third line and G on the fourth space of the bass clef.

Its double reed is assembled in the same way as the oboe's but is made of wider and thicker cane. Its tone production is more secure but not so sensitive as the oboe's, and the dynamic range is somewhat narrower. In regard to embouchure, the common defect is the same as it is with the oboe: a tendency to relax and produce coarseness in the lower tones and to "pinch" the upper tones, which may result in a thin, ineffective quality of tone. There is also a tendency to be sharp at the upper end of the compass, but this is not quite so pronounced as it is with the oboe. The bassoon has one superiority over all the other woodwinds except the flute: rapid passages requiring a separate tongue to each tone may be executed with greater security.

There have been various attempts to devise other instruments to serve as the bass of the family of woodwinds. One of these was a *serpent*—so called because the necessary length of tubing was formed in a spiral instead of being bent back on itself as with the bassoon. Some form or other of this instrument has been known since the sixteenth century, and it survived precariously as an orchestral instrument even until the middle of the last century. Mendelssohn prescribed it in his *Calm Sea and Prosperous Voyage* Overture, but its tone quality was never reliable. It seems that Handel on one occasion described it as "evidently not the serpent that beguiled Eve in the Garden of Paradise."

112

Of the composers of the last century, Mendelssohn seems to have been the most interested in experimenting with bass instruments. In his *A Midsummer Night's Dream* Overture there is a part for *ophicleide,* a keyed brass instrument which was devised in the early part of the century but obsolete almost as soon as it appeared. For the most part, whatever assistance the bassoon needs in the bass line is supplied either by the tuba or the contra bassoon.

As its name implies, the contra bassoon has a compass an octave below that of the bassoon, to which it is similar in most other respects. Because of the low tones with their rather slow rate of vibration through the double reed, it is almost useless in rapidly moving passages but excellent for long tones and slow passages, especially in cases where the bassoon tone may be thought to be too light and the tuba tone too heavy. It was infrequently used in the orchestra until about the time of Brahms, but its value is appreciated by many modern composers. Beethoven knew something of its possibilities. We find it in the last movements of his Fifth and Ninth symphonies.

FRENCH HORN   Like all things having to do with the organization of music, the order in which instruments are listed on a modern score "just growed." That the French horns are now usually placed between the woodwind section and the rest of the brass section is not due to any arbitrary decision but represents a general recognition of their tone quality and their relationship to the orchestra as a whole. In modern usage the tone is not "brassy" except when specially so directed. It is suave and rounded and can be combined effectively with either the brass, the woodwind, or the strings. Indeed it might be described as a sort of orchestral coagulant or, perhaps better, as a sort of solvent of the tone elements in the other groups.

Its name in English is a reminder that it came to England

from France about the beginning of the eighteenth century. It came to France from Bohemia via Germany, and its German name, *Waldhorn*, is a reminder of its association with forest hunting parties. The French called it *cor de chasse*, but it appears simply as *cor* in their orchestra scores nowadays.

It became established in the orchestra during the second half of the eighteenth century, when its shape became roughly the same as that of our modern instrument. At one time, about the beginning of the seventeenth century, its appearance was something like that of a large trumpet. The changes were gradual and are somewhat difficult to trace satisfactorily. It was only during the period when Bach was burgeoning as a composer that the method of holding the horn in the left hand, with the bell facing forward, was changed to that of holding it in the right hand, with the bell facing backward. Bach and his contemporaries would have known something of the effect of the older style of playing. When the bell is held forward there is an effect similar to that of a fanfare trumpet but somewhat coarser and certainly more "brassy" than the horn tone we are accustomed to nowadays.

There are controversies from time to time about whether music of the eighteenth century and earlier should be "modernized" or whether it should be "restored" to what is thought to be its original concepts. Music and its performance are, of course, a living art and whether we play eighteenth- or twentieth-century music the performance is always a part of our contemporary experience. To give too much attention to obsolete instruments and styles of playing may be against the best interests of the art. At the same time it may be useful to remember, for example, that J. S. Bach was accustomed to a much coarser horn tone than we know today. A conductor of a student or amateur orchestra may find himself with poor horn players but with good trumpet players, and it might be a pity if he decided against a performance of some fine music because of a reluctance to use, say, fanfare trumpets instead of horns.

When it came to be associated with the orchestra the question of using the horn with different tonalities arose. The difficulty was solved eventually by having a series of crooks: short tubes of various lengths which, when inserted, altered the over-all length of the instrument with a corresponding alteration in the fundamental tone and its related overtones. This method was continued until the beginning of the nineteenth century, when the valve mechanism, applicable to all brass instruments, was invented. Brahms, in the late nineteenth century, would still not accept the newfangled device. He thought it interfered with the free, open characteristic of the tone and he continued to write for horns in the old style, using crooks giving different fundamental tones. The modern practice is to play all parts—Horn in D, Horn in Eb, Horn in G, and so on—with the F horn. This requires some degree of skill in transposition and is one of the difficulties which beset a player coming newly to orchestra work.

Horns were at first used in pairs, as was the custom in orchestra music until about the end of the eighteenth century. From about 1730 onward there was a custom in the Paris Opéra of having four horns, not in order to provide a full chord—which is their principal use in orchestral tuttis now—but in order to provide with instruments of different length horn tone as required, whatever the tonality of the piece. This was common in operatic music until the early part of the nineteenth century but was not common in purely orchestra music. Mozart specifies four horns in his Symphony No. 25, but not subsequently. Beethoven uses three horns in the "Eroica" Symphony and four in the Ninth, but elsewhere he specifies two. It was not until after the invention of the valve mechanism in the 1830's that scoring for a choir of four horns became the standard practice. This is still the standard practice. The very large orchestrations requiring six or eight horns do not seem to have been permanently established in universal acceptance.

More than any other brass instrument, the French horn requires great delicacy of lip control. The length of the tube corresponds with that of an F tuba, but the diameter of the bore is nearer to that of a trumpet and the mouthpiece is very little bigger than a trumpet mouthpiece. All the other brass instruments are played in a compass using, normally, the first to the seventh overtones. Owing to the combination of a long tube with a narrow bore and a small mouthpiece, the horn normally uses these overtones and those up to the sixteenth as well. In fact, its normal orchestra parts lie between the fourth and the sixteenth overtones.

The following is a comparison of the overtones commonly used by the horn and the trumpet (or any other brass instrument):

EXAMPLE

*Indicates tones for which the notation can be only approximate.

From this it will be seen that it is but a slight exaggeration to say that for most notes written in the normal French-horn part almost any fingering will do; there are so many different tones which can be played by using the lip alone. This makes it imperative for the horn player, more than other brass players, to have an exceptionally good ear and to be able to imagine the tone clearly *before* he plays it, just as we do when whistling a tune; in so many cases the fingering used is almost irrelevant. Wrong notes by inexperienced players are more likely to occur in the horn section than elsewhere in the brass, especially in those

116

passages presenting rhythmic patterns with changing chords.

The horn is muted in two ways: either by inserting the hand into the bell, or by using a mechanical device similar to that used in trumpets and trombones. The insertion of the hand into the bell has the effect of shortening the column of air in vibration and of raising the pitch by a semitone. Before the invention of valves this method was used to play chromatic passages, but it was too clumsy for rapid passages. Its principal use nowadays is for the sake of the change in quality between a "stopped" tone and an open tone. There is, too, a difference in quality between a "stopped" tone and a "muted" tone. It is difficult to describe this difference in words, but the inquisitive beginner conductor will investigate it, no doubt.

TRUMPET   The quality of tone is related to the narrow bore, cylindrical through the greater part of its length. In fact, here is the essential difference between the normal orchestral trumpet and the English cornet (also the German *flügelhorn*). The cornet and the flügelhorn are conical through a greater part of the length of the tube, and the bore is a little wider. They "speak" more easily than the trumpet. The tone is attractive in smooth, *legato* passages but, although sweeter, it lacks something of the brilliant, exciting qualities of the trumpet. In the older scores the writing for trumpet indicates an intention of having it stand out from the surrounding texture. In modern times there is a drift toward a closer integration of the brass with the over-all tone in orchestral tuttis, and trumpets in some places are being made with slightly wider bores and larger mouthpieces. This results in a more rounded, "fat" tone, a little closer to that of the cornet, more flexible in dynamic range, and more gratifying to play in melodies that might be described as "lush." The merits of an increase in flexibility, and so on, at the expense of the dry, clean-cut brilliance of the true orchestral trumpet would seem to be a matter for controversy, but not here. Here it is enough to point out that such differences exist, and the thought might usefully be in the mind of a conductor planning a performance of a Haydn symphony or an excerpt from a Wagner opera.

Up to the early part of the eighteenth century trumpets were used melodically. They were seldom made in a key higher than F, and their use exploited the same series of overtones as did that of the French horn. In fact, many scores of the time carry the direction "Horn or trumpet" or "Horn or clarino," according to the range. From about 1740 onward, the trumpets—with the horns—were relegated to providing harmonic and rhythmic support. This relegation was due to the increasing weight of tone in string instruments and to more frequent changes to remote keys during the course of a piece. Harmonic and rhythmic support, principally in the tonic and dominant sections, was then their principal orchestral use for about one hundred and fifty years. In the last sixty years or so, there has been an increasing tendency to use them again as melodic instruments; but now, because of the use of valves and the chromatic possibilities they present in the lower overtones, they can be exploited in delicate, *pianissimo* passages. A reasonably good idea of the changing uses of the trumpet may be obtained by comparing the trumpet parts of, say, the Bach *Brandenburg* Concerto No. 2, a Mozart or Haydn or Beethoven symphony, and the first movement of *La Mer* by Debussy.

A common defect of a trumpet player who is inexperienced in orchestra work is to play too loudly, and to allow this to happen is a common defect in the inexperienced conductor. Both are inclined to forget that a trumpet can produce a *forte* or a *fortissimo* effect with much less effort than any other brass instrument because the tone can be penetrating as well as dominating. It is well to remember that dynamic marks are to be read in a relative and not in an absolute sense and that the over-all brilliance of an orchestral tutti is not necessarily lost by having the trumpets mitigate their tone as the balance of the chording might demand. When, as frequently happens, the orchestra platform is tiered, the place of the trumpet may be dominating too, and its tone may have a bigger effect in the middle of the concert room than the conductor may realize from his place on the podium. This point is not too important in works written up to the early part of the eighteenth century, and the position is usually safeguarded in modern works in which orchestration values have been calculated to a nicety, but it is an important point in dealing with works written between, say, 1750 and 1860, which covers the largest part of the normal repertory of the student or amateur orchestra.

TROMBONE In the trumpet and French horn the use of valves is to lengthen the tube and to lower the fundamental tone and its related overtones. The first valve lowers the series of tones by a whole tone, the second by a semitone, and the third by three semitones. All three together lower the pitch of the instrument by six semitones. The slide on the trombone fulfills the same function and, counting the closed position as the first, there are seven positions for the slide, each one representing a semitone. The slide can be moved freely to any part along its length but is intended to be used only in one or another of the set positions. A common defect is due to imprecise movement between the positions which results either in an insecure tone with a "muddy" effect or an unpleasant effect of glissando, comparable to "scooping" in a singer. Trombone players may use a slight vibrato in the hand working the slide. This is permissible within narrow limits; it keeps the tone lively, as does the left-hand vibrato of string players. It is not, however, a matter in which players should receive much encouragement, as it can be—and often is—so easily overdone. In any case, it is an effect which should always be used deliberately and should never become an unconscious habit or mannerism.

The principles of construction of a trombone have remained much the same since about the fifteenth century, and the only alterations since that time have been the result merely of refinements in manufacture. As it was capable of following the voice parts through the various tonalities, it was in use in the accompaniment of church music before any other wind instrument. It was used in opera orchestras in the seventeenth century and frequently occurs in opera scores of the early eighteenth century, but seldom as a solo instrument. When the orchestra began to have an existence independent of either church music or the opera the use of trombones was discontinued. Toward the end of the eighteenth century they began to reappear very occasionally in such works as the Mozart *The Magic Flute* Overture (still connected with the theater, as we may notice). Beethoven was among the first to use trombones in the orchestra in absolute music: three in the last movement of the Fifth Symphony, two in the last two movements of the Sixth, and three in the last movement of the Ninth.

The lip tension is naturally less in a trombone than in a trumpet, and it is easier to play softly in the upper part of the compass. Tone quality is variable at will, from a neat and rounded tone, possible even in fortissimo, to an open, "brassy" quality for which the embouchure is slackened slightly. It is well to know these differences in tone quality and to have them in mind, because the best effect in chord-playing—for which trombones are most often used—comes from a unified style between the players. The correct and precise matching of tone is one of the important things for a conductor to consider when he is training the brass section of an orchestra.

Because of the larger mouthpiece, the trombone does not "speak" quite so instantly as does a trumpet, especially in the lower tones. Because of this, the trombone may lag behind slightly in chords requiring both types of instrument. In the early stages of orchestral experience both conductor and player might have this in mind, but the player learns in time to adjust himself automatically to the circumstance. At any time, however, it is well to lead the trombone section with gestures that are especially clear in order to give them every possible assistance in playing with good precision.

Defects in trombone intonation are sometimes hard to trace. In common triads the defect is frequently traceable to whichever one is holding the third of the chord. Between the beginning of the seventeenth century and almost the end of the nineteenth all harmonic procedure was founded on the common triad, and the degree of a composer's skill was measured by his success in handling the "discords," those tones which were regarded as suspensions or anticipations of the "concords," the three tones of the triad. The third is the interval which determines whether the triad is in the major or the minor mode. It is the interval most commonly and naturally chosen by an untutored singer when he tries to improvise a "harmony," but with its comple- ment, the sixth, it is at the same time the most difficult interval to have really in tune. The use of the triad as the basis of harmony is expressed in the use of trombones in a group of three in the normal orchestration, and as trombones are mostly used for harmony and seldom for melody they need to give particular attention to their intonation, especially when one holds the third of a chord.

Another interval which may need attention is the fifth of a chord, not so much because of any problem of intonation, but because it is by its nature "dominant." In any full-orchestra chord it is almost certain that the fifth will be held by one or another of the tenor trombones, and it needs to be used carefully so that it does not become too prominent. In general it would seem best to regard the title of "first trombone" as being merely a matter of convenience, indicating the player who plays the tones that

121

may be the highest but not always the most important in a chord. The best results in tone quality and intonation will come by having the trombones regard themselves not as three instruments but as one.

Although previously trombones were made in many different sizes, there have been but two since the beginning of the nineteenth century. These are the tenor trombone and the bass trombone. The first overtone in the tenor trombone is Bb on the second line of the bass clef, and in the bass trombone it is the F, a fourth lower. The normal compass of both instruments is the same as the trumpet or the tuba: from the first overtone, with its lower extension of an augmented fifth, upward through the seventh overtone. There is also a "combination" trombone, which by means of a rotary valve operated by the left thumb may be used as a tenor or a bass instrument at will, but this is not regarded as a completely satisfactory instrument.

TUBA This instrument has no history before the invention of the valve system, and its appearance in the orchestra dates from the middle of the nineteenth century. The tone is round and agreeable in quality, especially in the middle part of the compass. It is not in any way penetrating and blends excellently with the other brass to which it supplies the bass. In most scores it is used in association with the trombones, but occasionally it may be used in combination with other instruments; a few passages in the first movement of Brahms' Symphony No. 2 provide a case in point. In more modern scores it sometimes attains to brief glory as a solo instrument: for example, in the *Overture to a Picaresque Comedy* by Arnold Bax.

Tubas exist in various lengths from the high Bb (baritone: euphonium), which is prescribed in some Wagner and Richard Strauss scores, to the double-Bb, an octave lower. The normal compass is the same as for other brass instruments: that is, from the first to the seventh overtone. The tubas principally used in orchestras are the double-Bb and the F, pitched a fifth above. The Bb tuba has naturally much more power than the F tuba in tones written below the bass clef, but from D on the third line upward the F tuba is more fluent and secure. As well as the difference in volume, there is a slight difference between them in tone quality. This is mentioned because the custom in this country is to use the Bb tuba, but in Europe, where most of the standard repertory comes from, the custom favors using the F tuba. There may be sometimes a problem in the balance of chords, but for the most part it makes very little difference. It is well to have the possibilities in mind, however.

The tuba has a fourth valve for convenience of fingering in rapid passages. Unlike the valve of the French horn, which raises the fundamental tone, the tuba's fourth valve lowers it by a fourth.

PERCUSSION   The principal function of percussion is in *support* of the musical text. Compared with other sections of the orchestra, the percussion section has not much to do, but this is merely a useless sort of statistic. The performance is the thing, and at a given moment a tingle on a triangle, given with precisely the right weight and timing, may contribute just as much to success as a whole section of first violins. There is much scope for good percussion playing at moments in a piece that are almost always important and sometimes very critical.

The percussion section comprises all those instruments which involve a striking movement for the production of tone. Its foundation is the timpani (kettledrums), which were the first to be used regularly in an orchestra, and the timpanist is the principal among the section of percussion players.

A timpani part implies the use of at least a pair. In scores of the last hundred years or so, the requirement is occasionally for three or more drums. Berlioz goes even so far as to prescribe eight pairs with ten players in his *Requiem Mass*, but the general usage since the eighteenth century is one pair.

The basic principle is that of a skin stretched over the top of what is similar to an old-fashioned boiling kettle. The skin is stretched on a wooden rim which in turn is pressed down over the rim of the kettle. The tension of the stretched skin is varied by turning a series of thumbscrews set around the rim, the pitch of the tone rising and falling with the degree of tension.

To change the pitch of a pair of timpani by twisting seven screws on each one is very cumbersome, and until the invention of a device whereby all seven screws were geared to one master screw a timpanist was not normally expected to change pitch during the performance of a piece. He was generally allotted the tonic and dominant of the basic tonality and made his entrances and exits with the trumpets and horns in tuttis. This restriction was no great hindrance to composers before the nineteenth century because their key schemes did not involve too frequently recurring excursions to remote tonalities. More modern scores have increasingly required alterations in pitch during the course of a single piece—especially since, besides the master screw already mentioned, timpani are being made with a pedal which can alter the pitch as readily as does the pedal of a harp. A pair of timpani, one larger than the other, covers the compass of an octave upward from about F immediately below the bass staff, each drum by itself having a compass of about a perfect fifth. Up to the beginning of the nineteenth century the regular procedure was to allot to a pair of timpani tones having the interval of about a fifth between them. Beethoven is credited with being the first to require that a pair of timpani be tuned at an interval of an octave (the *scherzo* in the Ninth Symphony) and also with being the first to use timpani with the effect of a solo instrument (slow movement in the Fourth Symphony and, to a lesser degree, the slow movement in the First).

No skin is ever perfectly uniform in thickness or texture, and the tension of a stretched skin is never uniform over the whole surface. For both pitch and tone quality the best effect is produced by striking the drum about three inches in from the rim.

So much of the timpanist's effectiveness depends basically on the result of continuous practice in his mastery of a roll that is close, even, and controlled throughout the whole dynamic range that there is little the average conductor can be expected to give by way of *ad hoc* technical advice. At the same time, there are many aspects of a timpanist's work with which the conductor ought to be familiar, and thereby conserve rehearsal time by knowing beforehand how required effects are obtained. One of these is the difference in timbre resulting from the use of drumstick heads of different sizes and consistencies. This is the most common consideration. How does a light stroke with a hard head compare with a firm stroke with a soft, almost fluffy head? What sort of drumstick head produces the best effect in the *andante* of the Beethoven First Symphony? In the *scherzo* of the Fifth? In the *scherzo* of the Ninth? At the beginning of the Rossini *Semiramis* Overture, and so on?

There are conductors who do not give much consideration to what is done in the percussion department and take notice only after something has gone wrong. Those who know something of a percussionist's techniques and let him see that they know may give him much confidence and encouragement, which are likely to produce better results in a section of the orchestra which is just as important as any other section.

SIDE DRUM, TENOR DRUM, AND BASS DRUM Beyond having the characteristic of being higher or lower, the tones produced by these instruments are indeterminate in pitch. The side drum is a shallow cylinder with two rims over which are wound two skins, usually sheepskin. These rims are kept in place by metal rods and thumbscrews which are used to regulate the tension. The upper side is called the "batter head" and the lower the "snare head." Across the snare head there is stretched the *snare*, a small number of strings which are sometimes of gut but more often of coiled wire. The contact of these strings with the snare head brings out that rattling timbre we are accustomed to associate with the side drum.

The roll is based on an alternation of single strokes on the timpani, but on the side drum it is based on an alternation of double strokes or, rather, a single stroke with its rebound. The stroke is made about one and a half inches in from the rim. In the course of a crescendo the best effect is obtained by allowing the point of striking to drift in from the rim toward the center and reversing the process for a diminuendo.

The side drum can produce many different qualities of tone by such means as the following: by slackening the snare instead of having it taut; by slackening the skin of the batter head; by muffling the batter head with a cloth; by using different kinds of timpani sticks instead of side-drum sticks; by flams, drags, and the many variations in the production of accent. It is possible that the combination of right- and left-hand strokes may need to be as carefully considered as a question of bowing on a string instrument. There is a clear distinction in the effect of the two examples following:

EXAMPLE (a) EXAMPLE (b)

There is also a subtle but easily noticeable difference between a succession of strokes played with one hand only, a succession played by alternating single strokes with each hand, and by alternating the strokes two at a time. An illustration of this is provided by comparing rehearsal-letter *K* in the last movement of the Rimsky-Korsakov *Scheherazade* and "Tambourin" from *Trois*

Danses pour Orchestre by Maurice Durufle. The combination of strokes used will make some difference in the effect in cases of this kind. No recommendation is made here except that the conductor consider before rehearsal exactly what he wants and how best the percussionist will satisfy him.

The tenor drum is similar to the side drum, but the cylinder is wider and there is no snare on the under-head. As its name implies, its tone of indeterminate pitch has a quality that places it between the side drum and the bass drum. It is not often prescribed in orchestra scores.

The orchestra bass drum is supported on a low cradle and is struck with a soft-headed stick. The best tone quality comes from a glancing blow across the center, but for an occasional special effect it may be struck directly to produce a dull, impacted tone quality. It was called the "Turkish Drum" until about 1800, as it had been introduced into Europe as part of the "Turkish Band." The other instruments in this group were the cymbals, triangle, gong, glockenspiel, and so on. At first these were used in operatic presentations to heighten the effect of "exotic" or "Eastern" scenes. They did not appear in scores of purely orchestral music until after the beginning of the nineteenth century, although they had been used in military bands before that. One of the first examples in orchestra music is the use of cymbal and triangle in the *alla marcia* variation in the last movement of the Beethoven Ninth Symphony.

The cymbals—a pair of circular, concave, metal disks—are sounded by being clashed across each other. A direct hit is never desirable. Besides the possibility of splitting the disks, the tone so produced is dull and unpleasant. Depending on the diameter of the disks, the tone may vibrate for as much as five seconds, and the usual method of terminating it at will is to bring the edges in contact with the player's chest. A wide dynamic range is possible. There is the rapid clash, followed by raising them above the player's head and facing them toward the audience.

There is a medium or a slow stroke, followed by lowering them to the player's sides. There is a clash by merely touching the edge of one against the edge of the other. An interesting variation is that recommended by Debussy for the end of the second movement of *La Mer.* Here the music has evaporated into thin air, as it were, and the last sound is a cymbal tone played *pianissimo.* He recommended placing the cymbals together noiselessly beforehand and separating them suddenly at the required instant. As a result of the sudden separation, they are set in vibration by the suction of air and there is brought into being a wonderful, gently pulsating tone just above the level of audibility.

Cymbal tone is sometimes required to be produced by having one disk suspended and struck by either timpani or side-drum sticks, either with single strokes or in a roll. If a *crescendo* roll is required, the effect is best produced by beginning the roll near the center and working out gradually toward the edge. This is, obviously, because the metal vibrates through a wider amplitude at the edge. Possibly the reverse process is useful if a *diminuendo* roll is required, but as a normal thing a *diminuendo* roll on the cymbal is scarcely a practical proposition.

Cymbals are made in various diameters from about eighteen inches to as small as three. For single clashes occurring at infrequent intervals, such as those made to reinforce a long-expected musical climax, the wider the diameter the better, because it produces more "tone" and less "noise." However, a too wide cymbal may be unmanageable, as for example in the rapid syncopations which come at the end of the Tchaikovsky Fourth Symphony; a smaller cymbal, even with a smaller tone, may be found more useful here.

Cymbals are made either by beating out a brass sheet to the required diameter or by beating a wire into a coil. A good beaten-brass cymbal has usually the better tone, but a good coiled-wire cymbal tends to last longer.

Gongs of various diameters are required also from time to time. These differ from cymbals in that the surface is not concave but flat and the edges are bent in at right angles to the main surface. The result is that the amplitude of the vibration is greater at the center and the process of producing a crescendo is the reverse of that with a cymbal. The gong is suspended by a line through an edge and is struck with a soft-headed stick in a manner similar to that of the bass drum.

Many other instruments find their way into the percussion department, such as the *tambour Basque,* castanets, tubular bells, sleigh bells, wood block and, less frequently, a wind machine, an anvil, a bull-roarer, and such devices as a pair of cannons for gala performances of the Tchaikovsky "1812" Overture. In more recent times the possibilities of the various types of percussion instruments in use in South American and Far Eastern countries have been explored by composers. It is not necessary to give much consideration to these, unless a specific performance using them is in mind, when the conductor will take care to inform himself beforehand of exactly the type of tone produced by each one. In the normal repertory the instruments most commonly used are those already mentioned: the timpani, the side drum, tenor and bass drums, cymbals, triangle, and gong.

STRING INSTRUMENTS As it is organized now-adays, the string section is the core of the orchestra. In fact, the orchestra is really a string orchestra to which other instruments are added in groups that are more or less stabilized but vary from one score to another. For that reason, the quality of an orchestra is principally determined by the quality of the string-playing. The technical problems involved in good string-playing are, of course, endless, but the principal problem for the average conductor is that of bowings and bowing style. Unanimity in the attack and release of phrases, all the variations in dynamic, all the requirements in expressive playing depend so much on having the parts bowed and played correctly.

Bowing is intimately related to a personal playing style, and a bowing calculated to produce the best effect with one player will not necessarily be the best for another. Indeed, it is not so frequently found that any one experienced player will agree entirely with another in a bowing detail. One of the more eminent conductors of our time has allowed his string players to bow at will. The results, although excellent, might better be ascribed to the very high quality of the individual players at his command than to the method of allowing them to bow at will. With the average professional orchestra and most certainly with the average student or amateur orchestra, the best effects are obtained by means of unanimity of bowing throughout the strings. Decisions on bowing and bowing style need therefore be taken in which the conductor must be the final arbiter because he is the one who is finally responsible for the effect of the performance.

For his effectiveness in rehearsal and especially in his preparation for rehearsal, the conductor needs a thorough knowledge of the effects of different bowings. Most bowing decisions will be obvious, but in borderline cases, unless he himself has had training as a string player, he ought to consult his concertmaster in an amateur orchestra or the string teacher behind a student situation. There is no abdication of his responsibilities involved in this; he is responsible for the results and for seeing to it that the means of achieving these results are correctly determined.

The ability of the players, some of whom may be good and some less good, needs to be considered in matters of bowing. Especially in non-professional situations, clarity and unanimity of style may conceivably have precedence over the higher aesthetic possibilities. It is possible to imagine choosing a set of bowings, ideal for certain passages and practicable with the first desk or two of a section but which, being beyond the skill of the back-desk players, would inevitably produce an effect of untidiness. The development of the player's skill by pressing him into practicing and achieving something beyond the current state of his technical ability is admittedly a most important objective for the conductor of the student or amateur orchestra. At the same time, the requirement of preparing for public presentation a performance which, although not ideal, is competent, tidy, and acceptable may reasonably introduce an element of what we may call "administrative caution" into his thinking on the subject of bowing.

Beginning at measure 17 in the first movement of the Brahms Symphony No. 2 in D, there is a long diminuendo phrase for the first violins. With really good players it is possible to take the whole phrase in two bows. It is a risky procedure, but when it comes off successfully the progressive attenuation of tone and the slight sense of anxiety that goes with it—communicable to the cellos and basses that come in later—produce with the *pianissimo* timpani roll at measure 33 a moment that is truly arresting and breath-taking. With less good players, bow changes will have to be indicated according to their ability in bow control and, although the changes will make for more security, the breathlessly dramatic quality of the diminuendo will be more difficult to realize.

Another example of a case in which it may be necessary to decide between what is ideal and what is practicable might be, say, measures 79 to 82 in the last movement of the Haydn Symphony No. 93. Here the question is whether *all* the players have enough control to play the staccato passage cleanly and securely by taking the notes in groups with a springing up-bow near the point instead of by using a thrown staccato with the more comfortable middle part of the bow. The primary consideration here is that of neatness, and to attempt the ideally feathery

131

quality of lightness without being sure of the neatness may be just so much waste of time.

The determination of bowing detail is very much a matter of individual opinion and, besides, it depends on circumstances which vary between one orchestral situation and another. There are, however, some generalizations which might usefully be considered here, together with an examination of the effect of the more commonly used bowing strokes. Many of these points will no doubt be already familiar to string players but not, perhaps, in their particular relationship to orchestra work.

One point is that there is no valid reason why the circumstances of playing solo or in a quartet or in an orchestra should make any real difference in the choice of bowing. Differences do exist, but primarily because soloists and quartet players are usually more skillful than the *average* string player in an orchestra and are, besides, more immediately conscious of the effect of small detail. Too often orchestra players feel they ought to produce a tone larger than life size. Perhaps this is because of the excitement of orchestra work and of a laudable desire to "give of their best." Perhaps it is because of a feeling that if they do not produce the volume of tone they will be overpowered by the woodwind and brass. Sometimes this fear is real enough. There may be too few strings in the ensemble, or there may have been a miscalculation in orchestration by the composer, but normally the fear is unjustified.

Every type of instrument has its natural maximum weight of tone, and any attempt to exceed this can only result in an overstrain and a deterioration in quality. The correct balance of tone between the different sections of an orchestra is a matter for the conductor to worry about and, if there is danger that a certain essential passage in strings will be obscured, he will be well advised to have the others play more softly rather than to have the strings press out their tone unduly. As we know, dynamic marks exist in their relationship to each other. They express

132

degrees of variation and contrast rather than levels of tone volume in an absolute sense. To have this in mind and to impress it on the string players will help them to avoid some of their more common hazards in orchestra work; namely, the progressive development of an individual coarseness of tone and an insensitiveness of phrasing. Besides, the control of tone in a pianissimo or a diminuendo is the most important element in good ensemble work. To play *forte* or *crescendo* always seems to come more naturally and easily—too easily, in fact. As a matter of drill and training it is normally better to encourage an orchestra to play on the light side during rehearsal. A continued bias toward lightness will draw their attention to the importance of observing minute detail and will help to keep in their minds the thought that the greatest part of good music-making is a matter of mental rather than physical effort.

In addition to forcing the tone, inexperienced players in an orchestra tend to forget what they have previously learned about using the different parts of the bow; they tend to use the middle of the bow altogether too much. This part is easier to control than either the upper or lower parts. Even when special bowings have been marked and rehearsed, student and amateur players— and, indeed, professional players occasionally—are inclined to revert to the more comfortable middle part. The tendency should be watched closely until good habits have been developed, until the players know their orchestra part as thoroughly as is usually the case with a solo or a quartet part.

When the bow is not drawn out freely in a *forte* passage there may be an overcompensatory pressure and a coarseness of tone. When too much of the bow or the wrong part of it is used in a *pianissimo* passage the pressure may be too light, and the results may be insecurity and scratchiness. Unless the players use the bow freely in every part of it, as they would expect to do in solo or quartet work, the over-all loss of vitality and expressiveness will defeat the personal force of even the strongest-minded conductor. There will be, to use Wagner's phrase, "no true forte and no true piano."

Another common tendency, especially but not exclusively with inexperienced players, is to begin every down-bow near the frog and every up-bow near the point, whether the phrase to be played is long or short, *piano* or *forte*. This defect produces dynamic variations that are unintentional and does more than almost anything else to spoil the shape of phrases and to give an effect of musical immaturity. A phrase such as the following, if played without due thought to the point of entry of the bow, is likely to sound as marked, whatever the conductor might do or expect:

EXAMPLE BRAHMS 2

Brahms: Symphony No. 2, Slow movement measure 27

This phrase has a gentle, nostalgic quality whenever it appears in the piece. The crescendo in the orchestra should be smooth at this point, but the violist has no need to worry about the volume of his tone. The whole effect of crescendo is really taken care of by the orchestration itself, principally through the trombone and tuba and through the successive entries of the second and first violins.

There is also a tendency, very natural and very common, to play any ascending passage with an involuntary increase of tone and a descending passage with a diminution of tone. Within reasonable limits this tendency should not be too much discouraged as it represents a natural instinct in preserving the vitality of the phrase line. It is possible that a too rigidly precise adherence to dynamic marks may produce a stodgy impression, and it is well to allow phrases to be developed with every natural freedom consistent with the context. That such a natural tendency exists, however, is something to keep in mind, because occasions occur when it is essential to have an ascending passage played without any hint of a crescendo and even with a diminuendo.

In theory, a player should be able to produce any dynamic level as well with a down-bow as with an up-bow. But the pressure of the bow is regulated by the index finger of the bow hand and, obviously, it is easier to exert pressure on the part near to the hand than on the part farther away. Solo players can concentrate on what they are doing to the exclusion of everything else, but orchestra players are subject to distractions of many kinds, and it is wise to have the bowing conform to natural, unthinking tendencies of this kind whenever possible. If no contrary reason appears in the context it is better as a rough-and-ready rule to have a crescendo played with an up-bow, moving from the point of the lesser to the point of the greater natural pressure, and to have a diminuendo played with a down-bow.

Most technical resources, however good in themselves, can be the basis of playing faults if they are not always used deliberately and for a conscious artistic purpose. It is in their habitual or unconscious use that the trouble lies. One of these faults is increasing or decreasing the tone involuntarily in the course of a single bow stroke. This may be due to an unconscious variation in muscular control or, perhaps, to misguided notions of what is "expressive" playing. Faulty notions of what is "expressive" playing may also lead to the *habitual* use of *portato*, a defect that is particularly tiresome to the listener. There is also the fault of a habitual accent at the beginning of a tone or a phrase, which is common especially among orchestra players who desire to make a "clean" beginning. On the other hand, there may sometimes be observed a habit of beginning too carefully and coming to the correct dynamic level only after the tone has been begun. In a *forte* passage players anxious to do their best may tend habitually to throw the bow onto the string from a slight distance above. Sometimes this is good, but there are times when it might be better—in the interests of precision—to take hold of the string by a slight bow pressure before the beginning of the tone.

Strong tone is produced either by little bow and strong pressure near to the bridge or by much bow and less pressure farther away from the bridge. Of the two, the first might seem to the player to produce the strongest tone but, if there can be a choice regarding the musical text, the second is heard more effectively at a distance. As the source of the second method is nearer the center of the string, the amplitude of the vibration is wider, and this gives the tone a greater penetrative and carrying power.

The following is a list of the more common bowing usages, with a short account of their effect in performance. No description, however clearly worded, can be a substitute for the experience of actual hearing. A beginner conductor who has not been trained in string instruments should seek every opportunity of becoming familiar with the audible results of the various types of bowing so that he knows exactly what he is about when he is preparing music for rehearsal.

Vibrato   This is a matter closely bound up with the personality of the player and, as it is so much a matter of personal good taste, it is one of the more difficult problems in string-playing. When overdone, it leads to a variation in pitch as unpleasant as that of a large but worn-out singing voice and, when underdone, to a tone quality that tends to be dull and lacking in vitality. At the same time, the deliberate and continuous use of vibrato in every context is a comparatively modern innovation. It was not yet accepted as a normal habit in the time of Leopold Mozart, and a conductor might do well to make himself familiar with the effects of *cantilena* passages played with and without vibrato. It is reasonable to think that what is good in Tchaikovsky is not always good in Corelli, for example.

Pizzicato This is more commonly found in works written since the beginning of the nineteenth century than in works written earlier. The best natural point for plucking the strings is just about two inches from the bridge. The tone has a hard and brittle quality nearer the bridge, and over the finger board the tone is weak. The volume of tone in a *pizzicato* passage does not carry any too well, and a common defect of orchestra players is to try to do too much with it when the passage is marked *forte* and over. If a *pizzicato* passage is not sufficiently audible against an accompanying orchestral texture, it is a matter for the conductor to work out in other ways. To pluck the string too violently can only result in the noise of its slapping against the finger board. At all times *pizzicato* tone should be produced by a left-to-right movement and not upward from below the string.

The principal and most easily noticeable defect in orchestral *pizzicato* passages is a lack of precision owing, in part, to lack of unanimity in playing style. Because the tiniest lack of precision is so much more noticeable in *pizzicato* passages than in bowed passages, the matter needs the special attention of the conductor, both by careful drill at rehearsal and by the extra clarity of his gesture during performance.

Martelé In French the verb *marteler* means "to hammer: to labor." In a musical context the word signifies the production of tone with a rigid, clearly defined quality. The bow arm is used without any separate wrist movement. If the resource is overused, as we sometimes notice in performances of music by J. S. Bach and his contemporaries, there is a loss in the lyrical qualities of a performance. As the style can be produced either with the top, middle, or heel of the bow with slightly differing results, it is well to make sure that for sake of unanimity each member of a string section uses the same part of the bow in a given *martelé* passage.

Staccato The varieties of staccato effects in bowing are almost endless, but the main division is between "sprung" staccato and "thrown" staccato. In a sprung staccato, as its name implies, the bow is allowed to spring, and the succession of tones comes from a succession of controlled rebounds. This style, obviously, is easier with the upper half than with the lower half of the bow and is also easier with an up-bow than with a down-bow. It is scarcely effective, of course, in a slow or a moderately slow tempo. The thrown staccato is more often used than any other kind because it is usable at any tempo and with any part of the bow, the bow being thrown, as it were, at the string with a quick wrist movement.

A conductor ought to be readily familiar, too, with such audible effects as the following:

Sul ponticello This indicates that the bow ought to be drawn across the strings near to the bridge with the intention of producing a thin, clear quality of tone.

Sulla tastiera The bow is drawn across the strings in the area of the finger board to produce a dimly outlined quality, useful in *piano* passages of a nostalgic nature. The tone quality might be described as something halfway between tone naturally produced and that produced with muted strings.

Col legno The bow is turned so that the wood, instead of the hair, is brought in contact with the strings. It is used only for staccato passages with rhythmic patterns and appears only at a tempo suitable for sprung staccato. It is a comparatively modern innovation and occurs only in modern scores. "The Wasps" Overture by Vaughan Williams and the last movement of the Rachmaninoff Piano Concerto No. 2 provide cases in point.

Al punta This indicates that the three or four inches near the point of the bow are to be used. It is applicable to any variation of *legato* or *staccato* style and is indicated in passages requiring a special delicacy and lightness in quality. It is a resource that is tiring for the player and should not be indicated for long stretches at a time.

Au talon This indicates using the bow at the part near the nut. With only moderately expert players there is an almost unavoidable tendency to play *forte*, but it is most useful in passages requiring a firm *martelé* or *staccato* quality.

These and other resources of bowing techniques are usually indicated in the scores of music composed during the last hundred years or so, when composers had become conscious of the value of a precise application to matters of detail in orchestra work. There are many occasions, however, when the addition of bow marks may help to clarify the composer's thought and bring it more securely to realization during a performance. This is especially true of music written before the middle of the nineteenth century, when composers paid little attention to bowing detail in orchestra work. Those eighteenth-century compositions which are now part of the modern standard repertory have been edited by many hands, some excellent and some less so. In dealing with modern editions of these works, it is well to remember that, while the bowing marks may represent the editor's views on good string-playing, they may also represent his views on interpretation of the music. A conductor who has difficulty in having a passage come out exactly as he feels it ought to may find that his difficulties disappear after a careful revision of the bow marks and their effects.

Bow marks are primarily intended to solve problems in playing and to clarify interpretative concepts. They might also be considered useful in making "foolproof" the achievement of certain intended orchestral effects. Even the best of players are subject to distraction and are liable to forget something during a performance. With a strict drill in the observation of bow marks during rehearsal, it might be hoped that the unconsciously used muscular memory may be there to support the consciously used mental memory during a performance. (There are, as we know, three kinds of memory: visual, muscular, and mental.)

If a *subito pianissimo* is indicated in the course of a *tremolando* passage, the addition of the mark *al punta* at that point, fortified by a little drill, may help to ensure that the effect comes off whether or not the player consciously remembers it at the fleeting instant of performance. Many other instances—such as the use of an up-bow in a phrase marked *crescendo*, of successive down-bows for an effect of deliberation in appropriate passages, and so on—will occur to the conductor who knows his bowing effects and who has them in mind when he is preparing the music for performance.

Programs

In a musically mature community the musician's reputation depends as much on the design of his programs as on the artistry and technical skill of his performance, for the design of his programs is a part of his art. In such a community he may rightly concern himself principally with the expression of his personal tastes. Etienne Gilson, in his *Choir of Muses*, touches upon this point when he says, "An artist makes things to satisfy himself and hopes that what he makes will afterward be acceptable to his public."

To adhere exclusively to his personal predilections in the matter of program design can be a practical proposition in the case of the individual artist. With the support of relatively small audiences he can at least hope to make his living, and small audiences can be expected to co-operate by their having a fairly high *average* of taste and experience. The case is not quite the same with the conductor of an orchestra in the social organization of our times. He needs to consider public support on a much broader basis, in which the average of taste and experience will

141

be much lower—outside the four or five main metropolitan centers of the world, at any rate. If he is the conductor of a community orchestra, the matter is further complicated by the need to consider what his players can do and, probably, to consider the present state and the future development of the audience's listening repertory.

In program design it is undoubtedly reasonable that a conductor should, as an artist, allow due weight to the effect of his own taste. At the same time, it is useful to remember that he is a leader and therefore a servant of the community in which he finds himself. This may appear to him to involve a compromise with his artistic integrity, but it is not necessarily so. To combine successfully the factor of his own taste with other relevant factors can be a project requiring a high degree of artistic perception and technical ability. John Ruskin (*Two Paths*, lecture ii) describes fine art as "that in which the hand, the head, the heart of man go together," and we might apply this description to the art of program design. In our context, "the hand" might be defined as the technical equipment of the conductor, the extent of his knowledge of the total repertory; "the head," as his intention of integrating that knowledge with the capabilities of his players and the *real* needs—actual and potential—of his audience; "the heart," as his general musicality and artistic integrity, qualities which would embrace and inform the other two.

The late Sir Henry Wood once made an interesting remark on this subject. He had a great skill in program design and in the development of program policy, and his career might be described as one of the principal sources of contemporary British orchestral activities. His London "Prom" concerts—begun about sixty years ago, and now with the collaboration of the British Broadcasting Corporation a permanent feature of English musical life—presented in the early days such items as "Trumpet solo: *The Lost Chord*" and potpourris of tunes from then

142

popular musical comedies. At the same time, his progressive policy embraced the first performance in England of many works by Wagner, Tchaikovsky, Debussy, and Sibelius, for example. In recent years the summer session of forty-eight concerts (every night for eight weeks) presents annually some fifty or sixty new works before audiences which vary between seven thousand on "thin" nights to ten thousand on a "Beethoven night." In contributing to this state of affairs, Sir Henry's central doctrine appears to have been: "A conductor is the leader of his musical community. If his ideas, however sound and progressive, are too much in advance of his followers, he loses contact with them. A leader who loses contact with his followers is no longer their leader."

It is not too customary to regard an artist as a realist. A "realist" is generally understood to be a person—usually a hardheaded businessman or politician—who grinds on ruthlessly toward an objective. In this sense, a conductor who thinks only of the box office may be described as a realist, as might also one who thinks only of himself, of his personal artistic needs and how to express them, of the development of his personal public relations. This concept of realism is not altogether valid, because it implies the selection of convenient considerations and the ignoring of those which, although quite important, may appear to be inconvenient for the time being. A true realist is one who neglects no discoverable factor relevant to a given situation, who makes no selection between them, but considers them all and integrates them all in order of their relative importance. This is what a true artist does in any art work. In this sense it may be thought that the truest artist is also the truest realist and, in program design, the one most likely to be successful in the long run.

The three main elements in the design of programs are the conductor's taste, the orchestra's ability, and the audience's requirements, all of which are about of equal importance. A conductor's preferences are entitled to much weight in the design of his programs and might, therefore, be considered first. A conductor prefers that music with which he feels the closest affinity, psychologically and temperamentally, and which is therefore that music most likely to receive the best performance under his direction. In allowing his personal preferences to inform his choice of items, he is beginning with "the heart" of Ruskin's description of fine art. He might therefore draw up the first draft of a program strictly according to his own preferences and without regard to any other factor. It happens so rarely as to be negligible, however, that a conductor's preferences are completely congruent with the players' abilities, through which the program is to be realized, and the capacities of the audience, for whom the program is given and without whom the orchestra cannot continue to exist. A second draft, and perhaps more, will be necessary, but by beginning with his own preferences a conductor's personal taste is felt all the way through to the final draft.

Although a consideration of the players' abilities would seem to be the next item on our list, we ought to consider first the audience's requirements. Otherwise we might find ourselves considering technical difficulties too soon, with the inevitable temptation to side-step them or be stopped by them, a procedure fatal to all enterprise. When we have achieved some correlation of the conductor's and the audience's requirements, we shall have an idea of what is necessary to be done. We may then approach the technical difficulties from another and better point of view; namely, how best we may get over and through them instead of how we may avoid them.

In these days of market analyses, referendums, and so on, there is much reliance on the evaluation of questionnaires and surveys as a means of discovering the public's desires in any given matter. It is probable (but perhaps not altogether certain) that the method is a reliable one in most cases affecting the sale of commodities, such as automobile accessories, cereals, and hotel accommodations. But items such as these have a limited and superficial effect on living and being, and their desirable attributes are comparatively easily assessed. To discover the *actual* and *potential* needs of the public in such a field as orchestra music is much more complicated, and it is unwise to place any sort of unconditional reliance on what are likely to be self-conscious replies to a questionnaire. In trying to evaluate the true needs of his audience, the conductor is not so much in the position of a market analyst as in that of a doctor required to make a diagnosis and produce a prescription. A doctor regards what a patient says as indicative rather than definitive, and a conductor's attitude must be the same toward specific requests for pieces of music; his closest approximation to what the audience really needs is based on the composite effect of what he hears rather than on attention to any one set of requests. His decisions on what to do about these needs are then based on his own professional knowledge and competence and, if possible, on previous experience of the same audience.

It is all very much a matter of good "intelligence work," of the collation of impressions and information collected as unobtrusively as possible from various sources on social and other occasions. In any case, to encourage specific requests and not be able to or not intend to comply with them exactly may easily leave a greater or lesser residue of disappointment and may, perhaps, end eventually in bad public relations.

Probably the best and largest single source of the needed "pointers" is to be found in the orchestra committee itself. The members are likely to be representative and to have a comprehensive view of the whole operation of the orchestra. What they have to say on program policy is likely to be representative, too. At the same time, this is a delicate area because in program design, as in other aspects of his art, the conductor, being an artist, will occasionally find himself in the position of knowing he is right without being able, altogether, to justify his views in set terms. Conflicts of view may and do occur. In such cases it would seem best that the conductor prevail or, at least, that the general attitude should be the same as in any other professional situation: either accept the advice or change the adviser.

All large groups, such as those that support orchestras, are divided into a small but vocal minority and a large but inarticulate majority. In small communities the minority comprises those enthusiasts who themselves perform or who collect phonograph records. In large urban communities we might add to these the "intellectuals" who frequent concerts and also the music critics, whose work in daily journalism is a comparatively recently added element in music-making. Because of familiarity with the details of works in the standard repertory and for other reasons, the minority group is inclined to seek for novelty and for new compositions. This in itself is good and sound and progressive.

It is likely that a conductor's acquaintances will be largely drawn from such a minority and that he will be in continuous touch with their views. At the same time, it is wise to keep steadily in mind that, although his professional reputation may depend on the minority, the support for his orchestra depends very much on the majority group—which, although inarticulate, readily recognizes when its real needs have been satisfied. The majority is never really satisfied by what we may call "pandering," but on the other hand it can be confused and discouraged by too much that is strange and unfamiliar. It is good, therefore, to be levelheaded and, if need be, courageous in preserving a balance between the pressures of both groups on the design of programs.

In every vital activity—and art work is nothing unless it is alive—the essential principle of growth depends on the critical balance between what is static and what is dynamic, between stability and mobility, between what is conservative and what is progressive, between what is proven and what is yet to be proved. New paths cannot be begun or explored or enjoyed unless against a background of familiar pastures. As the conductor is at the center of the activities of an orchestra, there are therefore many demands on his good judgment and common sense as well as on his perceptions as an artist in the design of programs.

A conductor might also regard himself as being somewhat in the position of a director of a museum of fine arts, but with the important difference that, whereas the museum director can display his masterpieces, both old and new, at the same time, a conductor may display the masterpieces of music only one at a time. When the members of the ordinary public go to a museum they may make their own choice of what they will look at; they may take their time examining the works in detail and return at will. Orchestra audiences can savor the pleasures of music and develop their listening repertory only through the choice made by the conductor—and the memorable qualities of his performance.

An inordinate desire for novelty and excitement is a mark of immaturity and adolescence, and the widening of experience does not necessarily mean the deepening of experience. Of the two, the latter is the more important for the artistic development of both performer and listener. That so many profess to be bored with so many of the standard classics is less a reflection on the works themselves than on the tendency toward routined, precisely machined performances. A freshness of outlook is welcomed by an audience at any time, whether the comparatively inexperienced audience of a provincial center or the sated, sophisticated audience of a large and concentrated urban area; and without being a mere innovator, without messing about with the tempo, it is still possible to produce a fresh reading of even the Beethoven Fifth Symphony.

In the field of unfamiliar works it is not always necessary to

147

produce those of which the style will be strange to the audience. Handel spent the greatest part of his life in writing opera for the London stage. There are many fine arias to be culled from *Solomon,* for example. How many can even name another of his operas, of which there are nearly fifty in all? It is possible to make interesting use of his twelve *Concerti Grossi* and of many other instrumental and vocal pieces without sticking monotonously to his *Messiah,* the "Water Music," the famous *Largo,* and the minuet from *Berenice.* There are six symphonies by his contemporary, William Boyce: lively, invigorating, and finely written works which are never heard of or, to quote W. S. Gilbert, "well, hardly ever." There is much delightful music by eighteenth-century composers which never appears in the concert hall but which is resurrected most successfully from time to time by compilers of ballet-music scores. There is an excellent symphony in D by Cherubini and also one in A by Boccherini, and three or four piano concertos by John Field, all charming and comparatively easy to play. Haydn, who wrote over a hundred symphonies, is represented in current repertory by four or five of the later ones. Even Brahms, whose music is pretty well represented in the standard repertory, still has something to offer. His two Serenades for orchestra are delightful works, not too difficult but seldom heard. There is also his *Rinaldo*— for tenor, male chorus, and orchestra—which, except for a performance about five years ago, has not been heard anywhere since the first performance.

There is a large list of fine works of composers whose names are bandied about in lectures and books of reference and which seldom appear on concert programs. They might be classed with the long list of literary masterpieces that nearly everyone knows about and can talk about but which very few have actually read. It is still quite possible to find good pieces of unfamiliar music which would not frighten off those "who do not know much about music but like a good tune," music which might attract those with some experience but not enough to give them a self-confident, healthy, and informed interest in unfamiliar music, and which may arouse the curiosity and interest of those who, a little preciously, may be "bored with Beethoven."

All this is by no means an argument against "modern" music. There is not, in simple, any reason why a program designer should classify works as "modern" or "old-fashioned," or otherwise. Either a piece is suitable for inclusion in a program or it is not. The only classification is whether a piece is "alive" and therefore worth the trouble of rehearsal or whether it is moribund. In this sense, *Tristram Shandy* is just as much alive as *Finnegans Wake* (and may possibly outlive it), and the works of Cimabue are as modern as those of Picasso. The Mozart masterpieces are as modern as the day they were written, but the symphonies of Stamitz would seem to have been dead with their first performance, just as many works produced in, say, the last twenty years. For inclusion in the common repertory of the players and the listeners, each single piece, "modern" or "old-fashioned," should be considered with an open mind and solely on its merits: Is it at least interesting enough to warrant its inclusion? Is its inclusion desirable now or at another time? Are the players equal to its technical demands? If not, are adequate rehearsals possible? How does it fit into the general scheme of the program or programs under consideration?

Because it tends toward a doctrinaire attitude, generalized publicity on behalf of contemporary music does more harm than good. It may result in a conductor being unreasonably pressured into presenting a poor work simply because it is "modern." At the same time, a really good contemporary work might miss adequate recognition by a public whose natural instinct is to resist overt general propaganda and pressuring, however noble the objective.

Having in mind these considerations and such others as may occur to him, the conductor may hope to reach a reliable estimate of the style and quality of programs which will best express both his own and his audience's requirements. The next step is to select the items which will best accord with this style and quality. In the average professional situation, with an experienced orchestra and conductor supported by what is probably an experienced audience, the selection of the items is comparatively easy, almost a matter of routine detail. But for the conductor of the community amateur-cum-professional orchestra or the student orchestra, there are still some matters to be carefully considered.

TWO

When describing the personnel of a community orchestra, the routine newspaper phrase has it that it comprises "a cross section of the community, doctors, salesmen, housewives and others who have come together for the enjoyment of good music." To the conductor this "cross section" comprises, not doctors and housewives as such, but persons who, as in every community, have greater or less skill as instrumentalists, who have greater or less inclination to practice between rehearsals, and whose taste in music may be much more highly developed than their technical proficiency. It is necessary to balance the ability with the desires of players who, after all, have no need to participate in performances of music they do not care for. A conductor must consider his own position, too, because as a conscientious professional he cannot ever afford to stand over a performance so technically inadequate as to be an outright distortion of the music selected. The "Interlude" and "Waltz Scene" from *Intermezzo* by Richard Strauss is much easier than, say, the *Rosenkavalier* waltzes, but might be expected to fill the same sort of audience and program requirement. (In fact, it might even be more interesting because less familiar.) A pressure for something from Ravel might be met with *Le tombeau de Couperin* (if the oboe player is up to it) instead of *Ma Mère l'Oie*, which may be too well known, or the *Rhapsodie espagnole*, which may be too difficult. By his knowledge of the repertory a conductor may hope to solve most such problems.

It is rarely found that a community orchestra is strong in every section. In the general interest, it may be necessary to decide whether to make the choice of pieces such as will either exploit the stronger section or give the weaker section an opportunity to work hard and improve itself. If the program requirement indicates a large and "exciting" work it is useful to remember that the average Sibelius symphony is less demanding on the technical dexterity of string players than is the average Tchaikovsky one but requires a somewhat higher degree of refinement in the brass ensemble. The string parts in a Mozart symphony are not usually as difficult as in one by Haydn, and the wind parts in both are easier than those usually found in J. S. Bach.

In general, the best scope for amateur players is to be found in music that depends for its main effectiveness more on the actual musical values than on orchestration values. With music that is within their executant ability amateurs, because of their freshness of approach, may hope to produce musical results sometimes difficult to realize on every occasion with professional players, for whom music can be a daily grind as well as an art and a vocation.

With the exception of the few who may be studying music as an agreeable pastime, the average student orchestra comprises those who, when they leave college, will become either teachers of music or performers of music, such as orchestra players. In either case, they will need a comprehensive idea of the orchestra repertory. The capacity of future music teachers to direct classes of music appreciation, for example, will be increased by the fact that their knowledge is derived from first-hand practical experience and not exclusively from analysis studies and from listening to records. Those students who propose to make their living as performers might well regard what they do in a student orchestra as the beginning of their "stock-in-trade," a knowledge of orchestral procedures and of the more routine aspects of the standard repertory.

Program policy for student orchestras will need to take this into account, and there are roughly two schools of thought about it. One is that a number of concerts should be presented annually for which the preparation should be as intensive as possible. This has the advantage of pressing the students continuously in the matter of accuracy. It has also the advantage that four or five annual concerts look well in the annual report of a school and attract favorable public notice to the school and its staff. It has the disadvantage of limiting the number of pieces brought to the practical attention of the students during the few years of their college life. The other policy is to have many rehearsals ranging over as wide a field as possible at which no piece would be entirely "finished"; with one or at most two annual concerts which would be the subject of a special effort. It may be argued that the passing from one piece to the next without "finishing" any may develop a sort of "Oh-it's-good-enough" attitude toward orchestra work. At the same time, it may be argued that the primary purpose of school work is to provide a rounded education for the student at graduate and undergraduate level, laying thereby a foundation on which each, according to his talent, might ultimately base his own state of perfection.

The series of programs for the year will then be planned to implement whichever policy is adopted. If he presides over a sloppy performance with a professional orchestra or if he selects works manifestly beyond the capacity of an amateur orchestra, a conductor's competency and good judgment are very properly called into question, but his professional reputation is not, or should not be, involved in the standard of performance by a student orchestra of selected works. There would be a teaching staff, it is assumed, to help with problems when somewhat difficult music is chosen. Students like a lively and large audience as well as any other group does, but unless the conductor is a candidate in a "most popular professor" contest, the development of the audience potential is not of primary importance with a student orchestra. The programs will, therefore, be related exclusively to present and future educational needs.

It is easy to find many works exemplifying varieties of techniques. Bowing styles may be investigated through, for example, any of the Bach *Brandenburg* Concertos; last movements of any of the later Haydn symphonies; overtures such as *The Silken Ladder* by Rossini, *The Secret Marriage* by Cimarosa; and, if a really difficult test is needed, the second movement of *La Mer* by Debussy. The orchestra's capacity to retain the shape of long, slow phrases might be tested by the "Good Friday" sequence from *Parsifal*, the slow movements of the Beethoven Sixth and Ninth symphonies, parts of Faure's *Pelléas and Mélisande*, the Delius *Walk to the Paradise Garden*, or the third of the interludes from *Peter Grimes* by Benjamin Britten. Brass chording might be developed through parts of the *Tannhauser* Overture by Wagner, the "March to the Scaffold" from the Berlioz *Fantastic Symphony*, the first and fourth movements of the Sibelius First Symphony, and the first movement of the Rimsky-Korsakov *Scheherazade*. General dexterity in ensemble might well be tried progressively with the march from the Tchaikovsky Sixth Symphony, the *scherzo* in the Sibelius Second Symphony, the same in the Vaughan Williams "London" Symphony, the Berlioz *Roman Carnival* Overture, the third dance of the first suite from the Falla *Three-Cornered Hat*, and so on.

For the sake of their general musical education, a good deal

153

of space in student orchestra work is, naturally, given to works written before, say, 1830. These works have one defect in regard to the training of an orchestra as a whole. Almost all of them keep the strings busy but provide comparatively little for the wind players to do and, except for one timpanist, nothing at all for a percussion section. This may be balanced by including in programs such works as the *divertimenti* for wind instruments by Mozart and Haydn, the Handel *Music for the Royal Fireworks* in the original version, the Wagner *Trauermusik*, the Concerto for Piano and Wind orchestra by Stravinsky, the *Missa Brevis* by the same composer, and so on. As the better string players are kept occupied with a little trio and quartet work, so there are many works—such as the *Kleine Kammermusik*, Opus 24, No. 2, by Hindemith—which can be found to keep the more proficient wind players out of mischief. For the percussion players there are usually suitable openings in works by Debussy or Ravel or, if something more "nineteenth-century" is in mind, in the works of Moussorgsky and Rimsky-Korsakov, to say nothing of Tchaikovsky, Berlioz, or Liszt. Attractive opportunities for percussion players may be found, too, among interesting South American composers such as Aguirre, Carlos Chavez, and Heitor Villa-Lobos. In the general run of the orchestra repertory it will be found that works composed since, say, 1850 will have the effort more evenly distributed over the whole orchestra than will works written before that time.

THREE

From our consideration so far of the various matters relevant to the design of programs it emerges that the solution of most problems depends on a knowledge of the repertory. The capacity to review in memory a large repertory can come only from that experience of rehearsal and performance which impresses each piece in all its details firmly on the mind. This capacity to work from memory not only facilitates the work of designing programs but tends to make the results better, more closely knit and more precisely graduated to the given requirements. The beginner conductor, however, will not have that experience, nor will his normally diversified college experience admit of his having even a nodding acquaintance with a large enough section of the orchestra repertory.

But it is necessary to be able to review a repertory when designing programs and, while the necessary experience is being acquired, it is well to keep a notebook, tabulated in categories of "overtures," "symphonies," "suites," and so on; something after the style of a library catalog. By having such a notebook, the beginner conductor would be able to jog his memory and review at one glance his information on the characteristics of, say, a dozen symphonies and so be able to make a more precise choice of what would fit appropriately into a given program situation.

Against each piece would be entered information such as may be useful when planning programs. Besides the title and name of composer, the headings might include: (1) information on timing; the over-all length of time and the timing of each movement; (2) the orchestration; peculiarities such as whether a harp (or two), a piano, or celeste or extra percussion players may be required and whether these are absolutely essential; whether the score involves special technical difficulties at rehearsal and for which sections; (3) general impressions; whether the piece is "exciting," flashy (a not unimportant attribute at certain points in a program), emotional, or intellectual in its appeal. The notebook could be built up gradually from pieces with which the student has become acquainted either through his general analysis studies, or by playing in an orchestra, by attending concerts, or by listening to records. Only those items which have been studied in detail should be entered. Otherwise, the notebook may degenerate into merely a catalog of names, representing no real acquisition of reliable information.

FOUR

We have been considering matters related to the development of program policy and its implementation in a series of programs. The internal organization of a single program needs some consideration also.

Music is described at various times as being cultural, educational, or inspirational, and so on. There may be a tendency to forget that the function of a program of music, in its essence, is simply that of providing entertainment. Sophocles' *Oedipus Rex* is entertainment, as is Shakespeare's *Much Ado about Nothing*, Verdi's *Sicilian Vespers*, a musical comedy, or an outdoor band concert. In this sense, a program of music needs to conform to certain basic requirements.

One of these is the time limitation set by custom, which may vary between one country and another and between one community and another. In this country the average length of any entertainment is about two hours, and in music programs a few minutes less rather than more. In the more leisurely times of about a hundred years ago people were, perhaps, less distracted by many things and therefore better able to concentrate for a long period. Over three hours was common enough for plays, concerts, and other entertainments but, for example, it would be a courageous composer who planned nowadays to write another "Mastersingers" lasting four hours or more, no matter how much his musical ideas bear the mark of genius.

Similarly, any entertainment will have regard for the principle of unity in diversity. This is generally covered by having one climacteric to which other, lesser climacterics will be related, and the placing of the point of climax in an entertainment is a matter of some consequence. Even in the old-style vaudeville shows, of which an almost totally unrelated diversity was a leading characteristic, there was a recognition of the need of having a point of peak interest and placing it correctly. The "star attraction" usually came just before the intermission or as the second item in the second half. If the "star attraction" was exceedingly prominent compared with the rest of the program, it was placed last and usually occupied the entire second half of a program. The avoidance of anticlimax is an essential principle in the design of an evening's entertainment, whether an old-style vaudeville show, a play, or a symphony concert, and the whole problem is one of correctly approaching and leaving the essential peak point.

In any entertainment, too, the question of a change of pace is an important one. The total impression of a program may be spoiled by a succession of pieces of equally high or equally low intensity. It may be ill advised, perhaps, to have the Beethoven "Eroica" Symphony and the Brahms First Piano Concerto on the same program. They are both on a heroic scale. They are both of almost equal length and, in view of the over-all time limitation, there is little scope to put in anything else for the sake of diversity. Such a program may do well enough with an experienced audience, but with an inexperienced one it might easily do a disservice to music and the enlargement of its influence. Equally, a program made up of lighthearted confections, without any one of them requiring much intellectual effort from either the players or the listeners, would be ill advised. It is normally best to have one main item to which the rest would be related, and this may be a symphony, a featured artist in a concerto, or the performance of a newly composed work.

When a diversity of style is being considered it is a good but rough rule of thumb to arrange that if the main item is in a style of composition characteristic of the last sixty years or so it ought to be balanced by something of an earlier period, and vice versa. Another rough rule of thumb is to arrange the pieces in each half in some sort of chronological order of composition. The reason for this suggestion is that a switching back and forth between sharply divergent styles may be disturbing and, perhaps, disagreeable. A program section comprising the Dvořák *Carnival* Overture, Delius' *Walk to the Paradise Garden,* and the John Ireland piano concerto might be reasonably satisfactory; as might also a section in a sort of reverse order, such as the Samuel Barber *School for Scandal* Overture, the *Fantaisie sur deux airs populaires angévins* by Lekeu, and a Mozart violin concerto. These lists are not presented as an altogether ideal assortment but to illustrate the point that variation in quality, in style, and in period should be presented as a gradation.

A section comprising a Handel *Concerto Grosso,* excerpts from *Wozzeck,* and a Bach violin concerto in that order may very well be disturbing. It would be better to put the Bach work as the second item. But perhaps the Bach work is being played by a featured artist, and getting him out of the way so early in the program might not be a very good idea, either. Perhaps the best arrangement would be to find something which in style would make some sort of transition between the Handel and the Alban Berg excerpts and to place the Bach concerto immediately after the intermission, following the well-tested psychology of the old-style vaudeville show.

For one designing programs, to have these and so many other thoughts may appear to be a little rambling and incoherent in tendency. After all, successful program design is a matter of delicate precision. But what is delicately precise in the end product very often involves an almost incoherent dwelling on all the relevant factors possible before allowing the mind to drift gradually toward definitive conclusions. An overly decisive, "Gordian knot" sort of attitude is seldom likely to be successful in the long run.

Rehearsal

IN GENERAL

It is said of the late Toscanini that, when in London in 1939, at one rehearsal he gave twenty minutes to the first four measures of the Beethoven "Pastoral" Symphony and somewhat less to the remainder of the first movement. For the first-class orchestra players at his disposal the technical difficulties of the work were "old stuff," and they were ready to respond to whatever he required of them. But the opening phrase is a critical one and delicate. In Toscanini's view, it needed some attention to make quite certain he could bring it off at the concert exactly as he wanted it.

To be unsparing of effort is essential in any kind of art work, and no good orchestra player, amateur or professional, resents demands on him that are well founded. At the same time, obvious waste of time and effort undermines all discipline. In any orchestral situation the respect of the players for the conductor and his real control over them depend absolutely on whether his demands—be they more or less exacting—are seen to be adequate on the one hand and reasonable on the other.

What is necessary and adequate and reasonable depends on the conductor's concepts of the music and on the ability of the players. The better the orchestra, the more direct will be the emphasis on artistic and other objectives. With less good orchestras, although the artistic objectives may be the same, the emphasis will lean more toward direct teaching. For example, in the opening of the slow movement of the Haydn "Clock" Symphony, it may be necessary to direct the repetitions in rehearsal simply at having the phrases played with the correct degree of precision and dynamic, in the hope that when the parts are correctly played much of the essence of the music will then appear. With a first-class orchestra the precision, the right degree of staccato, and all that, will be taken for granted, and the conductor may hope to proceed more directly to a consideration of other values; in this case, establishing securely an effect of what Cardinal Newman in another context calls "*acquired simplicity and innocence*" (as distinguished from the *natural* or naïve variety).

In the first half of the last century, when orchestra routines and standards of performance were not so clearly defined and understood as they are now, there was wide divergence in the view of what was adequate rehearsal time. Habeneck, with the Paris Conservatoire orchestra, studied the Beethoven "Eroica" Symphony for three years before he presented it in public. By modern standards he was unskilled as a conductor and lacked that analytical approach to conducting problems which we expect in any professional nowadays. But he was sincere, musical, and, above all, painstaking, and his personality was evidently such as to retain the good will of his players through all the repetitions he thought necessary to get the work right. In Vienna in 1824 Beethoven was at the height of his reputation locally, yet he had to see the first performance of his tremendous Ninth Symphony put on after only two rehearsals; the Kärthnerthor Theater orchestra was too busy rehearsing a new ballet at the

161

time. Although it contained many amateur string players, the orchestra for the *Concerts Spirituels* in Vienna during the same period presented itself in public without any rehearsals at all. On the other hand, Spontini in Berlin was able to require and get no less than forty-two rehearsals for his opera *Olympia* in 1821.

In general, there appears to have been in Europe at that time either too much or too little rehearsal. (We must remember that too much rehearsal may easily spoil the freshness and excitement of a performance, just as too little may spoil security in technical detail.) The situation seems to have been due to: (1) a wide divergence of view, in various centers, of what might be expected technically of an orchestra performance; (2) little experience or precise knowledge of what could be accomplished in a given time; (3) little knowledge of the details of all those works which we now regard as "standard" and which form the backbone of the present-day repertory of the orchestra player, amateur or professional; (4) incomplete understanding of the technique of conducting or of the need for such technique in any specialized sense; (5) little understanding among players of the personal discipline needed in the formation of an orchestra as a homogeneous instrument; (6) no established routines or general procedures, and so on. Nowadays the average musician, from the graduate student onward, will have a good idea of the routine difficulties of the items in a fairly large repertory. If he is especially interested in conducting, he will have, either directly from participating in college and other orchestral activities or vicariously from attending concerts, some experience of the time necessary to resolve these difficulties in different sets of circumstances.

It would seem that a correct assessment of what is a *necessary* amount of rehearsal time is a sort of synthesis of the artistic and technical capacity of the conductor, the ability of the players, and the difficulty of the music selected for performance in a program. Of course financial considerations are relevant to the assessment, but in a broad sense these might be weighed against the ability of the performers; the more expensive rehearsals would usually involve the more highly skilled players and conductors, who would be expected to produce more in less time. One thing is certain. Whether little or much, rehearsal time ought always to be *adequate* to the artistic purpose. Concerts with inadequate rehearsal are better postponed or redesigned in regard to the program. They do harm to music and are about as useless as a bridge built only part of the way across a river.

When we are thinking about the amount of rehearsal adequate to the achievement of an artistic purpose, we ought to keep in mind at the same time that good music is robust. While everyone concerned, amateur or professional, would aim at perfection, we must distinguish between perfection and that perfection-ism which can, in its way, be something of a vice. It is conceivable that an amateur orchestra giving its best and having a reasonable degree of technical proficiency might produce a concert more interesting artistically and certainly more exciting than a professional orchestra giving *less* than its best. The excited interest of the players in what they are doing is very quickly communicated to the audience, which in all normal circumstances will respond readily to the stimulus. This communication of excitement is the first attribute of a successful concert and should be the principal aim of a conductor when he begins a series of rehearsals.

How the conductor achieves this depends on his knowledge, his temperament, and his good judgment in the management of his players. The beginner conductor will likely have heard or seen something of the successful results derived from the tenseness and excitability of Maestro X or the calm impassiveness of Maestro Y, or the brutal dictatorship in the case of Mr. A, or the easygoing familiarity with the players in the case of Mr. B. As we know, the student of composition and related matters gains much from imitating good models, and the method is excellent as a form of mental calisthenics. But when a conductor is faced with the realities of directing others in any circumstances, any kind of imitation in regard to manner or method is useless at best and a faintly comic sort of attitudinizing at worst.

It is best for the beginner conductor to behave at all times exactly according to his own nature, to be as completely natural as possible in dealing with others. He may feel some diffidence at first, owing in some degree to an uncertainty of the precise effect of what he says and does and in some degree to a very proper appreciation of the gap between what he knows about the music and what he may yet learn. But a little courage, which is altogether different from conceit, and a confidence in the fact that players are usually persons of good will when there is no attempt to fool them will carry him through most difficulties. It is true that much of the excitement of a performance may derive from a conductor's personality but not all of it. It is not entirely subjective in origin. Good music well played is a common objective which can contribute much to such excitement.

Later on, when he has more of that assurance that comes from experience and from really knowing his business, a beginner can afford to exercise such pressure and force as has legitimately accrued to his personality. At all times, however, it is well to remember that, unless he has the misfortune to be associated with fawning and cowardly players, brutality and inconsiderateness are never either necessary or effective over a period of time. Brutality shows up in many ways during a performance. There may be, even inadvertently, a sourness in the general intonation that is hard to place; (players that enjoy what they are doing tend, as a natural thing, to play with good intonation). There may be completely unexpected errors because of a player's overanxiety. If there are no errors there may be, on the other hand, that inordinate, technical brilliance which obtrudes itself between the audience and the music.

Certainly, having regard to the occasional and very human tendency toward inertia when faced with hard work, pressure (and strong pressure) will be unavoidably necessary, but tenseness and excitability are useless unless the conductor knows exactly what he is doing and what he wants to achieve by it. As a professional man he is in much the same position as a lawyer in court or a surgeon in the operating theater. His sensitiveness and the strength of his emotions are useful and essential qualities but, unless they are conditioned by his professional and technical abilities and strictly directed to the task in hand, they may easily become a handicap. Even a pugilist in the ring, whatever the demands on his fighting spirit, cannot ever afford to lose control over his temper.

SCORE AND PARTS

Rehearsal time, whether ample or not, is always precious. To use it wisely and economically requires planning of some sort, and the basis of this is to sort out all those things which can be done before the rehearsals begin.

In studying the scores, the conductor will proceed somewhat on the lines indicated in the chapter "An Interpretation" not only by mastering the details but also by assessing and anticipating the probable difficulties of the players in rehearsal. When they are reading, conductors occasionally mark scores by underlining features which might accidentally be overlooked in the pressure of rehearsal and performance: *subito pianissimo* indications; places where there is a sudden change in pace or dynamic or both at the turnover of a page; entries into the text of instruments which, although very important, may be obscured visually in the text; and so on. This is a good idea for the busy conductor involved in the production of new music. It is also good for the inexperienced conductor who, in spite of a diligent application to his score reading, may not have thoroughly mastered the music and made it a part of himself. But the marking of scores can be carried too far. Too many such marks may induce a dependence on these aids, these crutches, and may develop a mechanical sort of attitude toward conducting. From the beginning, if circumstances permit, it is much better to try to depend on mental notes and to develop, in time, habits of memorizing which would make all such marks unnecessary.

Some conductors have an extraordinarily highly developed ability to memorize all the details of a score very quickly, but they are exceptional and we are here considering the problems of the average conductor and beginner conductor. Besides, it is consoling to remember that a ready memory for detail is not always the same thing as a true knowledge and deep understanding of the piece in question, just as a photograph is not necessarily as true a representation of a scene as an artist's painting might be. In fact, a too ready facility in memorizing may even be a handicap. It may easily prevent the exercise of that hard, patient effort which is essential to a real understanding of any great work of art.

There is also the rather widespread notion that a conductor takes a score that is new to him and reads it through with complete understanding, but this is completely untrue except in the most gifted and experienced cases. Even with a familiar score the experienced conductor is not so much taking in every note as he reads as he is reminding himself, as he goes through the pages, of what he already knows and remembers from previous readings or performances. It is a physical impossibility to read an *allegro* passage in a large score by, say, Mahler at the speed the music is intended to be played and to take in every note with its implications; the eyesight does not spread so widely and take in minute detail at the same time. Facility in score reading is mostly a matter of painstaking study and of the development of memory. When the mastery of the detail is complete the score is thereafter a sort of mnemonic.

To dispense with the use of a score once it is mastered is a practice about which there can be more than one opinion. A conductor directs, or should direct, mostly from memory, but the use of a score at rehearsal saves much time in many ways, such as by enabling him to refer quickly to rehearsal numbers after a stoppage. In a concert it is an added insurance against those normal and human lapses of memory which afflict even conductors from time to time, and everything which entails a risk, however slight, to the quality of the performance is better avoided. Conductors of virtuoso orchestras making a large tour with two or three programs can safely afford to do without the score, and the extra freedom may make, perhaps, for greater spontaneity of utterance. Doing without the score also may impress the more inexperienced music critics and those members of an audience whose minds are not entirely on what they are hearing, but players in resident orchestras, with many changes of program to produce, have been known to make remarks on the subject that indicated cynicism and disillusionment. With anything less than a first-class orchestra thoroughly familiar with the works being performed, the practice is certainly risky and becomes downright foolhardy if the orchestra includes players lacking in extensive experience.

The requisite concentration for score reading can come with progressive effort and experience. The cumulative effects of progressive effort and continuing experience are those which only time can bring, and meanwhile the beginner conductor will be faced with scores which will mostly be new to him; if not actually, then at least as far as the work of rehearsing others in them is concerned. When studying music that is new to him, he might find it an excellent idea to make himself a piano reduction of the full score. By doing so, he will force himself to analyze and dissect what he sees to a degree beyond his as yet limited capacity for unsupported concentration. Even the physical labor of writing it all out is an aid to memory; it is a matter of common experience that once a written memorandum is made on any subject, the memorandum almost ceases to be necessary. Another and more laborious method is to take the separate parts and recopy them into a full score. In this way he receives a special insight into the instrumental style peculiar to each instrument and, more importantly, an intimate acquaintance with the composer's thought. He will also know exactly how each part looks to the individual player and what special difficulties, if any, there may be in reading from it (poor manuscript, badly designed page turnovers, and so on). Wrong notes, which occur even in the best editions, may be picked up in this way, which saves much time and, as may very well be, some embarrassment during rehearsal.

In the course of the hard labor involved in a thorough mastery of the very many scores which will be new to him, the beginner conductor can console himself with the thought that his efforts need not be regarded as "current expenditure," something to be repeated each time he puts these particular works into a program. It should rather be regarded as the building up of a "capital asset." Every score mastered becomes a part of his stock in trade for the rest of his life and, granted reasonably good musical ability, he will need no more than a cursory glance at a future time in order to bring back the details clearly to mind.

In music written before about 1830 it is almost enough to have a clear concept of the melodic and harmonic texture. Orchestration as a musical specialty was then in a comparatively rudimentary stage. But in works written since that time it is necessary to be familiar not only with the actual musical material but also with the special effect of various combinations of instruments. This is an area in which the beginner may also find some difficulty, because when it comes to rehearsal he needs a precise idea of the orchestral "coloration" in order to reproduce it through the players. This is very much a matter of experience and the remembrance of previous hearings of similar combinations. The lack of experience may be made up by listening with a clinical ear to concert performances and, where this is not possible, to recordings.

It is useful to listen to recordings while reading a score in order to receive an impression of the effect of unfamiliar harmonies and orchestration procedures. In fact, to read a score while playing a recording through a few times is an attractive and easy way of getting an impression of the work as a whole. This method, however, should be used with some caution and reserve. It is best used only after there has been the hard mental labor of mastering the detail without an adventitious aid of this kind. Listening to a recording many times will undoubtedly give a good, even an excellent impression of the music, but "a good impression" is not enough for a conductor preparing himself for rehearsals. The possession of concrete, precise, and detailed information is an essential prerequisite of teaching others to their satisfaction and his own.

Next is preparation of the parts. The normal procedure in most orchestras is to have this done by the librarian, working from scores prepared by the conductor. The beginner, however, is well advised to do this work himself. By so doing, he gives himself another chance of assimilating more thoroughly the detail of the scores. He will also save much rehearsal time by having the parts correspond exactly with his score and with what he expects to hear when he waves his baton. By doing with the parts those many things which afterward save time in rehearsal, he will gain much in his professional knowledge. A list of these things would include: (1) picking up wrong notes; (2) clarifying defective print or manuscript; (3) making such additional notation as will help in an awkward page turnover; (4) writing in the minimum essential bowing for strings, and the tonguing marks for wind instruments; (5) writing in the occasional cue mark as a cross reference to the player in a complicated ensemble passage; (6) clarifying the phrase marks and possibly misplaced *crescendo* and *diminuendo* marks, and so on.

The degree to which bowing marks should be made on string parts might reasonably be graded to the proficiency and experience of the players. Too much "dotting the *i*'s and crossing the *t*'s" can be a mistake and, if carried too far, may even obscure the notation and diffuse the players' concentration. Besides, marking a set of string parts for good players with the same detail and meticulousness that might be necessary for beginners is useless and, quite understandably, irritating. So long as the conductor's intentions are clear, no more need be done, because marks are merely *aids* and not essentials. Marks should always be made lightly and clearly, never indelibly, because they are liable to be changed under different conductors or even under the same conductor, who may have changes of mind as a result of expanding experience.

REHEARSAL BEHAVIOR

A good rehearsal requires, naturally, a very high degree of concentration by everyone concerned, and any circumstances tending in any way to diffuse this concentration should be eliminated. As we know, prevention is better than cure, and it is always easier to maintain an effort of concentration than to recover it once it is lost. Everything not directly related to the work in hand (orchestra-administration questions, and so on) ought therefore be excluded from the rehearsal period.

It is also wise for the conductor never to approach the podium until everything is ready for him to begin; when the players have been seated, the parts distributed, and the main part of the tuning completed. This seems a pretty obvious point, but many beginner conductors seem to forget it. It is also wise to leave the podium, and perhaps the rehearsal room also, immediately after the rehearsal is over and to attend elsewhere to any matters arising. The value of this is that it tends to condition the players to associate a conductor's presence on the podium with a concentration on rehearsal work and nothing else. This, in turn, will contribute to the development of a habit of concentration during rehearsal and, as we know, the development of a work habit always means a reduction in tensions and fatigue.

It has not been entirely unknown for a player (especially in the back of the orchestra) to want to light a cigarette during rehearsal or have a quick look at the day's newspaper when he sees on his part rest marks to the value of a hundred measures or so. Obviously a practice of this kind should be discouraged. Whether seen or unseen by the others, behavior of this kind is no contribution to the general atmosphere of concentration. Besides, what a player hears of the music during his measures of rest will condition his own performance for the better when he comes to play, and the improvement is likely to mean one less time-wasting stoppage. Sometimes, too, players are inclined to converse during a rehearsal stoppage, very probably with the noble motive of clarifying their musical ideas to each other and improving the effect of what they are doing. What a conductor corrects during a rehearsal or leaves uncorrected until the next time is his sole responsibility, and conversations, even if well intended, are within reason better postponed; they have a tendency to be prolonged and to lead to a loss of time before resumption after a stoppage. There may also be the well-intentioned, if unmannerly, tendency of players to indulge in a little private practice while the conductor is discussing a fault in another section.

Whether his temperament is such as to lead him to roar at them as gently as any sucking dove or as 'twere a nightingale or, in emergencies, even as a raging lion, there must be a clear

171

understanding on all these matters from the very beginning, if time is not to be wasted and concentration spoiled. The conductor may make his personal contribution to the good atmosphere of a working rehearsal by stopping, as much as possible, only when he knows exactly what is wrong and what he must do to set it right, by confining his remarks to the technical matters under consideration, and by avoiding dissertations on aesthetic generalities.

REPETITIONS

In thinking beforehand about rehearsals, it is well to keep in mind the total number of rehearsal periods available, the ability of the players, and from preliminary studies the probable technical faults to be overcome before the music will be played to satisfaction. To attempt to plan beforehand the use of rehearsal time down to the last detail is not a practical proposition, but there should be some outline of a plan covering the series as a whole and certainly there should be three or four objectives clearly in mind before each rehearsal begins. It is useful to sort out which pieces in the program are the most important for the general success of the concert, which are likely to take the most time and repetition in rehearsal, and which are likely to be ready for performance with little effort. In a quiet little work such as the Delius *On Hearing the First Cuckoo in Spring* or the Moeran *Whythorne's Shadow*, it may be found that some attention to matters of intonation and chording is all that is necessary, followed by a run-through once. After that, if the conductor is convinced that the orchestra will follow him securely and correctly during the concert, it is unwise to spend more time on it, until the final rehearsal at any rate. It is probable that his rehearsal planning began when he was designing the program and that

172

such a piece was put in to offset the extra time seen to be needed for something else.

With a work completely unfamiliar to the players, especially one involving ensemble problems, it is a good idea to play it through once without stopping, and at the correct tempo, if at all possible. This is to give the players an over-all concept of the piece and of their own parts in relation to it and to reduce the need for generalized verbal explanations when the technical faults come to be worked over. This course may or may not be necessary with many works of the standard repertory whose outlines might be familiar already. Here the best method is probably to begin at once with difficult passages, leaving what is technically easy to a later time when a straight run-through might be hoped for.

Although the primary aim of rehearsal is to eliminate the possibility of faulty response to the conductor during a concert, an unrelenting persistence in drawing attention to every tiny fault the moment it occurs is not wise. It will be found that most players realize as quickly as the conductor does when they have made an error, and it is sensible to concede them the intention of avoiding that error the next time through. An error may be due to an obviously accidental slip, to a misreading unlikely to be repeated, or to a slight technical inadequacy which the player might be expected to make good unaided. On the other hand, anything that appears to be due to a basic misconception or to a lack of general proficiency should be attended to immediately and thoroughly.

Apart from the essentially negative function of eliminating faults, there is the positive function of helping the players establish a cohesive concept of the work and its different sections as a whole. It is therefore a good practice to store up two or three or more faults and to deal with them all at one stoppage; then to begin again, not where the corrections have been made but at some suitable earlier point. This keeps the broad outline

173

of the phrase or section in mind as well as the minor details. There is also the momentum, the general forward movement of a rehearsal, to be considered. Too frequent stoppages, even for good reason, may tend to defeat this. Even in one piece every single fault cannot be eradicated with certainty at one rehearsal. The correction may need time to settle in the players' minds and become part of them.

The principal faults to be attended to first are those which the players cannot be expected to observe or correct by themselves, such as: overemphasis of tone between sections, leading to imbalance in the chording; or an incorrectly understood phrase relationship in a contrapuntal texture. These are matters that cannot be clearly seen at first from the individual orchestra part. With passages offering problems in finger dexterity or in reading rapid successions of notes in unfamiliar or unexpected patterns, it will be useful, especially in string sections, to read the music through once or twice at a pace that is slower than ultimately intended; this to be followed by a reading at the correct tempo. To press players unduly, when all that is needed is a little consideration to enable them to see exactly what is before them, may lead to *unnecessary* tensions and may end in less rather than more accuracy. If, however, after a reasonable amount of repetition the passage does not come quite clear, it is advisable, if conditions permit, to put off further drill until another rehearsal. It would be assumed that the players would devote themselves to a little private practice in the meantime. It is never good for morale to give an inordinate amount of time to the correction of a fault in one section and leave the others idle. Moreover, there is a distinction to be drawn between what is an orchestral rehearsal, covering ensemble and general musical problems, and what is merely a supervised practice session for players that are technically deficient.

PITCH AND INTONATION

The scholarship and musicianship displayed in a performance may be brilliant, the interpretation may be deeply penetrating, and the execution of astounding dexterity, but if the intonation is not what it should be the music will fail to give pleasure.

Good intonation begins, obviously, with having the instruments tuned correctly. In tuning up, the usual orchestral practice is to have the A originate with the oboe, because of its penetrating quality of tone and its sensitive response to lip pressure in adjusting the pitch with precision. Before he produces the A the oboist always ought to take his tone from a mechanically fixed source; either a tuning fork or, as may be, an electronic device of some sort. There seems to be a natural tendency among all players to "climb" and, if the tendency is not checked regularly against a fixed source, it is surprisingly easy for an orchestra meeting daily to climb almost a semitone in a couple of weeks or so. That there is a natural and universal inclination to climb may be observed in the available information on the pitch of instruments in Europe during the eighteenth and nineteenth centuries, before the idea of a universally acceptable pitch had been established. Between 1700 and 1800 the pitch in most European centers appears to have climbed from approximately A-425 to approximately A-450. About 1800 there seems to have been a recession, probably owing to the complaints of singers, after which the pitch began climbing again until checked in 1895, when A-439.3 at a temperature of 59 degrees was universally adopted.

In the past forty years or so there seems to be emerging another tendency to climb. It is true that a piece played at A-443 or so will sound "brighter" and, as may be, more brilliant to ears accustomed to a pitch of A-440, but the effect wears off with custom and the seekers of "brightness" then need a new advance. Although everyone accepts A-440 as the norm, not every orchestra, piano, or organ in the country presents this pitch exactly. Many sources, if checked, will be found to be producing A-442 and higher. It seems that many ears have been conditioned by tuning at higher levels and that an orchestra which sticks rigidly to A-440 may run the risk of appearing to be "dull" at first hearing. This climbing tendency is to be observed in recordings too. Because of discrepancies in the manufacturing process, many of these reproduce a performance a shade quicker and "brighter" than the original source. Perhaps the recordings are more attractive and sell better that way.

Whether he prefers a pitch of over A-440 or not, the conductor should see to it that the tuning is kept at all times at the chosen level and that it is not allowed to drift. We know that, when a piano is retuned at its existing pitch, the tuning is likely to remain stable for some time, but if it is retuned to a lower or higher pitch the new tuning is likely to be unstable and to need rechecking pretty soon. This is true of other instruments and, curiously enough, the human ear is similarly affected. The hearing and the musical memory can become accustomed to a gamut based on A-440 or A-445 or any other level and, if it is left undisturbed, the sense of relative pitch can become secure and reliable. But when it is exposed to frequent variations, as for example a slightly different A every time there is an orchestral rehearsal, the sense of relative pitch becomes correspondingly unstable. This may very well account for orchestral occasions when the intonation is a little "off-color" for no traceable reason.

The instrumentalists themselves ought to be trusted to have their instruments correctly tuned but, when making a check, it might be remembered that wind instruments ought not to be finally adjusted until they have been blown upon and warmed to

176

the temperature at which they will be played. Sir Henry Wood used to have a tuning device in his dressing room, set at A-440 for string players and at A-436 for wind players whose instruments had not yet been warmed up. At one period he required every member of his orchestra to file past him and have his tuning checked against the appropriate device as he went on to the concert platform. It is not every beginner conductor who could manage to be as paternally tyrannical as Sir Henry, and on occasion players may be touchy on a matter of this kind, closely related as it is to their character and musicality. A conductor must use his own judgment about what is wise and necessary to do, keeping firmly in mind that a badly tuned orchestra—like everything else to do with the performance of the music—is his personal and inescapable responsibility.

But the correct tuning of the instruments is only the beginning of good intonation. In most orchestras an improvement in intonation is easily noticeable after the first reading of a piece. This is principally because during the second reading the players have a better understanding of the relationships of the phrases they play to the piece as a whole. Apart from presenting the notation accurately, the principal aim of rehearsal is to have the players listen critically to themselves, to listen and understand the relationship between what they are playing and what others are playing at the same time. The intonation of the ensemble as a whole depends very much on the extent to which the music is understood.

The concept "equal temperament," with arithmetically equal semitones, was a compromise for the convenience of keyboard instruments. That it is bearable is because we all tend to make unconscious adjustments, to substitute something of what we ought to hear for what we actually do hear. All the other instruments, although their basic tuning may correspond with one central tone (A-440 for example), do not have fixed-pitch tones in the sense that pianos and organs have them. A good choir singing well-written music from the polyphonic period will certainly not correspond to equal temperament, and an instrumentalist of good musicality will automatically adjust the pitch of any of his tones according to the context of the music.

All this becomes very obvious in a piano concerto, when the contrast of the piano tuning with the more "just" temperament of the orchestra is more sharply defined. The Schumann piano concerto, for example, provides many occasions which might be described as dangerous in regard to intonation. The first of these is the wind passage beginning at the fourth measure in the first movement. Coming as it does immediately after the piano in a solo passage, the contrast in intonation can be quite unpleasant unless the players listen most carefully to what is happening and make the necessary, if infinitesimal, adjustments. Another place in this work is the *duo* between clarinet and piano which begins at measure 152. Although he may be using a first-class instrument and although when playing by himself his intonation may be perfect, a clarinetist may find himself blamed for playing out of tune here if he does not listen to the piano and adjust his intonation accordingly. When the Mozart *Concertante* for oboe, clarinet, bassoon, and horn is played with a piano accompaniment, the intonation is seldom satisfactory throughout, even with the best of players.

Even without the piano as a complication, minor adjustments of pitch are always necessary. For the various instruments to be in tune within themselves in an absolute sense is excellent but, as has been indicated, good general intonation throughout an ensemble requires that the players be in tune with each other in a relative sense and ready to make such minute adjustments as may be indicated by the context. In the following simple examples there is a difference between the tones marked (a) and (b). In each case the tone marked (b), if not actually higher, will at least—to borrow a stock-market phrase—have a tendency to "harden," to press toward the high side. A player needs to be conscious of such tendencies in order to *harmonize* correctly with the other players; and a conductor needs to expect good harmonization in order to get it.

EXAMPLE 1

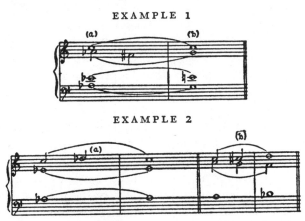

EXAMPLE 2

As we know, a mechanically accurate tone which does not vary, whatever the context, may tend to sound lifeless, if not indeed actually sour. It is possible that here we may find one reason why an orchestra performance, irrespective of the music, is always more enlivening and stimulating than an organ performance, however cleverly the stops are designed to imitate orchestra instruments and however cleverly the organist works out his registrations.

We are told in elementary textbooks that inverted chords are "weaker" than chords in root position, that a second is weaker than a first inversion, and so on. It is a commonplace device in the composition of music to use a succession of inverted chords to weaken an existing tonality in preparation for a change. The practical result of all this is easily seen when attending to the intonation of an ensemble. All players, whether consciously or unconsciously, tend to refer their own intonation to the bass line in any given passage. In a passage involving a succession of "weak" chords the intonation of the bass line is likely to be weak, too, in almost a physical sense; needing careful attention and nursing.

To describe a string bass player as an ex-cellist who found he could not play in tune is a very old joke. It is not very harmless, however, because it expresses a tendency, especially in amateur orchestras, to neglect intonation in the bass line, and in matters of intonation what the bass player does is often more important than what the concertmaster does. During a performance it may therefore be useful to allow some discreet prominence to the bass line, and during rehearsal it may be useful to have it played quite strongly occasionally. This may help the others to a clear realization of their place, for the time, in the harmonic scheme.

The passage already mentioned which begins at the fourth measure of the Schumann piano concerto opens with a 6/4 chord, the bass (French horns) carrying the E of the triad of A minor. Here the tone should be "bright" and firm, with an edge toward the high side. Any tendency to sag will adversely affect the quality of the "weak" 6/4 chord (to a degree more noticeable than if the E were a root). Another simple case in point is the passage at the beginning of the development section of the first movement of the Mozart Symphony No. 40. The bass F♯ in the fifth measure of this section is a chord root, but two measures later it becomes the seventh of a new chord. Because of the normal tendency of a minor seventh to fall, this brings about a minute but significant difference in the quality of the F♯ which the bass player should appreciate if his intonation is to be impeccable. The unthinking player is likely to play the E♯ in the next measure a trifle flat, perhaps because he has already given way to the falling tendency of the F♯ or because he does not realize that in this context the interval F♯ to E♯ is a very small semitone. Apart from the consideration that when the bass has the third of a triad it is better to play on the "bright" side (on the upper edge of the tone) in order to give good support to the upper parts, there is also the consideration here that the

180

E♯ has something of the feeling of being a leading note in the tonality of F♯ minor. As we know, the interval between the leading note and the tonic is the smallest in any diatonic scale. It is not too often understood that the bass line support may make an impression, almost physical, of underpinning a tangible weight, and upper-part players may occasionally be criticized for faulty intonation, when the cause is really traceable to the bass line. We may notice that from the fifteenth measure of this section onward, where the chording is more "solid" owing to the more frequent appearance of chords in root position, there is seldom much difficulty in securing accuracy of intonation.

"Playing by ear" is a sort of term of derogation because it usually connotes one who is musically illiterate, who can learn a tune by rote only. In the truest sense, to "play by ear" is the best way to accuracy and security of intonation. Any composer knows that his ear is the final arbiter in any musical problem with which he has to deal. The same is true of intonation problems, and players ought to be encouraged to play by ear, to listen to what they are doing at all times, and to appreciate the musical logic of it. This attitude is equally valid whether dealing with the music of a Corelli or a Stravinsky, a Stamitz or an Alban Berg.

RHYTHM

Rhythmic faults, too, often respond more readily and securely to an analytical approach than to repetitive drill. In the first movement of the Beethoven Seventh Symphony, the long-continued dotted rhythm presents such a problem. The difficulty does not lie in reproducing the simple figuration but in continuing to reproduce it securely over a long period. After a time some players are inclined to drift toward a pattern of equal eighth

181

notes or to the pattern | ♩ ♫ ♩ ♫ | instead of the pattern | ♩♫♫ ♩♫♫ | and the resulting combination of all three is certainly untidy. On paper the important sixteenth note appears to be related to the second eighth note of the triplet, but rhythmically the basic pattern is | ♩ ♪ ♩ ♪ | and the aural impression is that the sixteenth note is really a decoration of the third eighth note. It may seem to be a mere hairsplitting to regard the sixteenth note as coming not so much after the second as before the third of the triplet, but it is likely that if the players think of it in this way they may become more secure in the rhythm over a long period. Other methods, such as strongly marked, stabbing gestures by the conductor, may impress the required unanimity on the players, but it is better to train them to produce the rhythmic pattern out of their own personal conviction, with little help from the conductor. By an undue exercise of the force of personality there is a risk that the performance may evince a heavy-handed and overly vigorous quality. After all, the main objective here is to bring out that leaping, sprightly, unhurried, easy optimism which Beethoven has so wonderfully captured for us.

Most elementary rhythmic problems derive from notes and phrases beginning off the beat, and generally security can be achieved by relating them to the succeeding rather than to the preceding beat. This is quite obvious in a passage such as the following:

EXAMPLE

Although the short note must certainly be produced distinctly before the downbeat, the player's split-second decision on when to play it is not made until after the preparatory beat and *after*

the precise instant of the downbeat has been fixed irrevocably.

In the beginning (after the introduction) of the last movement of the Beethoven First Symphony the difficulty is not only to secure unanimity of attack but unanimity of tempo afterward.

EXAMPLE

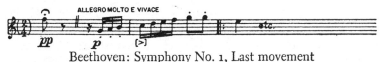

Beethoven: Symphony No. 1, Last movement

A new tempo is suddenly presented, and this is always a dangerous point no matter how well the passage has been rehearsed. To give two beats in preparation is not a solution. It is an incorrect representation of the score, and it is an inartistic exercise in caution because the extra gesture spoils the essential element of surprise. The best method is to use the upbeat only and to train the players to overaccent the C slightly. The aim is to have them together securely on this note and to have the preceding three notes fall naturally into place. In trying to have them concentrate on working to the upbeat, there is a danger of variation in what they will allow for the sixteenth note rest, with the inevitable scramble to get in on time. Besides, the listener hardly takes in the notes G, A, and B in a performance, but any imprecision at the note C and afterward is readily perceptible. Certainly the notes G, A, and B must be produced tidily and with rhythmic security but, paradoxically, the best way to achieve this seems to be to ignore them by having everyone concentrate on the succeeding whole-beat group to which they are best related. The same rhythmic problem comes in a more acute form in the measures 96 and 148 of this same movement, but the method of dealing with it is much the same.

ACCOMPANIMENT

The art of accompaniment, too often and quite incorrectly, is regarded as the Cinderella of music-making. "Well, at least he can become an accompanist" is an idea we may hear expressed when the future prospects of a student pianist are being considered. Of course the technical requirements of a pianist-accompanist are not quite so exacting as are those of a concert pianist, and what he contributes to a performance appears to be of a secondary nature. But in music, as in any human activity, one who appears to take a secondary part may nonetheless be doing what is of primary importance and, although the demands on manual dexterity may be less, the demands on the musicianship of the accompanist and on his sensitivity as an artist may easily be just as great as those of a solo performer.

Whatever may be said about a pianist-accompanist, the purely technical requirements of a conductor are greater in accompaniment work than in solo work. To collaborate with another artist in the production of a unified concept of a musical performance requires both greater firmness and greater fluency in the control of an orchestra. Compared with the pianist, whose fingers on the keyboard may be expected to react instantaneously to a received stimulus, the conductor has a more complicated situation to deal with. As we have seen, the basis of good ensemble work lies in the preparatory nature of his gestures, in giving the players at all times the essential warning of what is about to be required of them in tempo, in dynamic and in interpretation generally. For a pianist to follow a soloist exactly is satisfactory enough but, because of the slight time lag in communicating to others, a conductor who is content simply to follow will inevitably produce an effect of dragging. For this reason he must always regard himself as a leader even when he wants to produce an effect of following.

His function as accompanist may be approached from one of three angles which, like everything else to do with the performance of music, will "vary according to the context." He may regard the soloist as (1) just another performer in the total ensemble or (2) as a co-performer, equal in every respect or (3) as being paramount, with the orchestra simply as a supporting background. Although—in the usual way of human nature—the precise relationship of conductor and soloist is often determined by non-musical consideration such as the relative importance in the profession or in the public eye of those concerned, the best and most securely successful relationship is derived from an objective consideration of the purely musical elements of the piece in performance. Obviously, the soprano part in Hamilton Harty's *The Children of Lir* is just another orchestral part and should be so treated. The same might well be said of the baritone solo part in Delius' *Appalachia* or that viola part in Berlioz's *Harold in Italy* and, perhaps, of the *concertante* part in any eighteenth-century *concerto grosso*.

In a sense, the conductor's skill as an accompanist is called into play at all times, whether in a purely orchestral work or in any other kind, and his function is constantly varying through all the degrees of being leader, associate, and assistant artist. When he gives his attention to any one section of an orchestra during performance, it will not be invariably that which is the most important structurally. In the section that comes after the preliminary flourish in the Berlioz *Roman Carnival* Overture, the conductor is a simple accompanist, taking care that the rhythmic variations in the body of the orchestra are correctly related to the cor anglais solo. It is somewhat similar directing a performance of *The Swan of Tuonela* by Sibelius or of, say, the middle section of the Debussy *Fetes* where the strings are an accompaniment for the trumpets and later on for the wind

section generally. In Elgar's *The Dream of Gerontius* the
orchestra is merely an accompaniment for a chorus such as
"Praise to the Holiest"; both choir and orchestra have equal
importance in the Demon's Chorus and both are secondary
throughout the final song, "The Angel's Farewell."

At a given moment in any work a voice, an instrument, or a
section will be paramount, with the others as an accompaniment,
and a conductor's skill might be measured by the success with
which these shifting relationships are understood and brought
to realization under his direction. We might reasonably think
that his best attribute is his skill as accompanist and that no
basic difference in attitude is required in the direction of a performance of *Til Eulenspiegel* by Richard Strauss, "Iago's Creed"
from Verdi's *Otello*, or *The Four Seasons* by Vivaldi.

It is wise, too, to allow the solo parts, as they appear in the
texture, every latitude consistent with the spirit of the music
and with the general requirements of ensemble security and to
extend that latitude to the players themselves, to the enlargement of their personalities and their musical qualities.

The need for skill as an accompanist is, of course, much more
obvious in works in which a solo part is so extended and prominent as to warrant presenting the performer as a featured soloist,
and the element of personality becomes important here. Violent
clashes of personality are not utterly unknown in concerted
work, but a discussion of how to deal with them is better
reserved for a book on psychology rather than one on musical
matters. When such a conflict becomes unavoidable it is usually
due to what we might call bad preliminary staff work, or else to
serious personal and professional defects in either or both con-
testants. The result, whatever it is, is never good for music, that
harmony of spirit expressed in sound.

Everyone is a beginner at some time. When the soloist is a
beginner in concert work with an orchestra, he may learn much
from an experienced conductor. The same can be said of a be-

ginner conductor in his relationship with an experienced solo performer. If both are serious and high-minded musicians there is never any personal difficulty. It is good that there should be differences in concept and that they should be frankly discussed, but any "adjustments" ought to be made before rehearsals begin. One reason for this is the fact that the conductor must be in a position to direct positively the actual performance as agreed. Another and very important reason is the fact that extended discussion on points of interpretation during rehearsal keeps the orchestra idle and there is much waste of time. As we know, it is best to devote rehearsal time exclusively to those technical points necessary to the realization of previously established concepts.

In association with the human voice the orchestra part, however complex, is nearly always to be regarded as an accompaniment, as being subsidiary. This is due in part to the usual texture of the writing and in part to the fact that the human voice has always a greater impact on the listener than does any man-made instrument. When the soloist (or duo or trio) is not actually singing, the orchestra part usually bears the character of being a sort of commentary on the vocal phrases which have already appeared or are yet to come. This character may also be observed in the cases of instrumental concertos written before 1830 or thereabout. In the first movement of the average Mozart or Beethoven concerto, we find a sort of orchestral overture which exposes, in full or in sketch, the main themes to be heard later on, when the work might be said to get properly under way with the entry of the solo part. Thereafter, what the orchestra does is very much a matter of what we may call "intelligent and helpful commentary." In works written since that time there is found an increasing tendency toward a closer interweaving of what the orchestra and the soloist do. Both of the Brahms piano concertos, for example, are to be considered less as solo parts with orchestra accompaniment than as full-scale symphonies

187

with prominent and beautifully elaborated solo parts. It will also be found in many works that there are passages where the soloist becomes the accompanist; the César Franck *Variations symphoniques* come readily to mind, especially the two sections beginning at rehearsal-letter M in the Enoch edition.

We might describe the ideal relationship between conductor and soloist as a full freedom of association within the disciplines imposed by the text. The greater the freedom of movement, the more meticulously precise must be the understanding between them. This understanding comes out in many ways, mostly of a technical nature: by a matching of tone quality and bowing at the beginning of the last movement of the Beethoven Violin Concerto, with the soloist rather than the conductor setting the tempo in performance; by having the soloist work strictly to the conductor's beat in the beginning of the last movement of the Liszt Eb Piano Concerto; by developing a bravura quality in the introductory section of the first movement of the Beethoven Piano Concerto No. 1, as a foil for the rather "sweet" quality of the opening solo phrases; by carefully matching tempo and mood at the beginning of the second movement of the Brahms Double Concerto; and so on.

In the interests of freedom and spontaneity of utterance it is sometimes useless to count silent measures too precisely. In the *prestissimo* section of the second movement of the Tchaikovsky Bb Piano Concerto it is best for the conductor to know the passage completely by heart exactly as the soloist plays it, all mannerisms and idiosyncrasies included, and to train the orchestra to bring the chords on a single gesture with the minimum of preparation. The same thought might apply to such passages as those cadenza scales in the last movement of the Beethoven Piano Concerto No. 1. If the pianist here attempts any kind of *marcato* or division into groups in order to help the conductor to a precise re-entry by the orchestra, the essential and charming, free, *glissando* quality will be lost. Every soloist will have little personal mannerisms in passages of this kind, whether consciously or unconsciously. These are usually admissible within the true spirit of the music, and the conductor therefore needs an ear not only for the notes and for the musical nuances but also for those touches characteristic of the soloist's personality.

Security in the collaboration demands that, whatever is agreed, the performance should be reproduced exactly as rehearsed, but in the final analysis the success of a unified reading of the music in regard to both precision and mood hangs entirely from the conductor's gestures.

CHORAL WORK WITH ORCHESTRA

The principal technical aim in writing for chorus is that of exploiting the innate beauty of tone of the human voice, which can have a natural expressiveness and an effect on the listener that is more direct than any tone produced artificially with instruments. The texture of the writing is always less complex than that for instrumental combinations, and the singers, if adequately trained, will have their parts more nearly committed to memory than in the case of orchestra players. Because they have less to remember by way of complexities of texture, they can concentrate more on matters other than notation. As a result they can give more response to smaller gestures, and the relationship between conductor and singers can have a more intimate quality at times than that between conductor and instrumentalists.

We may notice that when dealing with a chorus *a capella* a conductor uses for the most part gestures that are smaller in scope and more cryptic in style than when directing an orchestra. The outline of the gestures seems frequently to be less clear also (to the audience, but not necessarily to the choir). This should not be taken to indicate that there is any fundamental difference

189

in the underlying principles of gesture in conducting a choir or an orchestra. In fact, it is rather a clear illustration of one principle: that all gesture should be *relevant* and minimum.

For the same reason, the scope of the gestures with a chorus and orchestra is likely to be larger than with an orchestra alone. Because of the larger numbers involved, the area over which the gestures must be visible and effective is larger. Under normal concert conditions, too, the chorus will be raised in tiers above the normal level of an orchestra, and it will be found that gestures formerly effective at waist level will have to be made at shoulder level. In working with large groups, the more impeccably clear the outlines of the gestures the better and, subject to the nature of the musical context, most gestures ought to be directed at the farthest ranks of the chorus. This has the effect of drawing everyone in the intervening ranks more closely within their influence. This is especially true of oratorios written up to the time of, say, Mendelssohn's *Elijah*. Whenever both chorus and orchestra are performing together in works of this kind, the orchestration is seldom more than a direct unisonal support of the various parts from soprano to bass, and if the chorus receives the exclusive attention of the conductor his gestures will most likely be ample direction for the orchestra players also.

The situation is somewhat more complicated in chorus and orchestra works written nearer our time. In works such as the Kodaly *Psalmus Hungaricus*, the Walton *Belshazzar's Feast*, or even the Brahms *German Requiem*, the orchestra part has frequently an independent significance which needs special attention from the conductor while the chorus is singing. But if the conductor knows his work thoroughly—as he should, if he has correctly assessed the shifting relationships between what is of primary and secondary importance as the work proceeds, if he appreciates the size and weight of the forces under his control and is not too shy to make the suitably large and expansive gestures, there should be no more difficulty here than in working with a chorus or with an orchestra separately.

The study of voice-training is about as complicated as the study of modern philosophy; there are almost as many "methods" as there are teachers. Happily, a consideration of the detail of voice-training is not too important in the rehearsal of a chorus. The conductor is more immediately concerned with the blend of the voices than with the training of the individual. Most composers of choral works have had in mind the normal choral society composed of amateur singers, and the very beautiful musical effects which they may hope for can be achieved with a group of singers whose voices taken one by one might not be very interesting.

Assuming that the part-writing is good, the basis of good choral singing lies simply in having all the singers know all the notes. As an idea, this could not be simpler but, it is not always too completely kept in mind, especially in large choral societies. Even as small a number of "passengers" as two per cent can do much damage in a choral group in regard to its ability to hold to the pitch, to have clarity in attack, or to maintain accuracy in chording. "Passengers" are principally those who sing well enough in the middle but who are uncertain of the beginning of a phrase or of the second note in an unusual interval and, as a result, depend and drag upon their neighbors. Uncertainty in three or four singers at a critical point can spread unreasoningly and unexpectedly through a whole group, just as panic may suddenly arise in a combat group in battle. In choral work, therefore, the first and most important matter to be attended to is a completely thorough drill in the notation.

In repetitive drill, however, it must be remembered that the human voice is more easily strained than the fingers or lips of instrumentalists. This is almost as true of professionals as of amateurs. It is all the more necessary therefore for the conductor to plan in advance what he intends to do at rehearsal, so that

191

he may avoid any unnecessary repetition of those passages and chords which can be easily realized by the singers and concentrate adequately on those sections in which difficulty and much repetition may be expected. The demands for volume of tone should be as light as possible during those rehearsals which are regarded merely as drill for the sake of the notation. This, too, has the advantage of enabling each one to hear what is happening in the other parts and will tend automatically to produce in the whole choir a good sense of the chording and of the correct balance of the various parts. Besides, a choir that has been trained to sing softly and without forcing is more likely to be under control when, later on, matters of nuance and interpretation generally are being worked over. In choral work, as in any kind of ensemble work, a lightness of voice in the early rehearsals can do much to maintain and develop a good over-all quality of tone. As we know, it always requires a better trained group to manage a *piano* or a *diminuendo* than it does to manage a *forte* or a *crescendo*. For a choir as for an orchestra, good music-making comes more from mental than from physical effort, and anyway, when physical effort of a sort is indicated in a climax, it is always the better for being controlled and directed.

When it is felt that everyone knows his notes thoroughly and that the chorus as a whole has a satisfactory sense of the chording and of the relative importance of the phrases, a conductor may proceed to draw out the other elements of the work. Most of these will be established through a thorough understanding of the verbal text, the words and their natural inflections, their emotional subtleties, and other implications. At this stage it is well to have the chorus read through the words aloud without singing, but in unison and at roughly the tempo of the music, and to offer such remarks as may be necessary to clear up doubtful points of meaning or inflection. It may be found possible to say something leading to a deeper understanding of their underlying import also. In, say, "All We Like Sheep" from Handel's

Messiah, something might be said about the impression of thoughtless levity we receive from the unpredictable motions of a flock of sheep. The aim of this would be to induce an attitude appropriate to that lilting gaiety of singing style in this chorus, which is so clearly indicated in the musical text and which serves to bring up all the more clearly the tragic situation of those who have foolishly "gone astray and have each turned to his own way." The dramatically breathless moment of sober realization that, as a result, "The Lord hath laid on Him the iniquity of us all" will then present little difficulty in regard to expressive singing.

In fact, a chorus should be trained to sing on the words in performance, because any composer intends his settings to be a clarification and an intensification of the meaning of the words. When a chorus has the words at the forefront of its consciousness and understands clearly the message they are intended to convey, it will be found that most basic problems related to phrasing and expressiveness will have disappeared. Obviously, clarity of diction is essential too, if there is to be successful communication with the audience. In English this takes the form, principally, of giving meticulous attention to the consonants, especially the last in a word. "The Lord is Great" from Haydn's *The Creation* provides a simple case in point. Even with a nice blend of voices, and so on, the complete attention of an audience may be difficult to hold if, for example, it is mystified by being informed that "The Law is gray and gray is my." Moreover, here the clarity of the enunciation will help the chorus to be secure in the rhythm and steady in the tempo in all those phrases beginning off the beat and thus to provide a solid foundation for the sixteenth-note decorations in the solo parts.

That he himself should know the words as well as the chorus does is a point sometimes overlooked by an inexperienced conductor. In any entry, and especially in a difficult one, the confidence of the singers is much enhanced if, besides indicating the musical phrase by his gesture, the conductor also indicates the words by his facial expression. As the singers express themselves through both the words and the music, they respond all the better when they are directed by one who has obviously the words in his mind as clearly as the music. This, too, is a guidance in the correct shaping of phrases, because it will help the conductor breathe with the singers and so keep them comfortable, confident, secure, and amenable as they follow his gestures.

Both chorus and orchestra ought to be thoroughly prepared separately before combined rehearsals take place. As has been said earlier, waste of time at rehearsal undermines all discipline and control, and it is not unreasonable to suggest that waste of time at a rehearsal with two or three hundred people is ten times more damaging than with twenty or thirty. Combined rehearsals ought to be devoted exclusively to establishing concepts of the spirit of the music. To keep the orchestra idle while drilling the tenors in a minor point of notation or to keep the choir idle while discussing a bowing with the violas is unwise. It will be found that too many stoppages of this kind inevitably defeat the conductor in his aim of presenting the broad sweep of a large choral and orchestral work. Combined rehearsals requiring specially large accommodation are also usually expensive but, if each group has been adequately trained separately and if the conductor knows his music and what he intends to do with it, it should never be necessary to have more than two combined rehearsals, even with the most complicated work.

There is no reason why any chorus should not be expected to be just as flexible in tempo, dynamic, and *rubato* style as any solo singer, and there is no reason why a large chorus should not be just as flexible as a small one. With many choral works it happens that the director is satisfied if the notes are sung correctly, if tempo and changes of tempo are managed securely, and if the dynamic marks are reasonably well observed. But these are only the bare essentials of the music, and much more is necessary, especially that "lift" and flexibility which are the principal marks of spirit and vitality in performance. Especially in the older choral works there are many performances which, although accurate enough in many ways, lack musicality and, as we may think, humanity to a degree completely unacceptable in a solo performer. A song is a song whether sung by one voice or by three hundred voices. It is most probable that this "four-square" attitude to choral work was principally responsible for the complete failure of Elgar's *The Dream of Gerontius* at its first performance; it was apparently beyond the understanding of worthy singers who had been accustomed to that stodgy, plodding style which used to disfigure, and still does, so many oratorio performances. During the last sixty years most choral composers have come to expect more from choruses by way of sensitivity of response to gradations of tempo and dynamic, and this is now reflected in what is required in readings of the older works also.

Singing pleasantly and well requires much less technical training than playing on any instrument with equal satisfaction. The amateur members of a choral society are not assumed to have an extensive musicianship. This notion is partly true but also partly misleading. Lack of formal training in music does not thereby mean that choir members have a lower order of musical instincts or that, as persons, they are in any way less intelligent or sensitive to musical and artistic impulses. Choral parts are less complex than instrumental parts, usually, and if each choir member knows his notes and is encouraged to sing with the same intelligence as he would as a soloist, the chorus as a whole will then be capable of answering to direction with as much flexibility as any orchestra, provided the conductor expects and demands it of them.

Coda

As the general aim in the preceding essays has been to consider some fundamental aspects of the work of a conductor and of his attitudes toward it, most of our attention has been given to the "Orchestra"; because it is the highest point which has been reached so far in the organization of the art of music and because it presents readily the greatest number and variety of fundamental problems, musical and otherwise.

But there exist many other kinds of ensemble, some of which are more likely to be met by the beginner conductor especially. That one or two of these are mentioned here and not in the body of the book does not mean necessarily that they are relatively so very inconsiderable artistically. After all, art work of whatever kind is a matter of quality and not of quantity: the scope of an activity is no absolute criterion of its excellence or of its artistic possibilities.

There are, for example, all those vocal ensembles, from "barber-shop" groups to Bach societies, which appear under different names, glee club, madrigal society, *Männerchor*, and so on. Whatever the size of the group or the style of program, they all have a common impulse; that of people who want to sing, first for their own enjoyment and then, if their skill and training and experience warrant such a hope, for the enjoyment of others.

Whether it is a large orchestra or a small choral group, there is no basic difference in attitude involved as far as the conductor is concerned. He needs the same judgment in the selection of program items, the same application to developing for himself and for his performers an accurate concept of the composer's intentions, the same methods in seeing to it that the concept is realized in performance.

One small point may be worth considering, however. A choral group usually performs in a smaller room and before a smaller audience, in circumstances more intimate than those of orchestras and larger combinations. During rehearsal and performance there will be somewhat more emphasis on minute detail and somewhat less on what we might call the "broad sweep" of the music, and, among other things, the conductor's gestures are likely to be more intimate and allusive in style. A good analogy is possibly the difference we might notice between the style of delivery of a lecturer in a small room and an orator in a large one; each equally effective but in a different way. (This analogy is applicable to any kind of chamber music, of course.)

It is desirable that small vocal groups should be trained to sing from memory at concerts. A large-scale composition, such as an important violin and piano sonata, does not suffer from the use of stands and music copies, but with the relatively short songs usual in an *a capella* choral program the effect of using music copies is the same as with a solo singer, that of interposing a barrier between the singer and the listener and of spoiling the immediacy and spontaneity of the communication. Besides, to expect the choristers to do without copies may at least be an insurance that they will know their notes thoroughly!

One very real difficulty in the management of amateur choral groups—and most choral groups are formed of amateurs—is that of reassessing the personnel from time to time. This is an area in which the conductor may be faced either with a progressive deterioration of standards or with the necessity of weeding out inadequate performers, the almost inevitable occasion of obvious psychological difficulties. It is a good idea, therefore, to have an annual test of *all* the members, given by a small choir committee, which would express opinions, and the conductor, who would take the final decisions. If the tests are applied to everyone inexorably for a few seasons, they then become an automatically accepted institution, to the great good of the choir as a whole.

As we know, the fundamental difference between a good choral group and one not so good centers simply on whether all the members know all the notes or not; the excellence of the performance thereafter being the conductor's responsibility. The test, therefore, ought to be based not so much on the quality of the voice, perhaps not even on sight-reading ability—although that has its importance—but simply on whether the choir member does or does not know his parts in the choir's repertory. Quality of voice, personal musical ability, and general potentiality can be a matter of *opinion*, but whether the member does or does not know his parts can only be a matter of *fact*. Unhappy decisions based on demonstrable fact are always easier to establish and therefore less likely to lead to those spreading dissensions so frequently a characteristic of a growing amateur musical activity.

With a newly formed singing group the first thing to seek to establish is the blend of the voices and the general group response to direction. Occasional moments during rehearsal when everyone feels that a chording or a contrapuntal combination has been perfectly realized are a not uncommon experience. Whether such moments of perfection are accidental or contrived, their value lies in the fact that they are unforgettable, and the memory of them becomes a sort of "capital asset." The more often they occur in the early days of a choir, the quicker will the important sense of corporate excellence come into being. For this reason, music of a too great notational complexity ought to be avoided at first. A vaulting ambition to work on, say, a five-part mass by Byrd or Palestrina or on a difficult madrigal by Weelkes or Gesualdo might be contained temporarily in favor of simple settings of folk song or of glees such as "The Cloud-Capt Towers." Besides, simple music beautifully sung is always more acceptable to an audience than difficult and "impressive" music programmed prematurely, and even a comparatively inexperienced group can, therefore, hope to give a really successful and enjoyable concert or two, even in its first season. When the blend of voices has been established securely and when the corporate quality of the choir has begun to emerge recognizably, it is then possible to contemplate a free enlargement of the repertory.

Another ensemble activity is the brass-and-reed band. In England the generic description is "military band" (in Germany, *Militärmusik*) because most such bands are maintained as part of a military establishment. This description is frequently used nowadays even when the band is made up entirely of non-military personnel.

The principal concert season for bands in Europe in general is the summertime, when concerts are given outdoors. Naturally programs designed for the outdoors, to be given maybe to haphazard listeners with limited musical experience, do not have on the average quite the same depth of artistic significance as have orchestra programs designed to be given indoors. They contain a good proportion of those pieces which do not require a too intense concentration from the listener, pieces which can withstand those distractions of sight and sound which occur outdoors. Most such pieces are categorized as "light" music, but there is no reason why programs of "light" or "popular" music should include items that are badly constructed or artistically negligible. The repertory available to bands nowadays is almost as big as that for orchestras, and there is plenty of good music to choose from when making the "lightest" of programs.

The band repertory consists mainly of transcriptions of orchestra works. It includes almost all the standard orchestra works on a comparatively small scale and also even very many of the great symphonies. Whether of "light" or "heavy" pieces, it will be noticed that the most successful transcriptions are of those whose effectiveness in their original form depended less on the beauty of string tone and more on variety of instrumentation. The *Lohengrin* "Prelude to Act III," for example, is more successful in transcription than the "Prelude to Act I." The Tschaikovsky Fourth Symphony is more successful than the Sixth and the Rimsky-Korsakov *Scheherazade* is more successful than either. In fact, there are very many people whose first introduction to the joys of great music came from listening, maybe as a child, to a band in a city park at a holiday resort.

There used to be many fine series of band concerts given outdoors in this country during the summertime, but there has been something of a change in this pattern during the last thirty years or so. When band concerts are thought of nowadays it is usually the "symphony band," commonly an offshoot of the football band maintained at high schools, colleges, and universities, which is in mind. As the members of these are seldom available after the end of the academic year the concert season is from the end of November when the football season is over until the end of May when the summer recess begins. The band concerts are, therefore, given indoors in circumstances comparable to those of an orchestra concert.

One effect of this is the emergence of unfavorable and perhaps unfair comparisons with an orchestra. Certainly no good band can be as attractive as an equally good orchestra in refinement of nuance and in general flexibility, but a good band is nevertheless a very important musical institution, capable of giving much pleasure to even an experienced and discriminating audience and capable of great good in the spread of musical education.

Most band arrangements—the European ones, at any rate—are intended for performance outdoors and a common characteristic of the instrumentation therefore is a doubling of the parts so that the part writing can be more immediately and securely apprehended by the listener. A phrase which might stand out clearly with, say, a couple of clarinets indoors may advisedly be scored for an additional couple of cornets for outdoor performance. In fact, the phrase might even be doubled at the octave with saxophones or, as may be, a couple of baritones. Instrumental procedures of this kind, advisable for outdoor performance, lessen the possibility of variety of "color."

A conductor of a band who is preparing an indoor performance therefore needs frequently to review the instrumentation in order to secure a satisfying balance between the various sections and the best possible variety of "color." Band instrumentations may need review also because the proportions of the various instrumental groups in a band have not been universally standardized to the same degree as in an orchestra. Every composer who writes for an orchestra has a more or less standard expectation of how the balance of the string groups with woodwind and brass groups will work out, but the component sections of a band vary from one country to another and even from one district to another.

The general formation of a band in most countries, however, envisages a fairly large proportion of clarinets and upper-register wind instruments which, roughly speaking, have a function corresponding to the violins and the violas in an orchestra. Because band concerts are given indoors and because of the possibility of unfavorable comparison with an orchestra, there is arising a new concept of the band not as a substitute orchestra but as a wind-instrument ensemble in its own right. The leading influence in this tendency is, I think, the Eastman Symphonic Wind Ensemble, which, although it uses all the instruments commonly found in the brass-and-reed band everywhere, uses only eight clarinets instead of the average fifteen or sixteen. The Eastman ensemble does not include in its repertory any of those transcriptions commonly used in Europe and confines its attentions exclusively to works originally conceived for wind instrument ensembles.

The development of the wind ensemble as a musical institution in its own right is an important one which offers a new and interesting outlet to the serious composer, an outlet which has produced, for example, a fine Symphony for Band by Hindemith, a charming suite by Poulenc, the Concerto for Piano and Wind Instruments by Stravinsky, besides many important pieces by American composers.

There have not been many compositions of the nineteenth century and earlier which were originally conceived exclusively for wind instruments (the Handel "Music for the Royal Fireworks" in its original version, some of the *divertimenti* by Haydn and Mozart, the *Trauermusik* by Wagner are cases in point), and the greatest part of the available repertory of such works comes, therefore, from contemporary composers. This will present something of a dilemma to the conductor of the average school or college band who may wish to adopt the newer concept of band organization. The repertory of contemporary works does not provide that wide variety of composition style required by one who is concerned not only with the production of a good band but also with the general musical education of those in his care. There are, as we know, many situations where the band is the only ensemble available. It would seem a pity if a bandsman went through high school and college without some of that really effective first-hand experience of Beethoven and Brahms and Wagner and, even, Johann Strauss which can be gained from band transcriptions.

Most bands are useful not only musically but also to enliven the intervals of football games and other festive occasions outdoors. Because of this, the qualifications of many band conductors emphasize their potentialities as producers of "spectacles" rather than as artists in music. Besides, most bands are made up of students, not all music students either, whose embouchure and general tone quality are not improved by a semester of appearances at football games. Because of these and other considerations there sometimes exists thoughtlessly an idea that when it comes to giving concerts the work of a band conductor is, fundamentally, of a lower order than the work of an orchestra conductor and that a lower order of artistic principles is involved. This idea is, of course, unsound.

It is true that, possibly because of this unsound idea, a higher proportion of trashy music appears in band programs than in orchestra programs. It is also true that band concerts may be the occasion of performances that, although correct enough technically, are dull and boring because they are artistically without inspiration. But good performances of trashy music and trashy performances of good music have been known to occur in orchestra circles, too.

It may be well for some band conductors to remind themselves that whether coaching a brass-and-reed band or a string quartet or a grade-school choir or a madrigal society or a large professional symphony orchestra, the conductor's work and his attitudes to it are fundamentally the same in every respect. The differences are a matter of degree and scope, not of inherent artistic principle or technical procedures. And so we might, therefore, conclude by defining a conductor simply as "one who coaches an ensemble of any kind," a good conductor as "one who improves the performance of an ensemble" and an excellent conductor as "one who can produce art work with *any* ensemble."

SUPPLEMENTARY READING

The following is a list of those books found most useful in preparing these essays. It is a short list but might provide a nucleus for a student conductor's personal library on the subject.

ORCHESTRA

Monteverdi: His Life and Work, by Henri Prunières (trans. Edward Lockspeiser), offers an excellent conspectus of music at a time when the concept of the orchestra as a formal organization was taking shape. *A New History of Music,* by the same writer, takes us up to the time of Mozart. *Bach's Orchestra,* by Charles Sanford Terry, and *The Orchestra in the XVIIIth Century,* by Adam Carse, give comprehensive but concisely presented information about the instruments and the organization of orchestras during that critical period in the evolution of the art of music. As a background for these latter two, it will be found useful to read *A General History of Music*, by Charles Burney, and, by the same writer, *The Present State of Music in Germany* (1789) and *The Present State of Music in France and Italy*. They give an excellent insight into the social background of musical activities in those times, as does *Reminiscences*, by Michael Kelly. There is, of course, an enormous number of books on the general history of music, but as a beginning the short *A History of Music*, by Cecil Gray, will be found useful. *The Orchestra from Beethoven to Berlioz*, by Adam Carse, takes us up to the beginnings of the modern orchestra. For developments in England *The Orchestra in England*, by R. Nettel, is excellent, and for the American scene the two most immediately useful might be *The American Orchestra and Theodore Thomas*, by Charles E. Russell, and *The American Symphony Orchestra*, by John Henry Mueller.

CONDUCTOR

Material useful to an understanding of the evolution of the orchestra is, of course, equally useful to an understanding of the evolution of the conductor's function. The article in Grove's *Dictionary of Music and Musicians* ought to be read, but it needs amplification. Wagner's *On Conducting* and the essay in Berlioz's *Treatise on Instrumentation* are worth having. *Vienna's Golden Years of Music*, 1850–1900, excerpts from the writings of Eduard Hanslick, provides a good background impression of musical activities at a time when "the conductor," in our modern sense, was beginning to appear. *The Perfect Conductor*, by Frederick Goldbeck, is an excellent book in which serious matter is presented in a lighthearted style.

INTERPRETATION

Any book or any idea whatever may very well be found useful grist for the mill of "Interpretation." *Interpretation,* by Arnold Dolmetsch, suggests a correct but too frequently overlooked meaning of the word. As we know, the foundation of an interpretation is really based on a combination of attention to technical minutiae with appreciation for the larger concepts. Reading the Dolmetsch book might therefore be balanced by reading *Greatness in Music,* by Alfred Einstein, or *Music, History and Ideas,* by Hugo Leichtentritt. *Symphonic Music,* by Homer Ulrich, might also be useful.

AN INTERPRETATION

Beethoven and His Nine Symphonies, by Sir George Grove, is a scholarly and painstaking work. *A Critical Study of Beethoven's Nine Symphonies,* by Hector Berlioz (trans. Edwin Evans), may be more stimulating and, at times, more amusing, but it is less informative: I feel it reveals to us more of Berlioz than it does of Beethoven. *Beethoven,* by Sir Donald Tovey, is an excellent, short but concentrated study of the relationship between the man and the music. *Beethoven's Sketches,* by Paul Mies, is also interesting, and *Beethoven Encyclopedia,* by Paul Nettl, is a most useful collection of Beethoveniana.

Supplementary Reading

GESTURE

Techniques of Conducting, by Benjamin Grosbayne, offers an exhaustive series of analyses, with diagrams, of movements in relation to various passages. Although it is not strictly a conducting matter, *Method of Eurythmics*, by Emile Jaques-Dalcroze, may provide some useful ideas.

INSTRUMENTS

The History of Orchestra Instruments, by Curt Sachs, and *Musical Wind Instruments*, by Adam Carse, are excellent books which give most extensive information in a concise and easily consulted form. Berlioz's *Treatise on Instrumentation*, brought up to date by Richard Strauss, and *Principles of Orchestration*, by Rimsky-Korsakov, are always useful to have, and of the very many more modern works on the subject a beginning might be made with *The Technique of Orchestration*, by Kent Kennan. More detailed information on the instruments themselves might be sought in *The Art of Violin Playing*, by Carl Flesch, *An Essay on the Construction of Flutes*, by Carl Böhm, *The Clarinet*, by F. Geoffrey Randall, *The Brass Band*, by Harold C. Hind, and similar diversified sources.

Supplementary Reading

PROGRAMS

Except for *The Art of Program Making*, by John W. Pierce, which deals with vocal works, I have been unable to find material on the specific point of the *design* of programs. For quick, if occasionally superficial, information about orchestra works which may be unknown to the student conductor, there are always those orchestra programs, with analytical notes, which are collected and preserved in most public libraries. I feel, however, that the best writing of this kind is still the *Essays in Musical Analysis* (6 vols.), by Sir Donald Tovey. Some useful ideas may also be derived from *The Education of the Concert-goer*, by Homer Ulrich, *The History of Music in Performance*, by Frederick Dorian, and similar works.

REHEARSAL

Handbook of Conducting, by Hermann Scherchen, is an excellent and exhaustive examination of the many problems involved in preparing music for performance. *About Conducting*, by Sir Henry Wood, and *A Handbook on the Technique of Conducting*, by Sir Adrian Boult, are shorter works but offer valuable insight into the work of a busy conductor and give excellent information of a thoroughly practical kind, expecially useful to students and beginners. There is also *The Way of the Conductor*, by Karl Krueger. *Choral Conducting*, by Alexander S. Davies, and *The Choral Conductor*, by Leslie Woodgate, contain much useful information about the management of choirs. There is also *Madrigal Singing*, by Charles Kennedy Scott, which is especially valuable. *Singer and Accompanist*, by Gerald Moore, and

The Well-tempered Accompanist, by Coenraad V. Bos, are both exclusively about piano accompaniment, but the basic information which may be drawn from them and the impressions they give of the attitudes of good accompanists are immediately applicable to orchestra work. There is a very large literature on the subject of pitch and intonation, but the average conductor is really more concerned with developing his own and his players' aural sensibilities than with the actual physics of tone production. However, an inquisitive conductor might begin with the excellent article in Grove's *Dictionary*. He might also look at *On the Sensations of Tone*, by Hermann Helmholtz, *The Physics of Music*, by Alexander Wood, or similar works. It is a most important subject and always worth investigating, although it is doubtful if problems of intonation can ever be settled on a purely scientific basis.

GENERAL

For his general reading the student would naturally follow his own bent in what is a very rich field indeed. It is probable that biographical knowledge is the best background for studies of the actual music of composers. In this regard we must avoid allowing too much weight to those charming but often misleading anecdotes which are so often presented as "characteristic" of various composers. There are, of course, very many first-class biographies in existence but, to develop his intuitive processes and for other reasons, the student ought to try wherever possible to read source materials such as collections of letters, autobiographies, and completely documented biographies. In *My Life*, by Richard Wagner, for example, there is not only an insight into his character and his ideas on music but also into the over-all picture of musical activities of his time. *Beethoven's Letters*, edited by Dr. A. C. Kolischer, *Mendelssohn Letters*, edited by G. Selden Roth, *Letters of Mozart and His Family*, edited by Emily Anderson, *Handel: A Documentary Biography*, by Otto Erich Deutsch, and of course *Bach*, by Albert Schweitzer, are all worth reading and having on the shelf for reference.

It is difficult to attempt anything like a formative list of books for more generalized reading. Perhaps a melange of such works as the following may do as a beginning and may lead the student to make further explorations for himself: *The Poetics of Music*, by Igor Stravinsky, *Monsieur Croche, Anti-Dilettante*, by Claude Debussy, *Choir of Muses*, by Etienne Gilson, *Music of the Western Nations*, by Hugo Leichtentritt, *The Mainstream of Music and Other Essays*, by Sir Donald Tovey, the collected writings on music by George Bernard Shaw, *Life and Letters of P. I. Tchaikovsky*, by Modeste Tchaikovsky (trans. Rosa Newmarch), *What is Art?* by Leo Tolstoy, *Notes Towards a Definition of Culture*, by T. S. Eliot, and, for lighter moments, *Rameau's Nephew*, by Diderot, or *A Mingled Chime*, by Sir Thomas Beecham.

CAPTURED BY THE ABNAKIS

CAPTURED
BY THE
ABNAKIS

BY CLEM PHILBROOK

ILLUSTRATED BY JOSHUA TOLFORD

HASTINGS HOUSE, Publishers · NEW YORK

To Dad and Madeleine

CAPTURED BY THE ABNAKIS

1

ISAAC BRADLEY swung his ax with uncommon vigor. There was a decided nip in the harvest-scented air. There was something else in the air too. Ike couldn't quite name it, but he could feel it.

Joseph Whittaker, Isaac's rotund companion, put it into words. "Trouble with Injuns is, they're sneaky," he said from his perch on a nearby stump. "They been peaceable quite a spell now. But that don't mean they'll stay peaceable, does it, Ike?"

Ike drove the bit of his ax deep into a pine and left it there, straightening to take a breather. Short, compact, quick of mind and body, Ike was fifteen. He tried to remember that Joe was only eleven, but sometimes it wasn't easy. Joe was extra big for his age—almost as big as Ike himself, who was extra small. But extra strong too, Ike was, and a willing worker. He could swing an ax from "daybreak to backbreak" with the best of them.

Joe was a neighbor of Ike's, and the two families often

9

swapped labor. First Joe would be loaned out to Ike's pa a few days, then Ike would be loaned out to Joe's pa in return.

No question who got the best of that bargain. Only thing strong about Joe was his tongue, everyone said. He could wag that just as long as a body would listen.

"The Indians were peaceable almost a year there, after signing that treaty at Pemaquid," Ike pointed out, "but look what happened up to Oyster River last year. And Salmon Falls before that, and Schenectady and Casco and Cocheco. They've attacked Haverhill before. Seems more'n likely they'll attack us again."

He saw the color drain from Joe's plump face and immediately felt ashamed. Joe was just a big baby. He had to remember that. "Here it is fall already," he hastened to add. "It's getting late. Soon there'll be snow on the ground. Everybody knows Indians won't come around then until spring."

He hitched up his buckskin leggings, spat on his hands. Then he dug his bare toes into the crusty fall earth and laid to the ax handle. "I don't reckon we've got much to worry about for some time."

It was a false statement, and he knew it. In this year of 1695, the settlers were never free from worry. Indians were wily and unpredictable. They were apt to strike anywhere at any time.

Joe seemed to take heart from his words. He got to his feet and reached for his ax. Plump, flabby, slow of mind and movement, Joe was in sharp contrast to Ike. Both boys wore buckskin leggings and gray linen shirts and wore their long hair clubbed in the back, but where Ike's hair was coal black, Joe's was brown.

"They sure better not come around," he boasted.

10

"They'll get more'n they bargained for if they do, what with our garrisons and the militia and all. We'll mow 'em down the same way we're goin' to mow down them pines."

He referred to the method of clearing they were engaged in. A settler's first problem, once his cabin was built, was to clear enough land to plant corn. If the settlers had cut every single tree all the way through, they never would have chopped their way out of Plymouth Colony.

They had learned quicker ways: for one thing, they girdled the trees. This meant cutting circles around them about a yard from the ground, then letting them rot.

Another way to speed up clearing was to take a whole row of trees, the same as Ike and Joe were doing. You went down the row, notching each tree. When you got to the last one, you cut it all the way through, felling it into the next tree beyond. This second tree, notched deep as it was, toppled into the third, and so on down the line.

It was like knocking down a whole regiment of soldiers. If you were skillful with an ax and planned it right, as many as a dozen or more trees could be brought down at one time.

And Ike Bradley was about as skillful with an ax as any man in Haverhill. He had been wielding one ever since he could remember. It was as natural to swing an ax as to eat or sleep or breathe. Like all pioneer boys, he early learned to "get up" and split the firewood. A few years of that developed rugged arms and a keen eye.

As a result, he was adept at games requiring strength, stamina and skill. The life of a settler was not all felling trees and planting corn. Come town-meeting time or a house raising, for instance, there was bound to be weight lifting and pitching quoits and running and wrestling. Ike had already made quite a reputation for himself locally as a runner and wrestler. Though small and light, he was cat-quick and wiry. On several occasions, he had thrown adversaries who outweighed him by fifty pounds.

"You better step back just a mite—and be ready to dodge," he cautioned Joe now, as he squared off to the last big pine in the row. "I expect she'll drop where I want her, but a little wind could put her in our laps."

Joe backed cautiously away. Bug-eyed with admiration, he watched Ike's ax bite pie-sized chunks out of the pine, spitting them six feet away. Under Ike's gray linen shirt, the muscles bulged like strands of rope.

"There she be!" Ike announced. The tree was notched deep. Now he moved around to the back side of it. The ax rose once more, glistening in the morning sun. Then it fell, severing the last tough fibers that held the tree upright.

The giant pine shuddered, as though dealt a mortal blow. Slowly, very slowly, its symmetrical green top began moving against the milky blue sky. With a swishing sound, it gathered momentum. Abruptly it crashed into the second pine, shearing off limbs.

The second pine now began moving, accelerating into the third. Even as it scattered limbs left and right, the first pine hit the ground with an earth-shaking roar. One after another the forest monarchs came toppling down, filling the air with debris.

It seemed to the spellbound boys that several minutes elapsed before the final tree came thundering to earth. They stood rooted to the spot, filled with awe at the mighty forces they had unleashed. The sounds echoed and re-echoed in the surrounding hills, and then all was still. It was a stillness all the more profound for the din that had preceded it.

"Jumpin' Jehosophat," Joe exclaimed, releasing his

breath. "That's the most I ever seen felled at one time. I counted thirteen."

"Fourteen," Ike corrected. It was the most he had ever seen felled at one time too. He was well pleased with himself.

"Listen," Joe said, cupping an ear. "Did you hear that? Sounded to me like a cowbell."

Then the sound came again—the unmistakable tinkling of a cowbell in a nearby thicket.

"Probably Betsy," Ike said disgustedly. "All that noise must've scared her into the woods." Betsy was always in trouble, Ike reflected. Only two days ago she had gotten bogged down in the cedar swamp, and he had had to rescue her.

But despite her waywardness, Ike was fond of the soft-eyed red calf, and she was a real bargain. A red calf came cheaper than calves of any other color. That was because wolves were apt to mistake them for a deer and kill them.

"Do you mind fetching her while I start in on another row?" Ike asked. "If I'm going to finish this north lot, I've got to keep swinging. I can't hang up every time ol' Betsy goes wandering off in the bushes. This makes three times in the last week."

"You leave her to me, Ike," Joe agreed with alacrity. "I'll fetch her outa there in no time at all." He was delighted to leave off chopping, even for a short time. Chopping winded him something awful. And if he worked it right, he could spend quite a bit of time down there in the woods, looking for Betsy.

Ike had half a dozen more trees notched before it came to him what Joe was up to. "Probably gone to sleep in the shade," he grumbled. "Laziest cuss I ever did see. No wonder he's so soft and flabby. I've got a good mind to go dress him down proper."

He was just about to holler when Joe hollered to him. Ike couldn't see him, but he sure could hear him. Joe sounded like a lost calf himself.

"Come on down here, Ike," Joe bleated.

"What's ailing you?" Ike shouted back. "I've got enough work to do without playing hide'n-go-seek."

The cowbell tinkled again, and Joe's voice this time sounded desperate. "It—it's Betsy!" he wailed. "She's gone and fell into a hole and—and busted a l-leg or somethin'."

Ike drove his ax into a stump and automatically reached for his ever-handy flintlock gun. If Betsy was hurt real bad, he'd have to put her out of her—no, he wouldn't think about that. Joe was excitable. Probably it wasn't as bad as he said.

Nevertheless, Ike was filled with concern as he ran down the slight incline toward the woods. At the edge of the thicket, he paused to peer intently into the dense undergrowth. "Speak up," he said sharply. "Where are you at?"

"D-dead ahead," Joe instructed him. "C-come right straight in."

Ike thrust the muzzle of his gun into the thicket and followed it through, stepping lithe as a lynx into a small clearing beyond. And there he came to an abrupt halt, every muscle in his body twitching. Each beat of his heart seemed like a sledgehammer driving home a wedge. He was staring directly into the bulging eyes of Joe Whittaker.

Joe's arms were bound securely behind his back. At either side of him stood a tawny Indian, head shaved except for the narrow scalping tuft. They wore snug-fitting buckskin leggings, laced at the sides and gartered above the

knees with deer sinews. Their shirts, too, were of buckskin, tied at the seams with thin strips of deerskin. Leggings, shirts and moccasins were all decorated with porcupine quills.

Even as Ike stood there, momentarily stunned, three steel-sinewed braves moved in on him, trying to pinion his arms. But before they could do so, Ike clubbed his gun and swung from the knees at the biggest one. The grim savage threw up his arms to ward off the weapon.

He was only partly successful. Though he broke the force of the blow, the gun butt made contact with his plumed head, hard enough so he staggered backward and fell over a log, landing heavily on his back.

But Ike's spunky stand was to no avail. The one-sided skirmish was over almost before it began. While he was occupied with the big brave, the two others flung him to the ground and swiftly bound his hands behind his back. There was no further chance to resist. All Ike could do now was open his mouth to scream the alarm.

As the Bradleys lived exposed near the North Brook, out there on the parsonage road, their house had been named a garrison by the Haverhill Committee of Militia. The trouble was, the house was in what might be called an unguarded state right now, owing to the long period of peace and quiet. The sentinels most likely wouldn't be at their stations; the gates would be wide open.

At least he could warn them. It might mean instant death to him and Joe, but it would give his father and the others a chance to defend themselves and their families. Better to lose two men than a dozen. Even that satisfaction, however, was denied him. A broad, dusky hand was clapped firmly over his mouth. In another instant a deer thong replaced the hand, gagging him effectively. Then he was jerked roughly to his feet.

Ike stood there helplessly, glaring at Joe. It was all Joe's fault—his and Betsy's. If Betsy hadn't gone and—puzzled, Ike looked around for signs of the wayward calf. She was in here somewhere, that was certain. Hadn't he heard her several times? Then he saw Betsy's cowbell. It was held aloft in the hand of a smug brave. Grinning broadly, he waggled his hand, and the bell tinkled.

"Kohokas, the owl, is too wise for the paleface," he said. In their dealings with the settlers, many Indians had learned to speak English quite well. Kohokas was obviously one of them. The tall Indian tinkled the bell again. "Kohokas has made the paleface stumble into a snare, like a blind rabbit."

Ike couldn't deny that. Usually he could recognize a cow by the sound of its bell. Each one sounded just a little bit different. If he hadn't been so cocky about felling fourteen trees at one lick, he might have noticed. Still, maybe not. Kohokas had done a good job of imitating Betsy's bell. Ike had been completely taken in by the ruse. Now he and Joe would have to pay the penalty.

He swallowed hard and looked away. This was only part of an attacking party, of that he felt sure. He only hoped his folks and the whole town of Haverhill wouldn't have to pay the penalty too.

2

Ike's concern for his family mounted as the Indians tightened his bindings. Joe watched the proceedings with terror-
filled eyes, trembling as though stricken with fever.

Ike felt a sharp stab of compassion for his companion
in misery. He held no ill will toward Joe for luring him into
ambush. Probably the Indians had put a gun to his head.
That was powerful persuasion.

When Kohokas was satisfied with Ike's bindings and
gag, he turned to Joe. "How many guns in the paleface
fort?" he demanded.

Joe, shrinking back against a tree trunk, glanced be-
seechingly at Ike. The broad-shouldered young Indian
whom Ike had clubbed down now planted himself squarely
before Ike. Hate smoldered in his small, deep-set black
eyes. The nostrils of his broad nose flared.

"Bomazine will make this one tell," he said.

The tall, stately Kohokas shook his head. It was obvious from his stern, inflexible manner that he was in

command here. Bomazine, Ike guessed, was about his own age. Kohokas was old enough to be Bomazine's father.

"No," Kohokas said firmly. He withdrew a tomahawk from his girdle of wampum. "Wees—the fat one—will tell Kohokas," he purred. "He does not want to get knocked in the head."

Joe tried hard, but he just wasn't up to it. "Fifteen," he blurted out. "Or—or maybe it's twenty."

There was this to be faced, Ike decided—he was in this alone. Not only was Joe fat and lazy; he was also a coward. Ike didn't suppose you could blame a body for that. No more than you could blame him if he had bow legs or big ears, but he would have to remember not to count on Joe for any help.

Kohokas nodded his approval. "Wurregan—it is well. It is a good thing Wees speaks with a straight tongue. Now Kohokas knows he can trust his paleface brother. Kohokas already knows how many guns are in the fort. We have been here in the woods for two days. That is how we know the calf gets lost. That is why we stole this." Grinning, he held up Betsy's cowbell and shook it.

During this exchange, Ike's ever-active mind was darting from one idea to another. He would gladly have given his life to sound the alarm, but bound and gagged as he was, he could think of no way to warn the garrison of impending attack.

"Got to be more'n these five Indians hereabouts," he reasoned. "They don't ever tackle a place unless they're sure to win."

In his next move, Kohokas confirmed Ike's suspicions. Replacing his tomahawk, he threw back his plumed head, cupping his mouth with his hands. There then issued from

20

his throat three raucous "caws" that would have deceived the most discriminating crow.

In a few moments, from across the clearing, a string of "caws" floated back. This developed into quite a crow conversation. And by listening very carefully, Ike finally solved their code to his own satisfaction.

The way he figured it out was this: three slow caws demanded a reply; six quick caws meant the other party was ready and awaiting further instructions; three, a pause, then three more meant it was time to join forces.

This information Ike tucked away on a shelf in his mind. At some future date, it might come in handy. You never could tell.

As the last "caw" died away, Ike's scalp prickled, for it came to him suddenly that he had been listening to these Indians for the last two days. Several times while chopping he had thought to himself that those pesky crows were awful noisy critters. If only he had known—

But he hadn't. And so there he was, captured by the Indians, standing helplessly by while his family and friends were about to be massacred or captured.

With a suddenness that startled even the impassive Kohokas, two sinewy braves appeared in the tiny clearing. It was as though they had materialized out of thin air, so stealthy was their approach.

"We have done well," Kohokas informed the cinnamon-colored newcomers in their own tongue. "Not only do we know the paleface strength so we will be well prepared to destroy them next summer, but also we have taken these two captives."

Ike had made friends with some of the Indians who came into Haverhill to trade. He was thankful that over the last few years they had taught him their language—

enough so that he could follow the conversation. He was even more thankful for the words Kohokas had just spoken. A wave of elation engulfed Ike. He blinked hard to keep back the tears of relief. This was just a small scouting party, laying plans for future massacres. They were not going to attack the garrison right away!

Ike's feeling of elation was short-lived. After another winter and spring free from attack, the settlers would tend to become increasingly overconfident and careless. Fewer watches would be kept, families would stray farther and farther from the garrisons.

Through a tiny break in the foliage, Ike could glimpse a corner of the garrison. So near—and yet so far—across the sun-drenched meadow.

Ike swallowed hard. He could visualize his mother bustling about inside their roughhewn home. This was baking day, and she would have the stone oven filled to overflowing with beans and brown bread, puddings and pies.

The girls would be carding and spinning wool when they weren't helping Ma with the baking. They would walk a good many miles winding the yarn before the day was over. They had some dyes to make, too, from the sassafras and goldenrod and pokeberry he and Pa had gathered for them.

Pa, he was gone for the day. It wasn't often he took time off, but today he had gone to dicker for a few more acres of land. He wouldn't be back until sundown.

No one would miss them until then at the earliest, Ike realized numbly. He and Joe had taken their lunches with them to the north lot. It was now only midmorning. By the time their capture was discovered, pursuit would be useless.

The swift-moving and tireless Indians would have an eight-hour head start.

"I'm afraid Pa'll have to fetch the backlog tonight," Ike thought wryly. Usually that was his job—his and his brothers'.

The backlog was the very foundation of the fire; a fire which, with luck, never went dead from early fall to late spring. Ike remembered sometimes they cut off a backlog so big and heavy it took four of them, harnessed to it like oxen, to twitch it into the house and over to the cavernous fireplace, where they heaved and grunted until it was rolled up back. Those times Pa was real pleased.

"If a man has a good backlog," he would tell them, "then he doesn't have to worry about the fire going out."

Pa used to say it other times too. When Indians struck at the settlements, there would be talk among the others of retreating, of forsaking the land they had cleared, abandoning the homes they had built. When Ma got a mite disturbed about it, as womenfolks sometimes did, she would ask Pa right out why *his* courage didn't flag in the face of such obstacles.

Pa's answer was always the same: "If a man has a good backlog, then he doesn't have to worry about the fire going out."

Ma would calm down then, because she knew what Pa meant. What he was saying was this, pure and simple: he had a good, strong reason for not giving up. He had purchased his land, fair and square. He had worked hard to carve a home out of the wilderness. And he would face any danger—even death—to keep what was rightfully his. That's why his courage didn't flag. That's why the fire didn't go out. He had a good backlog.

Ike's shoulders squared as he stood there, a prisoner of

the Indians. He, too, had a good strong reason for not giving in to despair. Somehow he must escape and make his way back home before next summer. He must survive to save his family and friends. It was up to him to warn them of the impending attack. That was his backlog. He would not let the fire go out until he walked back into Haverhill, a free man.

But the young Indian called Bomazine had other ideas. He wanted to slay the prisoners right then and there. His eyes, beady and unblinking as a snake's, never left Ike. "Let us kill them now and take scalps to French," he said in his native tongue. "They will never make long trip all the way up to Canada."

He jabbed his gun impatiently at poor Joe, whose knees were rattling like dried gourds. "This one too soft and fat." He turned and fixed Ike once more with his hostile gaze. "That one too small and weak."

One of the other braves grinned. "Him big enough to knock Bomazine down."

As Bomazine flushed in anger, Kohokas came to Ike's defense. "The small one is not weak," he asserted. "He is quick and strong, like brother Mosbas, the mink. Kohokas has watched him chop down the great pines. Kohokas has seen that he is brave, too. If his mouth had not been covered, he would have warned his people."

Bomazine loosened his tomahawk and moved toward Joe. "Let us knock this one in the head," he persisted. "Him too fat. Eat too much food."

Ike could not cry out in protest, because of the gag, but he could lunge for the big Indian youth, despite his bindings. Bomazine stepped nimbly aside and chopped at the back of Ike's neck with the edge of his hand.

Unable to protect himself with his hands bound be-

24

hind his back, Ike sprawled face down in the brush. For a few moments he lay there, stunned. Then he rolled over and got groggily to one knee, blood streaming from a gash in his chin. Bomazine stepped up to him and raised his tomahawk on high, but before it could descend, Bomazine's wrist was seized by Kohokas.

"Mosbas belongs to Kohokas," he said angrily. "Wees belongs to Kohokas too. We will take both with us. They will help to carry the load. If Wees does not keep up, then we will lift his scalp."

There were grunts of satisfaction from the five other braves. Glowering, Bomazine lowered his sinewy arm and stepped back, but he was destined to have some satisfaction as the northward trek began.

Kohokas himself led Joe by means of a deerskin thong, and Ike found himself lashed to Bomazine, one end of a thong tied securely to Ike's bound hands, the other encircling one of Bomazine's thick wrists.

It soon became apparent what the big savage was up to. Whenever he caught Ike off balance, he would jerk the thong with such force that Ike was sent sprawling. Since Kohokas was leading the procession Indian file, he was unaware of this duplicity. To the others, who saw what was going on, it was a big joke.

It was no joke to Ike. After half a dozen bad falls, he was bleeding from several cuts. His leggings and shirt were torn. His body throbbed with pain, like one big, jumping toothache. Yet each time he somehow picked himself up and staggered on.

"It wouldn't do any good to complain, even if I could," he reminded himself. He was an avid student of Indian lore. Wherever men gathered, he never missed an opportunity to listen in on their talk about Indians and their

25

ways. He had learned there was much to admire about these resourceful people. They were unsurpassed hunters, skillful fishermen and brave warriors. He would much rather have them for friends than enemies. He had hoped the day would come when they would live and let live together in peace, learning from each other, helping each other.

All of which didn't help much right now. That happy day was still a long way off. In the meantime, he was well aware that Indians were impatient with the weak or cowardly. He knew that you didn't cry out when they put the pressure on. You didn't lag. You didn't slow down their travel. You didn't make noises that might betray their presence to an enemy. You weren't weak or bothersome in any way—not unless you wanted to be tomahawked.

Most important of all, you didn't turn tattletale when the young bucks began goading you behind their elders' backs. This was common practice among the younger braves. Tattling only spurred them on to greater cruelties at the next opportunity. A captive's only hope was to bide his time, suffering in silence. Ike couldn't honestly say that he was shocked by this. He was sure that if the situation were reversed, he and Joe would not exactly coddle an Indian prisoner.

"Paleface fall down pretty soon, not get up," Bomazine taunted Ike, as he gave still another fiendish yank on the thong.

This time Ike tripped over a root, landing heavily on a jagged rock that took him squarely in the pit of his stomach. Searing pain shot from his groin throughout his body. He tried to rise, but this time he couldn't make it. His last ounce of resistance was gone.

Bomazine was right, he thought dimly. He had fallen once too often.

26

3

Something stirred deep within Ike. Then he remembered his resolution. He must survive! He must return to Haverhill before next summer to alert his family and friends, to help them defend their homes. Somehow he struggled to one knee.

Instead of a tomahawk, Ike felt a dash of ice-cold water on his face. Partially revived by the shock, he shook his head and stared up at Kohokas. The tawny chief held a dripping birch-bark cup in his hand. He had carried water from a nearby brook. Scowling at Bomazine, he unsheathed his knife and slashed the thong from Bomazine's wrist. Then he removed the gag from Ike's mouth. They were now far enough from the settlement so that any outcry from Ike would merely echo in the vast wilderness.

"What is the matter?" Kohokas asked Ike. "Why does the paleface keep falling down? Why is he torn and bleeding?"

In spite of the abuse he was absorbing, Ike remained silent. He knew better than to expose his tormentor.

Kohokas grunted in approval of Ike's stoicism. "No matter. Kohokas has eyes in the back of his head," he scolded. "He knows that Mosbas, the mink, is tougher than Wees, the fat one. Wees does not even puff, so why is Mosbas all scratched and torn? Because Bomazine is having much game with him, that is why."

So saying, he cut Ike's bindings, releasing his hands. "Mosbas will walk ahead of Kohokas. Kohokas will watch both palefaces, as the owl watches the mouse."

As he was moving forward, Ike had his first opportunity to speak to Joe since they had been captured. "How are you standing up?" he asked.

Joe gulped, and tears sprang to his blue eyes. Kohokas hadn't looked at Joe very closely, Ike decided. Joe was puffing, all right, and he was scared blue. Ike guessed poor Joe was on the verge of blubbering his head off.

That would never do. Indians would not tolerate weakness, in any form whatsoever. The weak, infirm or bothersome they disposed of, and of all signs of weakness, crying was the one they most abhorred—especially in a man.

"Don't fret, Joe," Ike whispered softly. "We'll escape somehow, just you wait and see."

A pair of tears splashed on Joe's fat, freckled cheeks, but he managed to keep silent as the march was resumed.

They were marching due north, close by the Merrimack River. It was a well-trod path they followed, now in the open along the broad river, now through dark forest aisles of stately pines. From listening very carefully to the Indians, Ike learned that this was the Merrimack-Winnipesaukee Trail. It would lead them past Watanic, or

28

Nashua, and then on to Amoskeag Falls. "Namis-kik—the fishing place," they called it. Amoskeag, as Ike already knew, drew hundreds of Indians from near and far every year, during the spring run of salmon, shad and sturgeon.

He also learned that their captors were Sokoki Indians of the Pigwacket tribe. The fiercest and most warlike of the Abnakis, they had long been allies of the French in their widespread massacres.

All of their strongholds were to the north; Pigwacket, St. Francis—and Quebec itself, where the wily governor of Canada, Count Frontenac, incited his Indian allies by the offer of generous bounties for English scalps. The French, outnumbered by the English in the New World, had won the Indians over to their side with flattery and conciliation and by living among the savages while leading them on forays against the English frontier.

If the French and Indians could get a toehold, they could consolidate their gains, bring in reinforcements and eventually drive the English into the Atlantic Ocean. This pressure had been growing ever since 1689, when King William's War had started. Across the ocean, they called it the War of the League of Augsburg, so Ike's father said. According to him, the whole British Empire was concentrating on the war in Europe, so the colonies in the New World were forgotten for the time being. Observing this, the crafty French had started a war in New England, aided by the Indians.

And he was a prisoner of that war, Ike reflected as they entered a brackish swamp. For a short distance they wallowed in mud to their knees.

Joe was puffing more now. He was stumbling, falling, beginning to sniffle as they prodded him time and again to his feet. Finally he went down and couldn't get up. He just lay there, moaning.

"I always thought you were a windbag," Ike flung at him scornfully. "You talk a good battle, but you haven't got any more spunk than a rabbit."

The stricken look Joe gave him almost weakened his resolve, but he knew that if Joe kept hindering the march, the Indians would lift his scalp. Even Kohokas was beginning to glower at him.

"I—I ain't had nothin' to eat since breakfast," Joe complained, getting to one knee.

"You can stand it," Ike retorted. " 'Twon't do you any harm to give up food for a spell. Maybe it'll take some of the suet off your ribs."

The Indians found this to be a big joke and laughed uproariously. Not only Kohokas but the others too understood English from trading with the settlers. Apparently nothing pleased them more than to have captives bicker among themselves.

"Ho, ho, Mosbas is right," Kohokas said gleefully in English. "The fat one does not need food."

"Him waddle like pig," another Indian sniffed.

Bomazine smacked his lips. "Him make good eating," he said. "Cook slow over fire, him make nice, juicy meat."

At that Joe sprang to his feet with an alacrity that inwardly delighted Ike. "I'll show you who's a windbag," he said defiantly. "I can keep agoin' just as long as you can— or them either, for that matter!"

Without another word, he struck off with a vigor which matched that of his captors. Before the seemingly endless afternoon was over, Ike did not know but what Joe had spoken the truth. He himself was so bone-weary he could scarcely summon the strength to place one foot in front of the other. His body creaked with fatigue, and his hunger was a constant, gnawing pain in his stomach. Twice during the long day the Indians had taken corn from their bearskin pouches, eating noisily, conspicuously, taunting their captives.

Ike and Joe were near collapse when dusk brought an end to the day's travel. Their captors selected a small, moss-covered clearing for their campsite and called a halt.

"I was just about ready to drop," Ike admitted to Joe.

"Me—too," Joe panted, sinking to the ground. He lay there on his back, eyes closed, arms outstretched, gasping noisily for breath.

When he finally got his wind back, he rolled over on his side and frowned at Ike. "I been thinkin'," he said. "You got me mad a'purpose, just to light a fire under me. Is that why you done it, huh, Ike?"

Ike chose to ignore Joe's question. It wouldn't do to admit the truth. He would probably have to light a fire under Joe again—and again. If he spilled the beans, it wouldn't work the next time.

Ike sprawled beside Joe, a sigh of relief escaping his parched lips. "Sure hope they give us a bite to eat," he said. "My belt buckle's scraping my backbone."

"If they don't," Joe said, "I'll never be able t'git up."

The words were hardly out of his mouth when Bomazine approached and stood over Joe. Suddenly he drew back a moccasined foot and planted it edgewise in Joe's ribs. Joe yelped in pain and doubled up like a kicked hound.

"Fat one go get more firewood," Bomazine sneered. "Him need plenty more exercise."

Ike came to his feet like a spring that had been released. Seething anger poured new energy into his weary

31

body. He knew that nothing gave a white man greater stature in an Indian's eyes than to best him at some trial of skill or strength. It sometimes turned out that the beaten Indian even treated his rival with greater respect thereafter.

If there was one trial of skill Ike was adept at, it was wrestling. Despite the overwhelming odds against him, Ike seized the big Indian's arm and spun him around. "If you want to pick on somebody, then pick on me," he said calmly. "I'll bet you anything I can throw you—two times out of three!"

Even as he said it, Ike realized what hung in the balance.

His scalp.

Bomazine was not caught unawares. His abuse of Joe was intended to spur Ike into action. Now he had an excuse to exterminate the pesky little paleface. When he kicked Joe, his hand had grasped his tomahawk firmly. The moment he felt Ike's hand on his arm, he spun with the weapon upraised.

Kohokas, however, was well versed in Bomazine's brand of cunning. Quick though the big warrior was, Kohokas was quicker. In one catlike bound he was behind Bomazine. His hand seized Bomazine's in a grip of iron. One deft twist and the hatchet thudded to the ground.

"Is Bomazine a squaw that he trembles before the little paleface?" he said sternly. "If Bomazine wishes to kill Mosbas, let him do so with his bare hands."

With a campfire piercing the gloom, the other braves drew into a semicircle about the combatants, making the forest ring with whoops of delight. Obviously there was nothing they liked better than a lively trial of rough and tumble. A great part of their lives was devoted to wresting a bare existence from the fields and forests; to planting and hunting and the warpath. Moments such as this were seized on with the greatest of excitement. Words of extravagant praise and encouragement were directed at Bomazine; verbal abuse was heaped upon Ike. Joe alone supported Ike's cause, and his feeble "You can lick him, Ike" was drowned out by the exuberant Indians.

Undaunted by all this, Ike warily circled Bomazine in a semicrouch, arms spread wide, crooked at the elbows. He could not help but feel somewhat like David going forth to meet Goliath. This was a story his mother often read from the Bible, a story Ike never tired of hearing. But David had one advantage over him, Ike reflected. He had a slingshot.

"All I've got is my bare hands," Ike thought, "but I'll lick him all right. I'll just move quicker'n he does."

At a signal from Kohokas, the two closed in battle, arms grasping the other's shoulders, heads down, butting against each other like two antlered bucks locked in combat. Ike watched Bomazine's feet intently. Any surprise move was usually betrayed by the lower extremities. To turn or twist, a man must either shift his feet or plant them solidly. It was that one false move, that single off-balance moment, that Ike waited for.

Bomazine, on the other hand, was no novice at this game. Despite his bulk, he was quick as a cat. His experience told him what Ike was waiting for, and it was his size and strength that enabled him to suddenly jerk downward with such force that Ike was thrown to the ground.

Hoots of derision greeted Ike as he got to one knee. "Paleface has big tongue," Bomazine taunted him. "Him talk better than him fight."

Ike's lip curled. "We ain't done yet," he retorted.

Kohokas nodded gravely. "It shall be done as Mosbas said—two out of three."

His hand descended abruptly in the signal to renew the battle. Ike sprang to his feet and came to grips with Bomazine with no preliminaries. Even as they made contact, Ike planted his right foot beside the Indian's right leg. Summoning all of his strength, he got the leverage for his specialty, a sudden "trip and twitch" that took Bomazine by complete surprise. With a look of disbelief on his bronze face he tumbled over backward, sprawling full length on the carpet of pine needles.

There was a stunned silence as he lay there on his back, staring up at Ike. Then the surrounding braves exploded in spontaneous approval of Ike's skill.

"Attaboy, Ike!" Joe cried delightedly. "I knowed you could do it. Now flip him again."

Ike would have liked nothing better, but he was not overconfident. He knew full well he had his work cut out for him. Bomazine did not look any too happy about being dumped by a man half his size. He was scowling fiercely.

"One thing's for sure," Ike reasoned. "He won't go down quite so easy next time. He'll be looking for the trip and twitch. I just better give him a dose of something else, like a good piggy-back ride."

To get away with this one, a man must be very quick. "I'll bet he's never had it pulled on him," Ike thought. Only a short, wiry wrestler could work it, and it was unlikely that anyone his size had ever seen fit to tackle the brawny Bomazine.

At that moment, Bomazine pounced on him, his big hands digging into Ike's shoulders. They grappled with each other, straining mightily to get the upper hand. A

34

hushed silence settled over the bystanders, broken only by the labored breathing of the fighters.

"Now!" Ike counseled himself. Immediately he relaxed his hold on Bomazine's shoulders, dropping into a deep crouch. At the same time, he twisted sideways, inserting his shoulder between Bomazine's legs. He was now in a position to be crushed by the red man, but the element of surprise was what he had counted on—that and agility. It was all done in an instant. In one swift, fluid motion he straightened up, and a sigh of relief escaped him as the Indian's feet left the ground. Bomazine had lost his leverage. He was at Ike's mercy. With a superhuman thrust of arms, back and shoulders, Ike sent Bomazine flying through the air. The Indian landed a good five feet away in the bushes, crashing to earth like a felled pine.

The evening calm was shattered by the whoops and cries of the braves. Such a demonstration of skill and daring against overwhelming odds delighted them. In that one brief moment, Ike was regarded as their equal.

Joe was beside himself with excitement. "By gorry, I was hopin' that's what you'd try, Ike. You pulled it off just as slick as a whistle."

Kohokas came over and patted Ike's shoulder. "Mosbas has done very well. He is as quick as the mink, as strong as the ox."

Ike accepted all of this praise as being fairly won, but more than anything else, he was anxious to learn Bomazine's reaction. He knew that the proud savage was in a position to make his life more tolerable—or unbearably hard. Most Indians accepted defeat without rancor, even with a certain amount of grudging admiration for their conquerors.

It soon became evident, however, that Bomazine was not of that breed. His face was twisted with suppressed rage as he crawled ignominiously from the bushes. Before he skulked away to nurse his wounded pride, he fixed Ike with a venomous glance.

Ike shook his head wearily as he watched Bomazine go. "I don't think he likes me," he told Joe.

Joe shrugged. "Why worry? Kohokas here likes you, don't he? And he's the boss." He smacked his lips greedily. "Seems like he might even give us a bite to eat after that performance of your'n."

Ike, too, was hopeful, but cloaked his feelings with an air of indifference. It was well that he did, for Kohokas now revealed that vacillation of character Ike knew was typical of the red man. Up to this point the chief had displayed a tendency to favor somewhat the two captives, especially Ike, but even though Ike had just displayed admirable skill and bravery, Kohokas turned away stonily. "Palefaces will not eat tonight," he stated.

It was not until Kohokas refused them food that Ike felt the full impact of his hunger. They had not eaten since breakfast. They had marched steadily all day, up hill and down, and he had just expended the last ounce of his energy in the battle with Bomazine.

"I—I can't stand it," Joe said. "I just can't go without food until morning."

Ike looked at Joe and saw that he was once again on the verge of tears and was actually drooling with hunger.

"Yes, you can, Joe," he said firmly. "You look here a minute, and I'll show you how."

As he spoke, Ike reached down and took up one notch in his belt. "All you've got to do is tighten your belt," he explained.

Joe stared at him as though he had gone quite mad.

37

"What good's that goin' to do?" he said irritably. "It ain't goin' to fill my stomach, is it?"

"No, but it'll make the hole in it that much smaller." Ike threw back his shoulders and took a deep breath. "I feel better already."

Actually, he didn't feel a mite better—worse if anything—but around the fireplace of a cold winter evening he had more than once heard his pa tell of the time he was trapping with a partner. Snowbound in a leanto, their provisions ran low. Game was very scarce because of the severe weather. The day finally came when there was not a scrap of food left.

As the snow piled higher, the two men took to tightening their belts, as many a desperate settler had done before them. Each day they took up one notch, until the last hole was finally reached. By now, both men were so weak they could scarcely stand. While they were in this feeble condition, a stray doe floundered by their leanto.

"We were both so far gone," his pa recalled, "neither one of us had the strength to lift a gun and fire."

Summoning their combined energy in one final effort, however, they managed to gouge one more hole in his pa's belt, and it took the two of them to draw the buckle into it.

"That gave me just about enough strength to lift my flintlock," Pa said, "and I dropped that doe in her tracks."

There was always a twinkle in his eye as he added: "A couple of hours later, our belts were too small to go around us."

That's what Pa meant by "tightening your belt." That's why he set so much store by hanging on, by keeping up your courage, no matter how grim the outlook. It was his firm belief that you could always take up "one more notch."

Standing there now, Joe was skeptically following Ike's advice. When he had tightened his belt, a puzzled expression creased his forehead. "Maybe you feel better, but I don't. Only thing that's goin' to make me feel better is some food in my stomach."

Their captors, however, gave no evidence of obliging. After gathering a few balsam boughs to cushion their blankets, they squatted beside the fire and proceeded to devour the smoked venison they had filched from their captives' lunch.

Already Bomazine was showing signs of resuming his harassment, although his companions had ceased taunting him over his defeat by Ike. There was a very simple reason for this, Ike knew. The rugged brave could throw any one of them, and if pushed too far he would do just that.

Bomazine ate noisily, sitting crosslegged close to Joe. He loudly smacked his lips and belched and licked his fingers one by one, all for Joe's benefit. At one point, he stood up and deliberately threw a scrap of meat aside, so that it fell within reach of the ravenous Joe. And when the drooling youngster clawed at it, Bomazine took one quick step and ground the scrap into the dirt with his heel. Then he reached down and tossed the grimy morsel into the fire.

This was more than Joe could bear. He threw himself down on the moss, buried his face in the crook of his arm and burst into uncontrollable sobs.

The harsh sound of his crying obviously irritated the lounging Indians. Finished now with their eating, some of them were relaxing on their blankets, pulling thoughtfully at their pipes as they stared stoically into the flames. Others sat about, mending worn moccasins or torn buckskins. More than one hostile glance was thrown at Joe's shuddering form.

For the second time that day, Ike found himself in the position of having to shock Joe out of his self-pity. The Indians would not long tolerate such a show of weakness.

"Think how you're going to look, all stuck up with flaming pine splinters," he told Joe, when the latter was catching his breath between sobs. "Just like a nice, fat pig being roasted."

Joe's shoulders stopped heaving. Cautiously he lifted his head from his arm and looked about him. In an instant his sobs were stifled. He rolled over and sat up, flashing a big grin. "You didn't think I was cryin', did you? Shucks, I was laughin' my fool head off!"

Ike admired Joe's quick recovery. "What were you laughing at?"

"I was laughin' at the way you fell on your face this morning, when Bomazine gave you a twitch."

Some nearby Indians laughed. "Him look very funny," one of them agreed.

Ike bridled. "Maybe I looked funny, but I got up, didn't I?"

Bomazine smiled at Ike's discomfiture. "Paleface wait few more sleeps, when we reach Pigwacket. There him run gantlet. Maybe then him get knocked down, not get up."

Ike faced up to him. "It'll take a better man than you to do it," he taunted. Turning on his heel, he went to gather spruce boughs to cushion his weary body. Shortly thereafter, Kohokas ordered that the two captives be bound and staked out for the night.

The fact that Ike and Joe chose to lie feet first to the fire was of great interest to the Indians. They themselves always lay around a fire with their heads to the heat and their feet outward. "Palefaces have cold heads and hot feet," they gibed.

40

"N-nothing hot about my feet," Joe chattered, as he curled up against Ike, trying to get warm.

Ike's feet, too, were far from comfortable. They felt like twin icicles, and they were sore as gumboils from walking barefoot over rocks and roots and blowdowns. More than once that day both he and Joe had eyed the protective Indian moccasins with envy.

There was an icicle somewhere down in the region of Ike's heart, too—an utter despair that had nothing to do with being bone tired and ravenous with hunger. All his life he had tried to live by the Bible, as he was brought up to do. Usually he could draw strength and inspiration from its messages. Everything had a reason, was part of some master plan beyond his control, so he was told.

"Even this was meant to be," he thought aloud. "We've got to accept it and find good in it somehow."

"Don't see how anything good could come out of misery like this," Joe grumbled.

"It doesn't always show, right off," Ike said. "You've got to think on it a bit."

And think on it he did. It was the last thing in his mind before he fell asleep from utter exhaustion. It was the first thing he thought of upon awakening next morning, stiff and sore in every joint. It was all he could think about that day, as they marched, Indian file, farther and farther from Haverhill. His mind kept asking, "Why? Why? Why?"

The answer that finally came to him was so simple, so easy to see, that he almost laughed out loud. It was Joe who unwittingly asked a question that supplied the answer he was seeking.

As they penetrated a seemingly endless succession of forests, rivers and lakes stretching northward, Joe looked about him in bewilderment, tinged with awe. "Golly," he muttered, "I sure would hate to be turned loose in this wilderness. Even if we could get away, what good would it do us? How could a body ever find his way back to the settlements?"

Herded in front of the others, Ike and Joe had frequent opportunities to converse in a low tone without being overheard. Sometimes they were clouted for it, but at other times the Indians paid no attention to them. At the moment, the nearest braves were talking among themselves in their own tongue. Ike decided it was perfectly safe to answer Joe.

"All you have to do is keep your eyes open," he said. He himself had been watching for trail markers right along. Of course some signs were simple, such as these: branches were thicker on the south side of tree trunks, and moss quite often grew on the north side. You could also tell direction by the sun—if it wasn't hidden by clouds. But there were other signs that weren't quite so simple, particular signs you had to bend your mind to. For instance, there would be a fork in the trail. Ike would carefully study the path the Indians took. He would notice a white birch split by lightning, or a tree with an odd-shaped bole, maybe. This information he would tuck away in his mind, without even knowing he was doing it, because that was his nature; alert, shrewd, observant.

"No matter how far they take us," he added, "I bet anything I can lead us back home. I bet I could even turn around afterwards and lead anybody right back up here to this very spot—"

Abruptly he broke off, staring open-mouthed at Joe. That was it! That was why the Lord had suffered them to be captured. It was so that he could learn the haunts of the Indians; their trails, their hunting grounds, their villages.

It was so that some day he could lead others—soldiers and rangers—back to rout the savages and bring peace to the settlements.

He hoped it wouldn't become necessary, that the pioneers and Indians would somehow settle their differences without further bloodshed. He would much rather return as a friend than a foe and use his knowledge to better advantage. Maybe if the settlers learned more about the Indians' way of life, they might get to like them.

If the war did continue, though, he would have laid the groundwork for a future career as a scout. Looking ahead to life as a captive among the Indians, Ike could even see it as an opportunity; a perfect chance to learn all he could about their habits, their strengths and weaknesses. Then, if it did become necessary later, he could more readily outwit them.

"W-what's got into you?" Joe panted, as they plodded along with their tireless captors. "You act like you're even enjoyin' all this."

Ike grinned. "Fact is, I am," he replied.

The hardships would be easier to bear from now on, because there was meaning and purpose behind them. Yes, he was actually looking forward to life among the Indians for a while—except for one thing. When they reached Pigwacket, he and Joe would be made to run the gantlet. Bomazine had assured them of that. This would be an ordeal, especially in their present state of weakness. The only sustenance they had received in two days was a few sips of water.

There was reason now to believe that they would not be fed until they had run the gantlet. Ike decided this was all part of some savage test of will and endurance. If he and Joe survived the trip to Pigwacket without food and successfully ran the gantlet, the test would be over. They would be fed. If. How much more of this torture could they stand?

Jaw set stubbornly, Ike reached down and took up another notch in his belt. As he did so, he noticed that it was the last one.

4

STEADILY THEY pushed northward in the four days that followed; through dank forests and sun-drenched meadows, wading chest-deep in ice-cold rivers, assaulting swamps, thickets and hills without a respite, from daylight to dark. Now the trees were bare, shorn of their bright foliage by slashing fall winds.

Through the day the party walked ankle-deep in once-vivid leaves grown sodden and brown. At night they slept on the frost-crusted ground. By day and night, Ike and Joe lived with hunger. Still their captors did not feed them, although the captives did manage now and then to conceal an acorn or ground-nut, which they furtively devoured after dark. The inner layer of birch-bark, too, gave them something to chew on, though there was no nourishment in it.

Ike was learning that there was almost no limit to what a person could endure if he had to. You could almost detach your mind from your body and ignore its demands for food and rest. All you had to do was concentrate hard on other matters. And so he watched the Indians and listened to them, absorbing things that might help him at some future date.

He learned, for instance, that the white man's Penacook was "Pen-i-kook" to the Indians. "Kook" meant "at the place," and "pen" meant "rapids"; the whole meaning "At the place of the rapids."

From Penacook they went on past Lake Winnisquam; "Winn" being the Indian word for "outlet," and "squam" meaning "salmon." Put together, it translated "Where the salmon waters flow out."

Next they skirted Lake Winnipesaukee, or "Wi'n-nip-pi-s-aki," meaning "Beautiful water in a high place." Here the Winnipesaukee Trail ended, and the Ossipee Trail began; "Awoss-sebi," or "The river on the other side of the mountains."

To the north of them could be seen the majestic, snow-crowned cones of the White Mountains. These the red men viewed with awe, tinged with fear. Ike saw them cast many an anxious glance toward the cloud-piercing peaks.

"Agiochook," they kept muttering, and Ike learned that this meant "Abode of the Storm Spirit." They avoided these towering mountains, believing them inhabited by evil spirits who gave vent to their wrath with violent storms that hurled thunderous landslides into the valleys below.

There were many legends concerning these mysterious mountains, especially the tallest of them all: Kodaakwajo, the Hidden One. Ike already knew that a man named Darby Field had invaded the Storm Spirit's domain, back in 1642. He was the first white man to ascend Kodaakwajo.

Kohokas confirmed this. "Your white man, Darby

46

Field, came to Pigwacket," he told Ike one day. "Two of our braves climbed the mountain of the snowy forehead with him."

He extended an arm, pointing. "Toward the sun setting, there is a great face guarding a deep valley," he said. "Here is an Indian Spirit one can see. He is reflected in a lake under his chin. He speaks in a voice of thunder. His eyes flash lightning."

Ike had heard of the great stone face to the west of them. Indians had carried its fame to the settlements. Ike hoped to view it some day—but right now there were other things to think about, because they had suddenly arrived at Ossipee Lake, after traveling steadily for six days. From here, Ike was told, it was but a one-day journey to their destination. Pigwacket would be reached on the morrow, via what the Indians called the Sokoki Trail.

"Now we see how fast palefaces run," Bomazine reminded Ike, with a cruel leer. "Tomorrow them run gantlet, get knocked down. Maybe not ever get up."

Ike didn't need to be reminded of the gantlet. He was already giving it a lot of thought. There was no point in getting panicky, he decided. You just had to face the facts. And here were the facts: Joe was near done in. Six days without food or adequate rest had taken their toll.

Of this, Ike was certain—after another day's travel, Joe never could run the gantlet. He would be struck down before he took ten steps.

There was just one answer to this problem. When they reached Pigwacket, Joe must not run the gantlet.

About midafternoon the next day, the Indians quickened their pace. Ike guessed that they were nearing their destination. They were eager to get home.

This was confirmed within a few minutes, as Kohokas

47

raised his voice in a blood-chilling war whoop. While the sound was still echoing in the forest aisles, he emitted a second whoop. When this had died away, an answering cry was heard in the distance.

"One war whoop for each prisoner," Ike speculated. "That must tell the other Indians to form the gantlet."

Bomazine revealed that this was true. "They make ready for Mosbas and the Fat One," he taunted.

Kohokas nodded. "The Fat One will go first."

Joe turned to Ike imploringly, a stricken look on his grimy face. His shoulders sagged, his arms hung limply at his sides, he was scarcely able to place one foot in front of the other. He was just about done in.

In a flash of inspiration, Ike saw the answer to Joe's problem. "The Fat One will not go first," he corrected. "The Fat One will not go at all. I, Mosbas, will go for him."

Kohokas scowled fiercely. "And who will run the gantlet for Mosbas?"

Ike glared back defiantly. "Mosbas will run the gantlet twice!"

A hubbub immediately arose among the braves, as they noisily discussed this proposal. Bomazine, Ike could see, was strongly in favor of it. There was a triumphant glint in his beady black eyes.

Ike had counted on that. Bomazine would relish two opportunities to strike him down. But how about the others? How about Kohokas?

The solemn chief studied Joe for a few moments, then turned to Ike. "Mosbas is brave," he admitted, "but Mosbas is also foolish. He cannot run the gantlet twice."

Ike's eyes held his. "The Fat One cannot run it once," he said flatly.

48

Kohokas stared at him impassively for some time. Then he inclined his head. "It shall be as Mosbas wants. He will run the gantlet twice—down and back."

Now that it was done, Ike began to doubt his sanity. What had he let himself in for? Most captives considered themselves fortunate to survive the ordeal once. How could he possibly survive it twice?

He was even more apprehensive a short time later when the well-worn path led them from the deep forest to the edge of a vast field. Before them lay Pigwacket, an Indian village of many wigwams, a council house, and a large stockade.

Whatever occupation the villagers had been engaged in they had dropped. Bronze young braves, wrinkled old men, squaws, children and dogs, all had hastily formed into two parallel lines, scarcely an arm's length apart and stretching from the center of the village to the very spot where the returning party had emerged.

The din was deafening; cackling squaws, shrieking children, taunting braves—all armed with sticks and stones, clubs and dirt—and all challenging the prisoners to run the gantlet. Dozens of yapping curs added to the confusion. For a moment Ike quailed before this dreadful sight. The thought of braving that narrow death trap even once was appalling.

"The best defense is a good offense." This was something Ike had long since learned in rough-and-tumble wrestling. The element of surprise was a very effective weapon. Without further hesitation, he snatched a stout club from the nearest brave in the line. Swinging this left and right, he darted down the aisle of bloodthirsty Indians, running low and fast, as though his life depended on it—which it did.

Some dirt was thrown in his face, a few blows glanced off his sturdy shoulders and back. But his gamble paid off. He had caught the Indians off guard. He reached the end of the line without a blow landing squarely.

He was hailed lustily for his daring feat. Cheers and jeers split the air; cheers for Ike, jeers for the glowering braves who had been outwitted. Above all the hooting and shouting, Ike could hear Joe's shrill voice: "Attaboy, Ike! They didn't lay a hand on you. Now do it again!"

Ike would have liked to do just that, but he wasn't counting on it. There would be no element of surprise this time. They knew he had to come back. Many of the old men and squaws were delighted by Ike's coup, but along that avenue of howling Indians were many young warriors whose pride had been stung to the quick. Their scalping tufts fairly bristled with anger as they took new grips on their various weapons and awaited Ike's return.

At the far end of the gantlet crouched Bomazine, a gnarled club grasped in his sinewy hands, a cruel glitter in his deep-set black eyes. Beyond him, taking no part in the proceedings, stood Kohokas. The stately chief was impassive, but Ike sensed a faint nod as their eyes met. Kohokas was wishing him well.

"I sure need somebody on my side," Ike told himself. Abruptly he charged down the shrieking line of Indians, but he was not so fortunate this time. A club caught him squarely between the shoulder blades with a loud "thump." Ike could barely restrain a cry of pain. Yet somehow he did, and even managed to run faster.

A sharp stone bounced off his forehead, and blood spurted into his eyes, impairing his vision. Still he kept on, his sturdy legs churning faster and faster.

He was halfway down the line of frenzied savages now.

Another crushing blow caught him on the shoulder, spun him around. Yet he righted himself and raced on. He was almost at the end of the line, and still going strong.

Then some crafty youngster managed to shove a stout stick between his legs. Tripped at full speed, he took a nose dive that carried him to the end of the line. He landed flat on his stomach at Bomazine's feet and rolled over on his side. For a moment he lay there, stunned, but only for a moment. The shadowy form of Bomazine loomed above him, weapon upraised. From somewhere Ike summoned reserve strength. One hand rested in the dirt, the other was plunged wrist deep in the dead ashes of an old camp fire.

Ike's fist closed on a handful of ashes. At the same time he twisted and rolled clear, scrambling to his feet. All in the same motion his hand came up, flinging the ashes full into Bomazine's face.

With a grunt of pain, Bomazine staggered back, dropping his club. As he clutched at his smarting eyes, Ike darted past Kohokas, and the Indians let out a mighty roar of approval that echoed back from the hills. "You done it!" Joe yelped, pumping Ike's hand. "You ran the gantlet twice—down and back!"

Kohokas met Ike's glance and nodded gravely. "Mosbas has the heart of a bear. He is worthy to live in the wigwam of Kohokas." He placed a hand on Ike's shoulder. "Now Wees and Mosbas will eat," he announced. "It is time for a feast."

They were the most welcome words Ike had ever heard.

5

In the days that followed, Ike gained weight and strength rapidly. At first, he looked down his nose at the Indians' food, finding the meat especially tasteless, eaten as it was without salt, or any other seasoning. But at least it was not spoiled. They smoked their meat by suspending it over a slow-burning mixture of dried leaves and pine boughs. After being smoked in this manner for a couple of days and nights, the meat became hard and seared on the outside and would then keep without spoiling for a year or more, so Ike was told. He soon found it as savory as any meat he had ever eaten, even if it was unsalted.

Nor was smoked venison their only food. Indian corn, or maize, was an important part of their diet. All told, Ike counted a dozen different dishes prepared from this one grain. Cooked together with beans, it made a delectable dish called "succotash." Pounded with a stone pestle into meal and then boiled, it became "hominy." Cut green from the cob and boiled, it was known as "samp." Then, besides corn, there were chestnuts and beechnuts and fruits. Ike found them all wholesome and tasty.

Joe was not suffering from malnutrition either. He early developed the habit of wandering from wigwam to wigwam, begging food wherever he went. His fat figure was a familiar sight, waddling along in a never-ending quest for something to eat. Most of the squaws had a weakness for children, regardless of the color of their skin, and they found Joe's chubby countenance and trusting blue eyes hard to resist.

"If you don't stop stuffing yourself, you'll be too slow to get out of your own way," Ike advised him one day. "How do you expect to escape when you're fatter than a pig?"

They were alone for the moment in Kohokas' big wigwam—alone, except for the papoose Mikowa, or "little squirrel." Strapped on a cradleboard that hung from a pole in the center of the wigwam, Mikowa was cooing away like a happy pigeon as he swung gently to and fro.

Greedily devouring a last bowl of popcorn, Joe licked his fingers. "The corn that flowers" was his favorite tidbit. "We're goin' to be here a long time," he sighed. "Winter's comin' on, and the snow'll be up to our armpits. We don't stand a chance until spring."

He smiled and lay back, clasped hands supporting his head. "In the meantime, we could be worse off, couldn't we? Kohokas and his squaw treat us real good, and it don't seem to me Indian boys have to work very hard. It's the girls who do all the chores. Shucks, we never had it so easy in our lives, did we? Back home, we had to chop wood and grub sprouts and milk cows—and—"

His voice trailed off under Ike's withering glance. "Now don't you go gettin' any crazy notions," he hastened

54

to add. "I'm just as anxious to go back home as you be, Isaac Bradley, but I ain't goin' to lie awake nights worryin' about it till the time comes."

Ike studied the buckskin shirt he was mending. It had been soaked and dried a dozen times, yet it still dried out as soft and pliable as velvet. No wonder white trappers had been so quick to adopt Indian clothes made of deerskin. Tanned properly, it would outwear the white man's cloth many times over.

He, too, was beginning to enjoy his stay with the Indians, but not for Joe's reasons. As he learned more about these people, his admiration for them increased. Their hospitality, devotion to family, and respect for the aged would surprise the folks back home. Never for a moment, however, did he forget that there was a war on, and that the Indians planned to raid Haverhill the next summer. It was his duty to escape and warn the settlers, to stand shoulder to shoulder with his family and neighbors.

He did not intend to let Joe forget it either. He had heard of boy captives—and girls too—who had adjusted so well to the carefree, nomadic life of the red man that they voluntarily remained with them all their days. He wouldn't let Joe become one of these.

"You've got to lie awake nights thinking and worrying about it now," he said slowly, "so's you'll be all ready when the time does come. We're a mighty long way from home. If we expect to make it back to Haverhill, we've got to plan every move we make."

Joe yawned and closed his eyes. "You're a lot smarter'n I am, Ike," he mumbled drowsily. "You go ahead and plan it."

Ike did. It was the last thing he thought of when he fell asleep at night. It was the first thing he thought of when he awakened in the morning. The conclusion he finally reached was this: he must throw himself wholeheartedly into the Indian way of life. He must eat with them, hunt with them, learn all he could about their language and ways.

The results would be twofold. First, the experience gained would be invaluable to him later on if the war continued and he became an Indian fighter and scout. Second, he would be accepted as a brother by the Indians. They would cease to be suspicious of him, to watch his every move. Then, when the time came to escape, they would be taken unawares.

"Mosbas will make a great warrior," Kohokas praised him a week after his conversation with Joe. They were sitting crosslegged around the evening fire. Ike had successfully bested Bomazine in a foot race that afternoon. The seething brave had challenged him to a shooting match the following morning.

"Mosbas will do well," agreed Kohokas' squaw, Silver Birch. Her shiny black hair, parted in the middle, hung down her back in two long braids. As she bent over the bubbling pot of bear stew, Ike could see vermilion stain where the hair parted.

"He is truly as swift as the mink," chimed in their fifteen-year-old daughter, Nolka, the deer. Admiration shone in her big doelike eyes. From her quill-embroidered moccasins to her plaited black hair, she was a smaller edition of her mother, and like Silver Birch she had become quite fond of Ike and Joe in the time they had lived in Kohokas' wigwam.

"When the rabbit chases the fox, then will Mosbas shoot straighter than Bomazine," commented Nolka's ten-

56

year-old brother, Sassup. A lean, lithe youngster, straight as an arrow, he gave promise of becoming a great warrior.

Joe, busily gulping stew, said nothing. Three weeks of sun and wind plus exposure to the grease and smoke of a wigwam had hardened both his skin and hair. A stranger might easily have taken Joe for an Indian youth, Ike reflected, and the change in Joe was more than skin deep. More and more he adapted to the languorous life of a young Indian. Their indolent mode of living seemed to suit him perfectly. Ike was beginning to suspect that in a few more weeks Joe might even hesitate to return to Haverhill.

"No danger of that, as far as I'm concerned," Ike thought. "At least I'm learning while I'm waiting, though." Daily he was absorbing more Indian lore; even the games taught him valuable lessons. Only that morning, he had learned something that might very well come in handy later on.

It had happened quite by accident. The Indian youths played a game very similar to the white boy's hide-and-seek. When it came his turn to hide, Ike had selected what he confidently thought was a perfect hiding place in a hollow log, but as he lay there congratulating himself, he heard a tentative snuffling sound, then insistent barking. The next thing he knew, he was being dragged feet first from the log, to the accompaniment of shouts and laughter.

Bomazine's big, thick-coated dog, Wokwesis—the sly one—had joined in the game of hide-and-seek. Guided by his relentless master, it had not taken Wokwesis long to track down all the hiders.

"We've got to remember what Bomazine did with Wokwesis today," Ike told Joe later, when they had a few moments alone in the wigwam.

Joe stared at him blankly. "What for?"

"What for, you fathead? Supposing we had escaped out there in the woods. Even if we were smart enough to hide some place that would fool the Indians, their dogs would sniff us out. Doesn't that teach you anything?"

Joe frowned for a moment, then brightened. "Yeah. Don't try to escape."

That was not what it taught Ike. He decided then and there that he must make friends with every hunting dog in the village. He must go out of his way to pet them, to slip them morsels of food—especially must he do this with Wokwesis. Then, if ever he should be trapped, he might stand a chance of diverting the dogs.

He was still mulling it over when Kohokas and the others sat down before the evening fire. "Mosbas looks sad," Silver Birch said, interrupting Ike's train of thought.

"Maybe he thinks of home," Nolka said, her big eyes filled with concern.

"That is bad," Kohokas said. "Mosbas would be better off to forget the weak palefaces. Kohokas will teach him to be a great brave. Mosbas is smart. He will be a great chief some day."

Nolka held out a tidbit of baked corn mixed with maple sugar—Ike's favorite. "Come, Mosbas, eat this. It will put a smile on your face. It will put a song in your heart."

Ike took the gift, and although it was not easy, he did manage to smile. But there was no song in his heart.

As the fire died down and those about him drifted into slumber one by one, Ike concentrated on the coming shooting match with Bomazine. When the day of escape finally arrived, he had no doubt that Bomazine would lead the pursuers. More than anyone else, Bomazine would be determined to track him down.

"I'm not going to fret about that now," Ike thought.

"The Good Book says, 'Sufficient unto the day is the evil thereof.' I beat Bomazine wrestling. I beat him running. And tomorrow I'm going to beat him shooting!"

Ike was not destined to test Bomazine's marksmanship. Shortly after sunrise the next morning, a runner arrived from a neighboring village with news that struck terror to every heart. A Sokoki warrior had been killed and scalped less than one day's travel to the west. On his chest was found a Mohawk war club, painted red. This was a challenge no self-respecting Indian nation could ignore.

Even the stoic Kohokas was concerned. "That is bad," he said, shaking his head gravely. "Kohokas had rather fight a she-bear with cubs than a Mohawk. A Mohawk is strong like the moose, brave like the bear, smart like the fox. He is a very fierce warrior."

And a valuable ally of the English, Ike knew. They could be thankful that the fearful Ma-qua-hogs, or "Man-eaters," were on their side, and they could thank the French for it.

The wily French had made one big mistake with the Indians, which would ultimately prove to be their undoing. Many years before, the French explorer Champlain unwisely joined the Hurons in a foray against the Iroquois, one tribe of which were the Mohawks. For this, the proud Iroquois never forgave the French. Ever afterward they were allies of the English, harassing the French at every opportunity and keeping them out of the Mohawk Valley.

"Let the Mohawks find our village empty," pleaded Silver Birch. "Let us go to Saint Francis. The French will protect us."

Sitting before the fire with his ankles crossed under him, Kohokas was deep in thought. When he finally spoke,

59

his voice sounded strange to Ike; infinitely sad and resigned.

"Pigwacket is our home," he said. "Pigwacket was the home of our fathers. Here we plant our corn. Here we hunt the moose and the bear and the deer. Here we were happy until the great canoe came from across the water, carrying the palefaces to our shores. Now they take our land and drive us back more and more."

"We didn't take your land!" Joe protested in the Indian language, which he was learning fast.

"Maybe a few white men cheated the Indians," Ike conceded, "but most settlers bought their land fair and square."

"We do not understand the ways of the white man," Silver Birch said. "Who owns the sea and the air and the earth? The Great Manitou owns it all. We do not own it. He has given our tribe the right to use this land. When we die, our children will have the right to use it. It has always been so. How can a single Indian sell what does not belong to him? Why does the white man not understand that a few Captured by Abnakis 11|13|23 El (2m par)—os (Hastings) trinkets and some rum cannot buy what belongs to the Great Manitou?"

"Most of the settlers are honest," Ike persisted.

An ironic smile touched Kohokas' dark face fleetingly. "My grandfather was there. He saw the first white men come in a big canoe. He told many times how the white men asked for some land to plant corn. Just a little piece, they said. Only as much land as the hide of a bullock would cover. When our people granted them this, with a knife the white men cut the hide into a long rope and claimed all the land it would reach. The palefaces cheated us then. They are cheating us now."

"It's a big country," Ike said defensively. He pointed

60

westward. "Out there is plenty of land for everybody, so the fur traders say."

Kohokas shook his head. "There is no land for the Sokokis. The Mohawks stand in the way and make war on us." He waved a hand toward the east. "The white man makes war on us toward the rising sun. What can the Sokoki do? Where can he go?"

Silver Birch pointed northward. "He can go toward the Great Bear. At Saint Francis he can join with his red brothers. He can get guns and powder from the French to fight the English."

"Are the Sokokis squaws, who run from the enemy?" Kohokas asked scornfully. He rose majestically to his feet. "No, we will go out to meet the Mohawks. Let everyone in the village come to the council house. We will hold a powwow at once."

The word spread rapidly, carried to every wigwam by Sassup, nimble son of Kohokas. Before the dazzling sun was clear of the horizon, everyone in the village had assembled at the council house. Crowded into the background, Ike and Joe nevertheless were in a good position to witness the proceedings.

Dominating the scene was the regal figure of Kohokas. Flanking him on either side were the older members of the tribe, their nut-brown faces inscrutable. Behind this group stood a trio of high-cheekboned squaws, their arms covered with jangling bracelets, their necks strung with beads. In their hands they held a long belt of black wampum with a conspicuous white figure in the center. It was the outline of a hatchet, signifying war.

"Those squaws keep track of what goes on," Ike told Joe. "I've heard tell about it. Of course the Indians don't have any written language, but they do draw pictures on birch bark and such, which is kind of a picture language. Their strings and belts of wampum tell them something too, but mostly their history is kept in their heads and passed on down, from one generation to the next."

"I should think they'd need awful good memories," Joe said.

"Seems like they do—leastwise the ones they pick to keep the records—like those three squaws. I'll bet you anything they can reel off the terms of every treaty this tribe has ever buried a hatchet on."

In front of the elders stood a long line of impatient warriors. Some held burning torches, others grasped tomahawks and knives, but all were painted for war. Here a shaved head was daubed vermilion, there one was smeared with blue. Of them all, Ike decided, Bomazine was the most hideous. One half of his cruel visage was painted red, the other half was painted black. On his heavily muscled chest was traced in black and white a grinning skull and crossbones.

Turtle-shell rattles were tied to the arms and knees of the warriors. Slowly at first they began to stamp their feet and brandish their weapons on high. The strong, insistent beat of a skin drum picked up the rhythm.

Sitting stiffly erect on their mats and skins, the dusky spectators began to chant in time to the throbbing drum. Gradually the tempo increased. Scalp locks bristling, the agitated warriors leaped higher and crouched lower, feigning great anger with one another. Scowling fiercely, they stabbed the air with their knives and swung their clubs threateningly, yet skillfully managed not to make contact. Now the braves became frenzied, their shrill voices rising and falling in the blood-curdling war cry. It was enough to make the hair rise at the nape of Ike's neck.

At this climactic moment, Kohokas arose and leaped nimbly into the center of the circle. As though someone had fired a warning gun, all sound ceased. Chests heaving, the painted braves fell back to observe their chief's next move.

Kohokas' sinewy right hand went to his wampum belt. It rose on high with a tomahawk grasped in it. With blinding speed it descended and the fingers opened, releasing the deadly weapon. Spinning end over end, it flew to its target—the large center pole of the council house. With a dull "tunk," the bit sank deep into the wood.

"Even so shall the sneaking Mohawks be struck down," he pledged. "The braves of Pigwacket shall hear them sing their death song."

He retrieved the hatchet and replaced it in his belt. "The bones of our brother lie exposed," he told the eager warriors. "We must seek revenge at once, that his spirit may rest in peace. Let us take provisions and snowshoes and go out to slay the Mohawks!"

Then they were gone. The last tawny warrior had departed. An air of desolation filled the council house. It was completely silent.

"The warriors are gone," Ike said. The words came unbidden to his lips, summoned by some deep, inner instinct.

"Only ones left is old folks and squaws and papooses," Joe muttered.

"And you and me," Ike added. "Old folks and squaws and papooses—and you and me. Every able-bodied brave is gone."

Joe was staring at him and he was staring right back. Only now were they beginning to perceive their good fortune. "We better not waste any time," Ike said. "You never know, they might even be back tomorrow."

64

Joe swallowed uneasily. "You—you think we can make it?" he blurted. "Don't forget, Bomazine warned Sassup to tie us up every night if the braves should go on the warpath."

Ike lowered his voice and looked around furtively. "Shh, not so loud. Of course, we can make it, you ninny. I'll take care of Sassup somehow. If we can't make it now, we'd better give up. We'll never have a better chance."

Joe's freckles stood out like polka dots. "Wh—when?" he croaked.

"Tonight, when Silver Birch and Nolka and Sassup are sound asleep. Don't worry, I'll let you know. All you've got to do is stay awake until I give the word."

Staying awake was no problem for Ike. He was taut as a bowstring as daylight waned and darkness crept into the forest. The chills that raced up and down his spine were not entirely due to the sharp, biting wind knifing out of the northeast. Throbbing with anxiety, he lay there in the flickering firelight of Kohokas' wigwam and waited.

Nolka was the first to fall asleep. It seemed like hours before Silver Birch followed suit. Their gentle snoring was sweet music to Ike's impatient ears. But Sassup was another matter entirely. He took his responsibilities seriously. He sat there crosslegged, blocking the wigwam entrance, his beady black eyes watching Ike with unwavering vigilance.

The minutes limped slowly by. Joe had feigned sleep for some time, striving valiantly to stay awake in the process. But at last he succumbed, his lusty snores drowning out those of the other two.

How long could Sassup hold out? Ike thought desperately. After all, he was only a ten-year-old boy. Through slitted eyes, while pretending to be asleep, he watched and waited for the first sign of drowsiness. Hour after hour dragged by, while the wind moaned through the forest and swished softly against the wigwam. Still Sassup sat there in an upright position; watching, watching, watching.

It must have been well past midnight, Ike guessed. Their chances for escape were growing slimmer by the minute. Was that hawk-faced little Indian made of stone? So far, he hadn't so much as flicked an eyelash. And then, at long last, Sassup showed the first sign of weakening. Ike's heart beat faster as the young Indian yawned. A few minutes more and his head began nodding. A surge of hope quickened Ike's senses, every muscle tensed for action.

Now Sassup began to sag, then suddenly he slumped over on his side, curling up on the furry deerskin. His snores were soon mingled with the others.

Hardly daring to breathe, Ike rolled over, wormed his way to a live coal. A few minutes of patience, a moment of searing pain—and his hands were free! His eager fingers soon untied his feet. In one catlike move he stepped to the entrance. Careful not to disturb Sassup, cautiously he pushed aside the bearskin covering to make certain there was no one abroad.

The sight that met his eyes literally chilled him to the marrow. Outside raged a swirling, blinding blizzard. Already the snow was piled to a depth of a foot, and it showed no signs of abating. Rather the storm seemed to intensify, even as he watched.

Stunned, Ike let the bearskin fall back into place. Even if the storm let up, a man without snowshoes would be floundering helplessly before he covered a hundred yards. At the rate it was now coming down, he would never cover a hundred yards in a straight line—even with snowshoes. He would be going around in circles.

Ike returned to his deerskin and sank down numbly on

his haunches. For the first time since his capture, he felt an almost uncontrollable urge to cry. Tears of anger, of frustration and hurt welled up, stinging his eyelids. Somehow he managed to blink them back. Then he sat there until dawn, staring unseeingly into the dying embers. It was going to be a long, cold winter, he decided.

6

THE WAR PARTY returned the next day. Their approach was first signaled by a faint war cry about midmorning. This alerted those in the village, who eagerly rushed from their wigwams to greet the warriors. It was Sassup who gave the answering cry. Almost immediately a string of piercing war whoops echoed in the snow-draped forest; one whoop for each Mohawk killed. "Red brothers do well," Sassup crowed. "Come back so soon with many scalps."

He glanced scornfully at Iko, whose hands were once again bound securely behind him. "Big celebration tonight. Paleface burn thongs, try to escape. Now we burn him."

"Mosbas did not go anywhere," Nolka defended Ike, her brown eyes troubled.

"That's right," Joe chimed in. "He never set foot outside the wigwam."

Sassup's lip curled. "That because snow too deep. No snow, no Mosbas."

Silver Birch said nothing, but her gaze rested sadly on Ike. She knew Sassup was right. Attempted escape was dealt with harshly. Once a prisoner showed he could not be trusted, he became a liability to his owner. In Kohokas alone might Ike's salvation lie. Kohokas had taken a great liking to the spunky white boy. If he so chose, he could save Ike.

Silver Birch stiffened as the shrill cries sounded again, nearer this time. Only now a new sound was added; a final cry that was louder and longer than the rest, finally dying out in a mournful wolf howl. This meant that one of the Sokoki warriors had fallen in battle. Along with Silver Birch, every squaw in Pigwacket would be praying to Manitou that the dead one was not hers.

Ike too found himself praying. Please, not Kohokas. Not his only friend among the warriors. He stared at Joe, and Joe stared back mutely. The moments dragged slowly, the tension mounted.

Then, abruptly, a shaved head emerged from the forest. A cry of joy, quickly smothered, involuntarily escaped from Weetamoo, standing nearby. That first warrior was her husband, Adiwando—very much alive.

Next came Hegans, gliding silent as a shadow from the forest on snowshoes. Canonchet followed him, and then Wexar. One after another, still maintaining single file, they entered the village. Scalp locks dangled from every belt.

Maybe Bomazine's ruthless father, Mugg, had been the victim, Ike speculated. No, there he was now. He wasn't the one. How about Bomazine? Could he be the— no, there he was, big as life, his snowshoes eating up the distance with prodigious strides.

Ike swallowed hard and looked at Silver Birch. Her face was inscrutable. There was no other warrior left. It

70

was Kohokas. This they all knew, even before the stoic braves came to a halt before the wigwam of Kohokas.

"The Mohawks were without snowshoes," Mugg grunted. "The Great Spirit sent an early storm to trap them."

"They floundered like frightened deer," Bomazine said.

"It was a proud day for the Sokokis," Mugg declared. "Many of our young braves proved themselves to be great warriors." He laid a hand on the broad shoulders of Bomazine. "My son kill four Mohawks all alone."

Then there was silence. Silver Birch raised her eyes.

"He who was our chief kill five Mohawks before he die," Mugg told her. "We bury him deep beneath the snow and cover the grave well. His bones rest in peace. They will not be disturbed. When the snow has gone, we will bring him to Pigwacket for burial worthy of a great Sokoki."

Ike had learned enough about Indian customs to realize that Mugg was carefully avoiding direct use of Kohokas' name. In their eyes, such a tactless blunder could only intensify the grief of his survivors. He further knew what the formal burial in the spring would involve. In the bark coffin would be placed weapons, pipe, tobacco, paint, tools and food. Indians believed that spirits continued in the land of souls the same sort of existence they had led in this world.

Ike marveled at Silver Birch's self-discipline. He knew that Indian boys were trained from infancy not to betray emotion. No matter what the misfortune might be, they must accept it without any change of expression. This was a supreme demonstration that squaws too could suffer stoically.

"Not only the Mohawks were trapped by the snow,"

71

Sassup announced importantly. "Mosbas tried to escape. Him burn bindings, get loose during the night, but big storm make him change mind. Now what we do with him?"

Bomazine's black eyes narrowed to slits. Instinctively he reached for his hatchet. "We will torture him at the stake," he said contemptuously.

In desperation, Ike held up a hand commandingly, palm outward. He knew that the warriors, still flushed with their victory, could easily be whipped into a lust for more blood.

"Is it up to Bomazine to decide the fate of the paleface?" he said in their language, with all the authority he could command. "Is it up to Sassup or Hegans or Mugg?"

His head moved gravely from side to side. "No, it is not for them to say. The one who has that right has not spoken. The one who now owns Mosbas has not even been asked." He swung around and inclined his head. "That one is Silver Birch!"

There was a murmur of grudging assent among the braves. In their desire for revenge they had temporarily forgotten tribal law. The widow of a slain warrior inherited all of his property—including his prisoners.

Silver Birch glanced at Ike. "Mosbas shall not be put to death," she said firmly. "That is the wish of Silver Birch."

Joe involuntarily let out a yelp of delight and hugged Ike tightly. Bomazine eyed them with a mixture of frustration and rage.

Silver Birch held up her hand, commanding silence. "But the hunter is now gone from Silver Birch's wigwam. For many moons there will not even be enough for Silver Birch and her three children."

72

Ike had heard Indian customs discussed on several occasions. When a brave died, his widow could not marry again for at least a year. Nor was she allowed to secure meat from anyone else. To do so would bring a curse down on the gun of the one who gave her the meat. In short, she and her children had to provide for themselves as best they could. It was not always easy, especially when one had a baby as young as Mikowa to look out for. Ike guessed what Silver Birch was about to say, hoping against hope that he was wrong.

Silver Birch looked steadily at Ike, her dark eyes filled with tenderness, her voice with regret. "Silver Birch has no choice. She must sell the captives so there will be two less people to feed."

Bomazine moved with the speed of a panther. In an instant he stood before Silver Birch. "Mugg will buy them," he said. "Him rich in dogs. Him give one of his best to help Sassup kill game."

Silver Birch shook her head. "That is not enough."

Bomazine scowled. "Him give two dogs then. But him not want Wees. There is not enough food in the village to feed the Fat One. There is no one who will take such a pig for a gift."

Silver Birch looked around, from one stolid face to another, and she saw that Bomazine spoke the truth. No one would take Joe.

Her lips tightened. "Silver Birch will keep Wees. But two dogs are not enough for a strong slave like Mosbas. Someone else will give more for him."

"Mugg will give three of his best dogs!" Bomazine added hastily.

Silver Birch considered this gravely. "It is done," she

73

said. "Mosbas is Mugg's." Without another word, she turned her back and stepped into the wigwam.

Then Ike got a mild taste of what was coming. With a triumphant sneer, Bomazine gave him a violent shove that sent him sprawling headlong into a snowdrift.

Even as he rolled over and pulled his knees up under him to arise, Ike realized that he was now facing his greatest trial. At last, Bomazine had him at his mercy.

Ike was roused at daybreak the next morning by a moccasined foot thumping his side, none too gently. He opened his eyes to see Bomazine glowering down at him. "We go now," he said. "Paleface get up quick, help dogs carry load."

Before Ike got to one elbow, he heard a rending sound overhead. Suddenly a portion of wigwam was torn loose and flung aside, exposing the stern face and tufted head of Mugg. "The Frost King has come down from the North," he said. "It is time for winter hunt. We leave today—now."

It was not unexpected. Ike had heard the Indians discussing this many times. When nights grew long and days grew short, when deep snows sent the forest creatures into hibernation or confined them to browsing, the Indians split up into families or small groups, ranging far and wide to forage for food.

"Each of our people need much meat," Kohokas had explained to him, only the week before. "Our hunters must kill many deer every week—or many, many rabbits. If we stay in one place, all the deer and rabbits are soon killed. So Sokokis must split up and go to many hunting grounds until planting time in the spring, when the new Indian year begins."

74

Just thinking of Kohokas now made Ike's throat tighten.

"Mosbas run fast, wrestle good," Bomazine taunted, as Ike got stiffly to his feet. "Now we see how him survive winter; much cold, little food. We see if him tough, like Bomazine, or weak like little papoose!"

Ike shivered as a bone-chilling wind sluiced through the opening made by Mugg. It was a bleak landscape that greeted his eyes. Overnight, it seemed, winter had sunk its sharp talons into the vulnerable earth. The ground was blanketed with two feet of snow, the mounded evergreens sagging under its weight. But the dogs seemed to enjoy it. They looked very much like big, gray wolves, Ike thought, with their pointed muzzles and bushy, curled tails.

They were responding to the toe-tingling air with sharp barks that echoed back from the hills. Wokwesis—the sly one—bounded over to nuzzle Ike's hand. This was the one that had invariably exposed Joe and him when they were playing hide-and-seek. True to his vow, Ike had gone out of his way to make friends with the dogs—especially Wokwesis. He had slipped them morsels of food. He had even trained the dog to return to Bomazine, his own master. If Wokwesis searched Ike out when they were playing hide-and-seek, Ike learned to bribe the dog with morsels of food. "Bomazine," he would command, using a hand signal. "Go find Bomazine!" When the dog did as he was told, Ike would slip him his reward behind the mystified Bomazine's back.

Standing there now, Ike saw that even Kogwa, Wokwesis' mother and oldest among the dogs, was frolicking like a puppy. She dashed up to Ike suddenly, planting her forepaws on Ike's chest and licking his cheek with a coarse, wet tongue.

75

This show of affection, insignificant though it was, warmed Ike's heart, but it was short-lived. In one catlike bound, Bomazine reached Kogwa's side and planted a foot in her ribs. The poor dog was sent cartwheeling through the air, writhing and yelping, and disappeared from view in a deep snowdrift.

Ike checked an almost overpowering impulse to fly at Bomazine. He must watch himself more carefully. He belonged to Mugg now, which was the same as belonging to Bomazine. The big savage would be egging him on at every opportunity, just waiting for a chance to get even. And there was no Kohokas any more to insist on fair play.

No, Bomazine had thrown down the challenge in so many words. The sole way to survival in the next few weeks was perfectly clear. No matter what the provocation, Ike must control himself.

Instead of tackling Bomazine, Ike turned away deliberately and watched Mugg's activities with feigned interest. Having stripped the bark wigwam, the tawny brave now disassembled the pole framework. Next, he hitched the four dogs, one ahead of the other, to a wooden sledge. About eight feet long and turned up in front, this sledge was bound tightly together with buckskin thongs.

Finally he and his fat squaw, Onux, loaded the sledge with goods, lashing them down securely. When the sledge was heaped too high to hold any more, Mugg turned to Ike. "Here, paleface, eat," he commanded, holding out a clenched fist.

Ravenous, Ike eagerly extended his hand. Into it dribbled half a dozen kernels of parched corn. Not a very hefty breakfast, Ike reflected. Still, it was food, and he was grateful for any nourishment. This would be all he would get until evening. He opened his mouth hungrily to pop the kernels in, but they never reached their target. As Mugg turned away, Bomazine jostled Ike's arm, and the precious corn flew astray into the deep snow.

Ike whirled on the smirking Indian, uttering a low cry of anger. Mugg heard him and turned around. And Ike was dimly aware that Onux had observed the incident with toothless glee. At the last instant, Ike checked himself—for the second time that morning. Losing his temper would be foolhardy.

"We have come to say good-by," someone suddenly spoke up behind Ike. He turned to face Nolka. Before he could say anything, she reached out and took his right hand in both of hers. "Do not bother with Bomazine, Mosbas," she whispered hurriedly. "Slip this into your pouch when he is not looking, and eat it later, when he is not around."

Ike's hand closed over a generous helping of corn meal. "Hello, Nolka," he smiled gratefully. "Hello—and good-by. My masters arise with the sun. They are ready to leave. See, all of their belongings are piled on the sledge."

"Mosbas is wrong," Bomazine corrected. "The sledge will not hold everything. Mosbas himself must carry the rest." So saying, he proceeded to pile clothing and blankets and other goods on Ike's back, securing the load with a buckskin tumpline, the broad part of which encircled Ike's forehead. While the load was well balanced and not too heavy at the moment, Ike knew that it would become almost unendurable before the long day was over.

Joe stood forlornly behind Nolka. Ike could see that his eyes were red-rimmed from crying. "I—I sure wish't I was goin' with you," Joe managed. His lower lip quivered as he spoke. Ike was afraid he might burst into tears at any moment. More of that and one of the Indians was sure to knock him in the head.

"I can't rightly say that I feel the same," he retorted. "It's going to be tough pickin's as it is, without toting the likes of you."

"Ho, ho, Mosbas speaks with a straight tongue," Mugg agreed. "Wees—the Fat One—would eat more than the rest of us put together."

Taken aback, Joe looked at Ike in bewilderment. Then he scowled and turned away. "Well! If that's the way you feel about it, then good riddance!" Without another word he waddled off.

Ike watched him go regretfully. He would have liked to console the forlorn youngster—to assure him that everything would turn out all right. But sympathy wasn't what Joe needed right now. He had to grit his teeth and take up another notch in his belt. Maybe insulting him would make him do just that.

A sharp "crack" exploded behind Ike suddenly, accompanied by the stinging lash of a buckskin whip. With a yelp of pain, Ike leaped forward, stumbled, slipped and went down beneath his topheavy load.

It was Onux who pulled him roughly to his feet and tightened the goods again. Bomazine stood watching with a smirk on his face and the whip in his hand. When Ike's load was once more in place, Bomazine sent the lash whistling out over the team of dogs. Instantly they strained forward, putting the sled in motion.

"See, even the dogs do not stumble and fall down," Bomazine taunted Ike. "Only Mosbas fall down, like a feeble old man. One dog worth more than two palefaces."

"Ho, ho," Mugg agreed. "Bomazine right. One dog worth more than two palefaces."

Ike bent silently to his load, falling in behind the sledge. Nolka trotted beside him a few feet. "Good-by,

Mosbas," she cried. "We will see you in the spring, when the new Indian year begins. Then we will all be together again."

"Good-by, Nolka," Ike panted. "May Manitou fill your wigwam with good health and much food."

Ike had never dreamed that he would ever regret leaving the Indian village, but such was the case now, as the white-mantled forest swallowed them up in its immensity. He was alone with three hostile Indians. Never in his life had he felt quite so defenseless.

That first day, Bomazine complained constantly about their slow progress. "Paleface slow, like tortoise. Him hurry up—or get knocked in head."

Ike couldn't believe he was that much of a hindrance. Back home, he had used snowshoes many times running a winter trapline. It seemed to him he was doing all right, despite the fact that he was traveling on an empty stomach. All he could do was place one foot ahead of the other until they told him to stop—or he would drop in his tracks from hunger and exhaustion. He could not even have the satisfaction of answering Bomazine's frequent jibes in kind.

"It takes two to make a fight," his pa used to caution Ike and his brothers, when they got into a hassle. "One can't fight alone, no matter how hard he tries. Just keep your mouth shut when you start boiling, and see how quick you simmer down."

That was the course he must follow. He couldn't risk any more open hostility with the savage. With no Kohokas Captured by Abnakis 11|13|23 El (2m par)—os (Hastings) to intercede, Bomazine might very well sink a hatchet in his head in a fit of anger. No, he must content himself with the single spark of hope that some day, somewhere, somehow, an opportunity to escape would present itself. When it did, he would have his chance to outwit Bomazine, once and for all.

Even as the thought of escape entered his mind, he noticed that they were snowshoeing southward, at least for the present. Every step in that direction brought him closer to Haverhill and home.

When they continued southerly on the second morning, Ike's hopes began to rise with the sun. "If they just keep on going in this direction," he reasoned, "my chances will get better all the time. Sure as shootin' they'll slip up, sooner or later, and I'll have a chance to escape."

It was a beautiful morning, warmer than the day before. Not a cloud marred the deep blue of the sky. With half a dozen kernels of corn under his belt, Ike felt stronger. There were fewer disparaging remarks from Bomazine that morning. As a matter of fact, the three Indians were hard put to keep up with him.

"Little Mink is well named," Mugg admitted grudgingly, about midday. "Him quick and strong. Make good hunter some day."

"Feed him too much," Bomazine grunted. "Paleface travel too fast on six kernels of corn. Tonight him get only three." He watched intently for Ike's reaction, but Ike did not so much as flick an eyelash. He was learning well the Indian trait of stoicism. "If Bomazine thinks he can goad me into a showdown, he's got another think coming," was his inner reaction. Instead, Ike quickened his stride. That was one way he could challenge Bomazine. "Let the big bully keep up with me, if he can," Ike thought.

· He did, and so did Mugg and Onux. Ike marveled at their endurance, and that of the dogs as well. Without respite or food, the sturdy animals had been bucking deep snow since sunup, pulling a load of three hundred pounds.

It was about midafternoon that Mugg abruptly called a halt. Then he threw back his head, cupped his hands and gave voice to the sharp, prolonged wail of the wolf. The call echoed back from the towering white hills and was swallowed up by the winter stillness. Quiet as a statue, Mugg awaited an answering call. When there was none, the journey was resumed.

Before long, Mugg called another halt and repeated the performance, and this time, from afar, came an answer. Then began a series of calls and answering calls, establishing each other's identity, while Mugg and his party pressed onward.

Soon they came to a well-trodden path among the pines. Following this a scant hundred yards, they emerged into a sizable clearing that held a score of wigwams. Smoke was streaming straight upward from their vents into the still winter air.

Here Ike received his first news of the colonies. There were two white captives in the village; a man named Jonas Tarbell and a boy named Samuel Ladd. Left alone temporarily, while the Indians held a powwow in the council house, the white prisoners had a chance to talk freely. Seated around a crackling blaze in one of the wigwams, they eagerly swapped experiences.

"Where was you taken?" Samuel asked Ike. He was about sixteen, Ike guessed; a tall, frail boy with lank brown hair and a nervous habit of glancing apprehensively over his shoulder at the least sound.

"Haverhill," Ike replied. "How about you?"

"Oyster River in New Hampshire," Samuel said.

"During that attack a couple of years ago?" Ike asked.

Samuel nodded. "That's right. They come on us in July."

Ike frowned. "You've been with 'em near two years, and you haven't had a chance to escape in all that time?"

Samuel cringed and glanced over his shoulder. "Shhh," he said, putting a hand to his lips. "I don't even think that word, let alone say it out loud."

Noticing Ike's scornful look, the older man spoke up. Jonas Tarbell was about fifty, Ike decided, a thin, balding man with a hangdog look of servitude, but he appeared to be a man of some learning; a man of the gospel, maybe.

"Samuel, here, and I have good reason to be cautious," Jonas said. "Samuel's brother got it into his head that he could make it back home. Not a month after we were taken, he tried it one dark night."

He paused, and Samuel added for him, "They brought him back before noon the next day. The dogs tracked him down in a hurry."

"They won't track me down," Ike boasted. "I've made it a point to be friends with 'em. I pet 'em a lot and sneak scraps of food to them every chance I get."

"Samuel's brother wasn't the only one," Jonas said. "In our wanderings, we have heard of many others who have tried to escape, but so far, we have not heard of anyone who has made it."

He smiled indulgently at Ike's look of skepticism. "Ah, but the dogs are the least of it, my boy. There's this cursed wilderness to contend with." He shook his head. "No, you'll never make it. Give up the idea, for your own sake. T'would be better if you wait until your loved ones redeem you, or possibly the heathens will sell you to the French in Canada."

"Or maybe they'll just keep you, like they have us,"

83

Samuel said. "Maybe you'll have to live and die the life of an Indian. But even that's better'n being tortured to death by them savages."

Ike's mouth drew to a determined line. "I'd rather die right here than give up," he said. "Somehow or other, sooner or later, I'll escape and find my way back home to Haverhill."

Captured by Abnakis 11|13|23 El (2m par)—os (Hastings)

Jonas frowned his disapproval. "I admire your spirit. We fervently pray that you will be reunited with your loved ones, but we beseech you to wait patiently on the Lord. Do not attempt to escape. It would be suicide."

"Mosbas not want to escape any more now," spoke a voice from the wigwam entrance.

Startled, Ike half rose to his feet and turned to face Bomazine. How long had he been standing there? Ike wondered. How much had he heard?

The grim-visaged brave crooked a finger. "Paleface come," he commanded.

Silently, but with thudding heart, Ike followed the young Indian past the row of wigwams. What form of abuse did Bomazine have in store for him now? Ike asked himself. Whatever it might be, he was determined to take it like a man.

Before the council house, Bomazine halted and stepped aside, drawing back the bearskin covering the entrance. "Mosbas go inside," he said. "See what Indian warriors do to white men."

Although he cringed inwardly, Ike stepped in with a bold stride. No one paid any attention to him and Bomazine as they entered. Legs crossed under them, the braves sat about, conversing solemnly, drawing now and then on their long-stemmed pipes.

84

But it was not the braves who held Ike's eye. His gaze was drawn to the center of the room. There, dangling from three poles, was the grisliest sight he had ever seen.

Black scalps, brown scalps, blond scalps—scalps of every size and description hung there.

"Our Indian brothers raid Haverhill, kill every paleface there," he heard Bomazine say triumphantly. "Warriors, squaws, papooses—everybody killed and scalped. Now Mosbas has no family to go home to."

Ike fought desperately to retain his composure. Of all the blows Bomazine might have struck, this was the cruelest of all. Despite his every effort to absorb the shock, he was convulsed with grief. Whirling, he fled blindly from the council house.

At that moment, Ike no longer cared whether he lived or died.

7

Now BEGAN for Ike a period he would not soon forget. Dazed by what Bomazine had told him, stunned by the sight of all those scalps—was that tiny blonde one his baby sister's?—he could not eat or sleep in the days and weeks that followed.

From that first Indian village they wandered on to others, with no apparent destination in mind. It was a helter-skelter existence at best. At its worst, it developed into a bitter struggle for survival. As the snow piled higher in the woods, game grew scarcer. The Indians became gaunt and ill-tempered, but it mattered little to Ike. You had to fight, when there was something to fight for. You made ambitious plans, when there was something to plan for. But what did you do when your incentive was destroyed? When your loved ones were gone, and there was nothing left to cling to?

Ike did what so many tormented captives had done before him. He lost heart. He moved like one in a trance, scarcely aware of the specter called starvation that stalked their camp day and night.

Always before he had been able to dredge up some inspiration, some advice of his father's that sustained him in the face of adversity, but now he was sinking into an apparently bottomless pit of despair. His pa was dead, his ma, his sisters and brothers. His home was destroyed. He could not rouse himself, could not even generate any interest in survival.

"Mosbas does not eat enough to keep a sparrow alive," Onux said one evening before the fire. "If him not eat, North Wind will blow him away. Him very thin. When him move, Onux hear bones rattle."

She extended a steaming bowl of broth to Ike. The hunting had not been good for several weeks. They had been eating less and less in January, February and March. Now, early in April, they were reduced to the barest of fare.

This broth, for instance, was merely water thickened with meal that they had ground from the bark of a maple tree. Even in his despair, Ike never ceased to marvel at the Indians' ingenuity. In a pinch, they would even throw a few pine needles into boiling water, just to give it a little flavor, and make a meal of that.

When times were bad, they made use of everything. From a deer they obtained not only food but hide for moccasins and clothing, glue from boiling the hoofs, tools made out of bones, bowstrings from sinews, arrowheads and tool handles from antlers.

Ike had even seen them make use of some old, smelly bones they stumbled across in the forest. First, they separated them at the joints. Then they scalded them to drive out the maggots. Next they boiled them and gulped down the broth. Finally they pounded the bones to powder and ate that.

It had been a nauseating performance, but it had not concerned Ike. He took no interest whatsoever in food. To placate Onux, however, he now took the proffered bowl and dipped into it halfheartedly. The broth warmed his stomach, but did not in any way revive his spirits.

Onux leaned over and placed a hand on Ike's forehead. "Mosbas is hot," she said sharply. "Him not well. Onux has snakeroot here. Onux give Mosbas medicine very soon now or him die."

Bomazine grunted. He had become increasingly irritable as the food supply diminished. "Let him die," he said.

"Then we cannot redeem him or sell him in Canada," Onux protested.

"Can sell him scalp," Bomazine pointed out. "The great French warrior, Frontenac, will buy it."

The mention of Frontenac's name kindled a faint spark in Ike's misery-glazed eyes. He had almost forgotten any other world existed outside this cold-manacled prison of tall pines, hunger and fatigue.

He had forgotten that King William's War was still being waged; that Count Frontenac, governor of Canada, was inciting the Indians to raid the English frontier settlements. Englishmen—and women and children too—were being led off like animals into captivity. Others were being scalped without mercy—like his loved ones.

It was bad enough to fight the Indians. How could the English fight them and the Frenchmen too? What chance did the scattered and vulnerable pioneers stand against the swelling tide of French and Indian attacks? No doubt about it, the settlers were taking a licking.

"It's one thing to lick a man, but it's something else to

conquer him. The French and Indians will find out that the only conquered Englishman is a dead one!"

Ike's father had often spoken these words. Whenever he heard of another attack, he would clench a big fist, shake it at the dark brooding forest and shout his defiance.

The words struck a responsive chord. For the first time in weeks, something stirred within Ike . . . faintly, but unmistakably. The tempo of his eating increased and he soon cleaned up all of his broth. At least there was one consolation, he thought grimly. He was not conquered. He was not dead yet, though he felt close to it. For two days now they had been traveling in a cold, steady drizzle. The snow was soggy on top and rotten underneath. It was treacherous footing on snowshoes. In his weakened condition, burdened with a heavy load of furs they had taken, he had fallen a lot in the slush. As a consequence, he was soaked to the skin most of the time.

Now all the weeks of adversity were telling on him. That night he alternately shivered uncontrollably with the chills, then broke out in a cold, clammy sweat. He was on the verge of pneumonia.

By morning, Onux was adamant. When Mugg and Bomazine would have moved on, she stood her ground with the ferocity of a she-bear defending a cub. Long before daylight she was boiling roots to make medicine.

"Mosbas not move today," she told Mugg and Bomazine firmly. "Him stay with Onux. Onux make him all well. One more sleep, maybe two, him be all right."

"Only two, maybe three more sleeps and we reach Pigwacket," Mugg retorted. "Let him wait until then."

Onux shook her head. "Mosbas not move today," she repeated stubbornly. Turning her back on the two braves,

90

she knelt down and propped Ike's head up in her lap. Then she put a cup of vile-smelling liquid to his parched lips.

Ike rejoiced faintly that they were near Pigwacket. Joe was at Pigwacket. Since he had been told of the death of his family, Joe had become even more important to him. Joe was just about the only friend he had left in the world. Aside from that weak response, however, Ike was only dimly aware of the controversy between Onux and her menfolks, and he was too far gone with fever to care.

They were wasting their breaths anyway, he thought dully. Why, he could no more get to his feet and push on than he could fly. So he lay back and relaxed under Onux' ministering hand. Sick as he was, he could appreciate the luxury of a day of rest. He knew that Onux only wanted to keep him alive so they could sell him for a fat profit, but he was grateful that someone was concerned over him, no matter what the motive.

Bomazine, however, was not yet convinced. At his best, he was none too agreeable. When he was hungry, he was brutal. "Mosbas is a weakling, like all other palefaces. Him no stronger than Wees, the Fat One. Bomazine does not want to wait here. Him want to reach Pigwacket as soon as possible. Maybe there is food there for all of us." Scowling, he loosened his tomahawk and stepped forward. "Let us knock him in the head and go on to Pigwacket."

Onux snatched up a hatchet and turned to face him, her dark eyes flashing. "Onux did not ask Bomazine and Mugg to stay here. It would be well if they did go on to Pigwacket. When they have found food and rested, they can come back. By then, Mosbas will be ready to travel."

Mugg reached out and laid a restraining hand on Bomazine's arm. "Onux is right," he agreed. "We will go on to Pigwacket. They will stay here."

Reluctantly, Bomazine yielded. But he raised a threatening fist even as he backed out of the smoke-filled wigwam. "If Mosbas is not ready to travel when Bomazine returns, Bomazine will scalp him and feed him to the dogs."

"If Mosbas is not ready to travel when Bomazine returns," Onux promised, "then Onux will scalp him herself."

Though he clung desperately to consciousness, Ike felt himself slipping into delirium. Would he ever come out of it? he wondered. And if he did, what fate awaited him? Reunion with Joe—or a tomahawk?

When Ike came to, it was broad daylight. How long had he been delirious? A day—two days—maybe three?

That final scene between Onux and Bomazine came back to him with the vividness of a nightmare. "If Mosbas is not ready to travel when Bomazine returns," the brave had threatened, "Bomazine will scalp him and feed him to the dogs."

Impulsively Ike tried to get up, only to fall back, exhausted. The fever had left him as limp as a rag doll.

"Wurregan," a voice said, "it is well. The evil spirit has left Mosbas. Him get better fast now."

Ike glanced up to see Onux standing over him. She sat down on her heels, carefully balancing a steaming bowl of stew, and extended a spoonful toward him. "Mosbas eat this. Make him strong like brother Maqua, the bear. Him be ready to travel when Mugg and Bomazine return."

Ike's heart beat faster. "How long have they been gone?" he said anxiously.

"Three sleeps," Onux said. "They will return today. Mosbas must be ready to start for Pigwacket. Him stop talking now, start eating."

Somehow Ike managed to get to one elbow, and with the first spoonful of thick, meaty stew, strength began slowly to seep back into his system. The stew was delicious; piping hot and filling. It was the most nourishing food he had eaten since his capture.

Where had Onux obtained such fine meat—and so much of it? How had she succeeded where Mugg and Bomazine—both mighty hunters—had failed?

These were but fleeting questions, and he was too famished to seek the answers. For an hour or more he alternately ate and rested. Onux was too wise in the ways of starvation to let him glut himself. After such a prolonged hunger, he might easily have gorged himself to death.

Gradually, too, hope began to stir within him again. Oh, he was far from well, he knew that. Every move he made told him he had been mighty sick, but it was as though the fever had purged him of the grief and despondency that had gripped him all these weeks—ever since Bomazine had told him about Haverhill. Given half a chance, he might have accepted his loss and surmounted it somehow, but there had been no respite from cold, hunger and weariness until now. This was the first real rest he had been given in weeks. And the first solid food.

"A little rest and a full stomach can do more for a man's morale than all the sermons ever written," Ike murmured aloud.

Onux fixed him with her shiny, birdlike eyes. "What is Mosbas saying?" she asked.

Ike smiled and shrugged. "Something my pa used to say. I'm just coming to realize what he meant."

Onux placed a wrinkled hand on his forehead. "Is cool. Mosbas is all right now?"

Ike nodded and struggled to his feet. Once upright, he

felt surprisingly steady. The strength was fast surging back into his sturdy frame. "Mosbas is all right now," he assured her. And he was. He was ready for anything—Mugg, Bomazine, the trip back to Pigwacket—Joe.

Joe! In all the misery of the past few weeks, he had hardly given Joe a thought. Now excitement flooded through him at the prospect of seeing his friend again.

Wees—the Fat One. Ike smiled fondly. How had Joe fared on sparse winter rations? His mistress, Silver Birch, was kindly disposed toward him, and Joe was no slouch at ferreting out food. Ike was willing to bet that Joe had wintered as well as anyone at Pigwacket.

They would be together again—temporarily, at least. Long enough to plan their escape, and long enough to carry it out this time!

Ike's excitement continued to mount. Soon the snow would be gone. Yes, the time to escape was at hand. For the first time in weeks, he had enough strength and courage to give it serious consideration. And the more he thought about it, the more he realized it was now—or never.

Mugg and Bomazine had been discussing a trip to Canada in the early spring. There they planned to exchange the furs they had taken that winter for guns and powder and tobacco. They had also let slip that they intended to sell him into slavery up there.

Ike's fist clenched. "I'd rather die!" he said aloud fiercely.

Onux was at his side in an instant. "Mosbas not die," she said, patting his hand reassuringly. "Him strong and tough as the oak. Him live a long time."

Ike was glad that Onux had not guessed what was on his mind. He would have to be more careful from now on.

94

If she did guess his intentions, she would tell Mugg and Bomazine that he was getting itchy feet. Then they would be watching and waiting, laying for him, ready to pounce.

Ike nodded. "Yes, I'll live a long time," he agreed. Long enough to escape. Long enough to lead some rangers back into this country, if necessary. Above all, he hoped, long enough to see the settlers and the Indians living together in peace. There had been enough misunderstanding and bloodshed.

Stepping outside, Ike took a deep breath of pine-scented air. "It's great to be alive," he said. "I haven't felt this good in a dog's age."

A cold, wet muzzle was shoved into his palm and he looked down. "Speaking of dogs, look who's here," he laughed. He leaned over and scratched Wokwesis' shaggy sides. He was shocked to feel every rib in the dog's body. "Why, you're nothing but skin and bones!" he exclaimed.

Quickly he stepped into the wigwam, seized the largest chunk of meat in the kettle and hurried back.

"No!" Onux cried, rushing out and reaching frantically for the dripping meat.

But it was too late. Ike had already tossed it into the air. "Catch!" he commanded.

Wokwesis caught it all right, but then a strange thing happened. Almost immediately he dropped it on the ground. Whining deep in his throat, he backed away from it.

"Now what in tarnation ails you?" Ike demanded. "Just when did you get so all-fired persnickety?"

He retrieved the piece of meat. "Oh well, if you don't want it, I'll give it to your poor old mother. I'll bet she won't turn up her nose at it. Here, Kogwa. C'mon, Kogwa."

95

He was soon holding off the other dogs, but no Kogwa. She was nowhere in sight.

He turned to Onux. "Where's Kogwa?" he said.

Onux was staring guiltily at the chunk of meat in his hand. Then it struck him. A spasm of nausea gripped him, and he flung the meat away. The other dogs did not hesitate. They were upon it in an instant; growling, snarling, rending it to bits that they gulped down greedily.

This, then, was how Onux had succeeded in providing meat where Mugg and Bomazine had failed.

Onux laid a hand on Ike's shoulder. "Kogwa was very old and very tired from many winters on the trail. She would have died in another day or two anyway. Do not be sick, Mosbas. The food has made you much stronger. The life of Kogwa has saved yours."

Her hand stiffened as a wolf howl issued from deep in the forest. Kogwa, nausea—everything but that mournful, long-drawn-out cry was swept from Ike's mind. It might fool anyone else—even a wolf—but not him and Onux. That double inflection near the end was the signal. Mugg and Bomazine were returning!

The wolf cry sounded again, nearer this time, and placing her hands to her mouth, Onux expertly answered in kind. From the forest a short time later emerged two lithe figures in buckskin—Mugg and Bomazine.

"Mosbas is standing," Mugg greeted them as the two braves snowshoed up. "Him must be much better. Onux mix good medicine."

Onux nodded. "The evil spirit is gone. Mosbas is well again. We are ready for the trip to Pigwacket. When does Mugg wish to leave?"

"Bomazine wishes to leave now," her strapping son

96

spoke up brusquely. "There is much good food in Pig-wacket. Two moose were killed yesterday."

"Our people there are well?" Onux asked.

Mugg shook his head. "They have had a bad winter. Much cold, little food. Many of them lie buried beneath the snow."

"How about Wees?" Ike spoke up anxiously. "Is he well?"

It was Bomazine who answered him. "Him well done," he replied. "Before brother moose killed, Indians thin, starving. Wees fat, like pig. Indians hold council, decide to kill Wees, cook'um."

He rubbed his stomach, smacked his lips, rolled his eyes. "Him good eating too. Nice and tender. Yum, yum."

For the second time within the hour, Ike fought a wave of nausea. But this time it was worse, because he was sick at heart, as well a sick to his stomach, and filled with raging anger and loathing. Joe's loss was a staggering blow. First his family, and now his only friend out here in the wilds. Ike didn't feel he'd ever get over it. Yet somehow he must.

There was only one thing to do, and he did it. Ignoring Bomazine's leering face, Ike reached down and took up a notch in his belt.

8

IT WAS early afternoon before they broke camp. That meant only half a day of travel. By nightfall, Ike was grateful for this. He had misjudged his strength. The fever had left him weaker than he realized, but a good night's sleep accomplished wonders. A savory stew, prepared from moose meat brought by Mugg from Pigwacket, revived him further. He was ready and eager to hit the trail at sunrise. He refused to let himself think about poor Joe. His impending escape was all that occupied his mind.

"Mugg is glad him did not knock Mosbas in the head," Mugg said with satisfaction that night, after a full day's travel. They had marched Indian file from sunrise to sunset, and the footing was none too good. Rapidly melting snow made the ground soggy. Yet despite this, Ike was still going strong when they halted.

"Him bring much more than scalp money," Onux said. "We go to Canada soon. French pay two—three times more for strong young slave."

Bomazine grunted. "Him not strong. Him get sick, almost die. Him weak, like little papoose."

He flexed his brawny arms, strutted before Ike as they made camp. "Bomazine not get sick, like paleface. Him twice as strong as Mosbas."

Ike let it pass. The big Indian was spoiling for a fight. He would not rest easy until he had settled the score. Too many times had he been bested by Ike, disgraced before his people. Sooner or later he must have his revenge. Not now, though, Ike decided. His energies weren't quite back to normal. He had lost weight. No, he certainly would be no match for the rugged brave at this point.

"You'll have your chance, redskin," Ike reflected, as he turned his back on Bomazine to help Onux erect the wigwam. "And it won't be long now either. We'll be matching wits just as soon as I gain me a few more pounds. And this time it will be for good!"

His every thought now was focused on one thing. He still would not let himself think about Haverhill, or his family, or Joe. There was no yesterday, no today—only the day of escape. And that day would see his final contest with Bomazine. The moment his absence was discovered, there would follow another game of hide-and-seek. Only this time the penalty for being caught would be death at the stake.

Calmly and efficiently, Ike reviewed his plans before he went to sleep. He had absorbed much on the grim march from Haverhill to Pigwacket. He had learned even more about this remote wilderness in their wanderings this winter. When he struck out for the settlements, there would be no guesswork. He knew exactly what direction to take, what trails and watercourses to follow. Everything waited now on favorable weather. That and a little more rest, a little more strength. And the opportune moment.

100

Morning gave promise of soon fulfilling the first condition; favorable weather. Overnight, it seemed, spring had burst forth in all its rejuvenating glory. The mountains were still capped with snow, but down there in the lowlands, the snow was melting fast under a brilliant sun. Brooks were swelling into rivers, rivers into streams. Oaks, elms, birches, maples—all were beginning to show green buds. Birds were flocking northward by the thousands, from dainty bluebirds to wedges of honking geese.

"The new year has begun," Onux said. "Soon we will start for Canada."

"Not me," Ike thought. "I'll be on my way to the settlements."

He paid close attention to their surroundings as they resumed the march. By late afternoon, he began to recognize landmarks he had filed away in his mind last fall, when they made the trip to Pigwacket from Haverhill.

This stand of birch they were passing through was close to Pigwacket, of that he felt certain. The thought had no sooner crossed his mind than Mugg gave voice to his distinctive wolf howl. There was no answer immediately, but at least it confirmed Ike's suspicions. They were nearing Pigwacket.

Yes, and there was another spot he remembered, right there by that uprooted pine. Joe had stumbled and fallen there, he was sure. Poor Joe. For the first time since Bomazine had told him of Joe's appalling fate, Ike let his thoughts dwell briefly on his unfortunate friend.

Abruptly Ike wrenched himself away from such emotional upheavals. He needed all the mental and physical vitality he could summon to plan and execute his escape.

"You've got a lot to be cheerful about," he reminded himself. "For one thing, good weather is here. The snow's going fast, and you really know the lay of the land around here. You guessed we were getting near Pigwacket. I reckon that's two mighty good omens."

There was a third omen to come—the best one of all, but it was several minutes later before Ike learned of it. That was when an answering wolf howl ushered the returning party into Pigwacket.

The comparative hustle and bustle of the Indian village was a welcome change after their solitary wanderings. The air was sweet with the odor of boiling sap. Ike's mouth watered at the thought of that Indian delicacy called maple sugar.

Several braves, painted and dressed for a ceremonial dance, were filing into the council house. There was Silver Birch, standing at a wooden mortar, grinding corn with a pestle. Now she saw Ike and her teeth flashed white in her dusky countenance.

And there was Sassup, patching a leak in his birch-bark canoe with tree gum. He was taller, but much thinner, his young body showing the ravages of hunger. He had not seen Ike as yet.

Ike found himself searching quite eagerly for Nolka. Yes, there she was now, just stepping lightly from their wigwam. Nolka too was taller—but very slim. This only served to accentuate her natural grace and to enhance her delicate features.

She caught sight of him and let the moose hide drop back into place. With a cry of joy, she came bounding toward him.

Then came the third omen—the best one of all. Around the corner of the wigwam, big as life, waddled— could it be?—yes, it was Joe Whittaker! A bit taller and thinner, dark as an Indian, but still very much on the roly-poly side.

He could move fast, though. Spying Ike, he let out a war whoop and made a beeline for him, and he reached Ike one step ahead of Nolka. A lump formed in Ike's throat as he hugged his old friend. For a moment he couldn't trust himself to speak, but he didn't have to. Nolka and Sassup and Silver Birch were greeting him all at once, and a dozen yelping dogs added to the confusion.

When Ike finally did find his voice, he held Joe at arm's length. "You—you're alive!" was all he could say.

Joe grinned. "If I ain't, then we're both dead and in the Happy Hunting Grounds."

"But—but Bomazine was lying. He told me you were dead!"

Joe scowled. "And he told me the same thing about you!"

Together they turned to face the big Indian youth accusingly. Bomazine stared back defiantly, his lip curled in disdain. "Bomazine test palefaces. Wees, him cry like little papoose, boo-hoo! Mosbas get sick to stomach. Both palefaces weak. Not strong and brave, like Indian."

Despite the consequences, Ike would have turned on Bomazine but for Nolka's hand firmly grasping his arm. That moment of restraint was all he needed to bring his anger under control. He was too close to freedom now to destroy his chances in a temper tantrum.

With a triumphant sneer, Bomazine turned on his heel and stalked regally away toward the council house. Onux and Mugg followed him, the latter a bit shamefaced, it seemed to Ike, and yet he could hardly blame Mugg for not exposing Bomazine as a liar. Young braves, especially, could do no wrong in the eyes of their fathers.

"I should have known better than to believe him in the first place," Joe grumbled. "All Injuns are liars. You can't never trust 'em."

Nolka shook her dark head. "Not all Indians," she said gently. "Nolka speaks with a straight tongue, and so do Silver Birch and Sassup."

Ike was staring after Bomazine, a faint spark of hope fanning to life within him. "If—if he lied about you, Joe," he mused, "then maybe he was lying about Ma and Pa— about Haverhill."

"What about Haverhill?" Joe said.

"Bomazine showed me some scalps, way back in the early part of the winter. He told me they were taken at Haverhill, that everyone in town was killed or captured."

Joe and Nolka exchanged glances. "Bomazine spoke with a crooked tongue again," Nolka told him. "Not ten sleeps ago, a white captive stayed overnight here in Pigwacket, on the way to Saint Francis with his master."

"That's right, Ike," Joe added. "They just come from a raid on Lancaster, where this fellow—Jeb Stevens was his name—was took. He said everythin' was fine and dandy in Haverhill. Ain't been a shot fired there all winter."

Nolka reached out and patted Ike's shoulder. "Mosbas and Wees have much to talk over. Nolka and Silver Birch and Sassup go now, prepare feast for their friends."

Ike was grateful to be alone with Joe. Overwhelmed by this latest news about Haverhill, he swallowed hard and gave silent thanks to the Lord. Then he squared his shoulders and faced Joe. All the omens were in their favor. This was the opportune time to escape.

"What's going on in the council house, Joe?" he asked, lowering his voice. "Are they gettin' ready for a big powwow?"

Joe nodded. "Big feast and ceremonial dance. Goin' to celebrate killin' them two moose, and the end of winter. Then, too, some of the Injuns is leaving for Canada to trade their furs for guns and tobacco and such. They got to have a farewell shindig for them. It's more'n likely we're goin' to Canada too. Mugg and Bomazine plan to sell us up there."

"Then tonight is the night," Ike said. "All the omens are good. No need to waste any more time."

"What you talkin' about?" Joe asked.

"I'm talking about escaping, what else?" Ike told him. "Are you with me?"

Joe turned pale, glanced about uneasily. "G-gee, I dunno, Ike," he stammered. "Y-you really think we can make it?"

Ike nodded. "We'll never have a better chance," he said grimly.

"W-what time?" Joe said.

"Whenever they all fall asleep," Ike said. "You might have to stay awake half the night, and you've got to be sure not to make a sound when I give you the signal. You think you can do it?"

Joe's vanity was pricked. "Course I can do it," he bristled.

"You'd better," Ike warned him.

He let it go at that. They both knew what the penalty for failure would be.

9

THE CELEBRATION went on far into the night. Everyone in the village was present, including the two prisoners. Ike and Joe were ordered to feed a big, open fire, over which large slices of moose steak were kept sizzling.

Braves, squaws, children—even the snarling dogs—gorged themselves on the bountiful fare. Some of the Indians ate themselves into a stupor, falling asleep where they sat. Others retired to their own wigwams.

But many of the braves were imbibing rum, which they had obtained recently from a passing war party of French and Indians. Various hunting songs were chanted, to the monotonous beat of a skin drum. Then the frenzied dancing began. The heavily painted braves were attired in their finest, with rattles tied to their arms and knees.

Intently Ike watched and waited for the least sign of negligence, and as the hour grew later, there were more and more indications that the dancers were letting their guard down.

At first the rum had served to excite them. It caused them to leap higher and whoop louder, their antics creating grotesque shadows in the flickering firelight. But as they continued to drink the fiery liquid, one by one they staggered off and lay down, falling almost immediately into deep slumber.

Only the hardiest of braves were still standing, and finally there was only one left—the hardiest of all. That one was Bomazine. But even he was groggy from several hours of strenuous dancing and from the paralyzing effects of rum. He finally reeled up to Ike and stood over him, breathing heavily. Ike saw him coming and feigned sleep.

"Mosbas not reach Canada alive," Bomazine muttered thickly. "Bomazine not forget what happen long time ago. Never forget. Soon—him—get—even—with—"

His voice trailed off and Ike heard a thud. Opening one eye cautiously, he saw that the Indian had collapsed in a heap nearby. Already he was sound asleep, his chest rising and falling rhythmically.

Now! Ike's breath quickened. This was the moment he had been anticipating for six months—and now it was here. He was aware of the perils involved. The odds were against them. Two boys, pitted against the stamina and cunning of two score savage pursuers, who were as skilled at tracking as the dogs they hunted with.

But Ike did not think of that, except fleetingly. He pressed his palms to the earth and raised himself up, getting a knee under him and rising stealthily to his feet, remaining in a crouched position, scanning the lodge carefully, making certain he was unobserved. Not a soul stirred —not even Joe. Ike felt a sharp stab of annoyance. Joe couldn't fake that well. He had fallen asleep! Ike was so angered he had a good mind to leave Joe behind.

Dismissing Joe for the moment, Ike deftly removed Bomazine's bearskin food pouch. He had observed earlier that Bomazine had stuffed it with dried moose meat. Moving as silently as a shadow, he appropriated Mugg's powder horn and gun from where the elder brave had laid them aside.

Scarcely daring to breathe, he stepped from the council house out into the cool night air. Golden moonlight flooded the village, making it nearly as light as day.

"That's sure in our favor," Ike thought, concealing the gun and pouch in a clump of bushes. "We ought to have a good head start by sunrise."

He couldn't dwell on that, though. He still had work to do. Joe had to be roused. "I ought to leave him where he lies," Ike reflected. "If he doesn't care enough about getting out of here to stay awake, then I don't know why I should bother."

Briefly he considered escaping alone. He knew Joe would be a hindrance, from start to finish, but almost immediately he abandoned the idea. Ever so cautiously he re-entered the council house and crept to Joe's side.

"Hey, Joe," he whispered softly.

There was no answer. Gingerly Ike reached out and tugged gently at Joe's arm.

With a snort, Joe rolled over. "What do you want?" he said loudly.

Disturbed, a nearby brave stirred in his sleep. Quick as a flash, Ike threw himself down, his heart beating like a drum, but in a moment the brave resumed his snoring. When Ike was satisfied that it was safe to move again, he made his decision; much as he hated to, he must leave Joe.

"No point in taking another chance like that," Ike thought. "He's sleeping like a log again. It'd be better to have one of us get away than to have both of us lose our hair here and now."

With even greater care than before, he stole out of the lodge into the moonlight. He had just reached the bushes where he had concealed the gun and pouch and was already thinking of going back to the lodge again for Joe, when a twig snapped behind him.

Ike froze in his tracks, fully expecting a tomahawk in the back of his head. Instead, he felt a light tap on the shoulder.

"It's me, Ike," whispered Joe. "I didn't fall asleep. I was just playin' possum, same as you."

Ike was so relieved he could have hugged Joe, but this was no time for sentiment. Their battle wasn't over; it was just beginning. This was the easiest part of their escape. Threading one hundred and more miles of dense forest without getting caught was another matter entirely.

Ike started to hand the food pouch to Joe, then shrugged and kept it himself. No sense taking chances. If Joe got really hungry, he might be very tempted to sneak a little. And once he got started, it was hard for him to stop. Next thing you knew, they would be cleaned out of what little they had. No, there was no sense tempting Joe. He just couldn't be trusted around food.

The powder horn Ike slung over one shoulder, the gun he held in his right hand. It would be better if he carried everything, he decided. Joe would need all his strength to keep up.

Then, after a final look at the slumbering village, Ike and Joe turned and melted into the forest.

Once they were among the trees, there was no guess-work. This was no spur-of-the-moment thing. Ike had pains-takingly been studying the lay of the land ever since last fall. In his mind, he had plotted every move.

The easiest route would be southward, toward Ossipee Lake. It was a route he was familiar with, since he and Joe had been brought that way after their capture. It was also the one most commonly used by the Indians and there-fore to be avoided.

The southeast was a country of many lakes, threaded by the meandering Saco River, a major Indian canoe route to the sea. In spite of the dangers this presented, it was a country that offered ample concealment, and Ike did not plan to follow the river until they neared the settlements. They would stay off the beaten paths.

This southeast route was the one he had decided on long since, and he knew a lot about its geography both from first-hand observation and from listening to the Indians. What he could not know was this: at what hour would the fierce Sokoki warriors awaken? He would give a lot to learn the answer to that question.

"Maybe it's just as well we don't know," he muttered aloud. "No danger of our getting overconfident this way."

"Wh-what you mumblin' about?" Joe wheezed. He was panting like a hound in August.

And no wonder. Ike was setting a blistering pace. Five minutes from Pigwacket, he had led them into a cedar swamp. There they had broken into a trot. Not a jog, either. A good healthy trot. That was two hours ago, and they were still moving along, briskly as ever. If anything, Ike was step-ping up the pace a bit.

"Never you mind what I'm mumbling about," Ike said. "Just you shake a leg, you hear? Far's we know, they might be on our trail already, and the way you're draggin' along, even a feeble old squaw could catch us."

"Least you could do is travel on dry land," Joe complained bitterly. "With all them hard-packed trails to run on, I still don't see why we got to flounder around in swamps and bushes."

Actually, Joe was exaggerating. Oh, there were plenty of bad spots. Before they got out of the cedar swamp, they had briefly sloshed along in water up to their knees. Aside from that it was thick, with lots of alders and blowdowns and brush, but you could make good time if you watched your step. Of course your face and hands took an awful beating, from the whiplike action of bushes and limbs. Both Ike and Joe were cut and bleeding in half a dozen places.

But they had no other choice. On the deer runs and hunting trails the redskins would ambush them for sure. Their only hope was to stay in thick cover.

"By the time you did see," Ike told Joe, "it would be too late. The Indians would have your scalp."

There was silence for a while after that. Moonlight gilded the trees about them with a golden sheen. Not a bird twittered, not a twig snapped, not a leaf stirred. It was as though every living thing throughout that vast forest was watching and waiting with bated breath, aware of the unfolding drama.

With the moon still an hour high, they came to a sprightly brook, swollen to twice its normal size by ice-cold runoff water. And here, for the first time, Ike came to a halt, but only long enough to step on a large boulder and remove his moccasins—standing first on one foot, then the other —and to sling the moccasins around his neck.

"Take your'n off, too," he directed Joe.

Joe sank down on a fallen tree trunk, panting heavily. "If you think you're goin' to talk me into goin' barefoot, through the woods, at night, when I got a perfectly good pair of moccasins—"

"Take'em off!" Ike's voice carried the sting of a whip. "And stop plankin' yourself down where you leave signs!"

Sullenly Joe obeyed, finding another flat-top boulder and removing his moccasins, as Ike had done. Even as he did so, he began whimpering. "I got to have a rest, Ike. I'm all done in. I just got to have a rest—an'—an' somethin' to eat."

"You'll have a rest soon enough," Ike told him. "We've only got maybe an hour until daylight, and then we've got to hole up, whether we want to or not. We can't take a chance traveling in broad daylight—not yet, leastwise—not until we put more distance between us and them."

He then stepped directly into the ice-cold brook, without so much as drawing a quick breath. "We couldn't help leaving a lot of signs back there in the underbrush," he explained to Joe, "but going barefoot in a brook, a man doesn't leave any trail. It's our good luck we struck one that's flowing our way, but that doesn't mean they can't find us. Those dogs of theirs could track a ghost."

He started off down the brook at a brisk pace. "And it doesn't mean we can dilly-dally either. If you're coming with me, you better hop to it—and step careful, directly into the brook!"

Joe stood there for an indecisive moment, shivering uncontrollably as he contemplated the cold, dark waters, but as Ike rounded a bend, he hesitated no longer. Inadvertently taking one step along the bank, he plunged into the brook ponderously, with a sharp intake of breath. Teeth chattering like gourd rattles, he splashed after his companion.

For an hour they traveled southeastward, in the bed of the brook. They were now well beyond the area with which Ike was familiar. Never had they hunted this far from Pigwacket. Farther along, as they approached the settlements, he might tell where he was. Maybe he could here, when he got on one of the hunting trails, but in the meantime, they were mere dots in a boundless forest. All Ike could be sure of was that they were traveling in the right direction. The moon's position told him that, as it slowly dipped toward the west. Even without it, he was constantly in touch with their position by the growth of moss on the tree trunks. He couldn't have been more certain of their course if he had been carrying a compass.

The first streaks of dawn showed that east was exactly where it should be. As the golden sun peeped over a distant snow-crested mountain, Ike came to a second halt. Joe was slowing down considerably, panting, stumbling, in danger of falling. It was time for a respite.

Standing on one foot, Ike slipped the other into a moccasin. Stepping ashore to a large flat rock on this moccasined foot, he withdrew the other and put the moccasin on that.

Then he turned to his sagging, forlorn companion. "Do as I just did," he ordered. "Mind you don't plant a footprint on the bank, where they can see it—that's it—careful now—lemme give you a hand."

Once out of the numbing water, toes tingling, Ike gingerly led them away from the brook, cautiously picking the way on stones and boulders for some distance. Then he began searching for a proper hiding place. This first day, it was too risky to travel in broad daylight. There was no telling how far they had come. A mile in the underbrush always seemed like ten miles on a good trail. The place could be swarming with Indians in an hour, for all they knew.

Oh, they would fan out all over the place. Some would spread out on the footpaths, others would take to the brush. A crushed leaf, one clear imprint, and they were hot on the trail. The dogs didn't even need that. All they needed was a faint scent.

Then there was always the danger of other Indians. Small villages dotted this whole wilderness. Tribes were stirring from their winter quarters, on the move; to Canada, to their planting grounds, to the sea.

Yes, it was far too risky to travel in broad daylight. "Time to get some rest," Ike told Joe. "Either we gave 'em the slip, or we didn't. Ain't much we can do about it now. And if we didn't, we want to be fresh so's we can give 'em a good run for it."

Joe perked up a bit. "Now we can eat, huh, Ike?"

Ike shook his head firmly. "Not moose meat, if that's what you're thinking. We've only got one big chunk, and that'll have to last us a spell. If you want something to eat, chew on some of that birch-bark for now." He kept right on going, casting about with his keen dark eyes for a suitable hideout. Up the hillside a way he paused, appraising their immediate surroundings with something akin to satisfaction.

Before them lay a huge hollow log—it must have been a primeval oak—its top well covered with green moss. Ike crawled in and looked around. It was as dry as a bone in there, and plenty large enough for the two of them. Also, it lay parallel to the brook, on the brow of a knoll, commanding a good view of the small valley. In a matter of minutes Ike had pulled a dozen pine seedlings. These he

116

carefully placed to screen the log entrance, tamping them into the moist earth. When their hideout was camouflaged to his satisfaction, he motioned Joe inside and crawled in after him, careful not to disturb the screen of seedlings.

"Don't know as we could do much better than this," he said, "and besides, it's high time we hid somewhere. Sun's up an hour or more now."

"Wonder if the redskins is up too," Joe said.

Ike wondered the same thing himself, as they settled down to a long, tense vigil. He could envision the hue and cry at Pigwacket, when the Indians discovered their escape. It wouldn't take them long to hit the trail, bent on running down their quarry. And the finest hunting dogs in the village would help them do it. Wryly Ike recalled his many kindnesses to Wokwesis, the long hours he had spent trying to train Bomazine's big dog. It was ironic that this same animal might now prove to be his downfall.

But of all these vengeful savages, none would be more tenacious and formidable than Bomazine. He would leave no stone unturned in his quest for Ike's scalp.

How long they lay there, waiting, they could only guess by the sun. It was directly overhead before Ike noticed that Joe was sound asleep. He himself had not closed his eyes. White-throated sparrows broke the silence with their plaintive call: "Old Sam Peabody, Peabody, Peabody." A big-antlered, ten-point buck came to drink from the brook and passed on, every movement a study in caution. A saucy red squirrel scolded from a nearby limb.

Ike was only dimly aware of these things. He could think of nothing else but Bomazine and the other Sokoki warriors. Where were they now? What were they doing? Were they hot on the trail, or were they cold? Near or far?

Hope began to stir within Ike. The sun was now dropping in the sky. The day was more than half over. A few more hours and they could travel once again, under the protective cloak of darkness. A second night of travel would greatly enhance their chances of escape.

Soon thereafter it clouded up and a light drizzle set in. This, too, was encouraging. Rain would tend to wash away their scent, handicap the Indians and their dogs.

Then, as Ike himself finally began to drowse, he heard a sound that made him come to life with a start, every nerve taut. Had he been dreaming? He fervently hoped that he had. Breathlessly he waited, as the minutes dragged by. No, he had not been dreaming. There it was again; faint and still far away, but unmistakable. To the unpracticed ear, it would have been the mournful howl of a wolf, but Ike was not unpracticed. He had carefully listened to the Indians' calls, marveling at their authenticity, yet becoming, through close study, aware of slight faults and variations which identified each imitator.

And he was not fooled by the call he had just heard—a call containing undertones of savage triumph. He would stake his life on it. That call was made by Bomazine! It was not hard to imagine what had happened. Somehow, somewhere, one of that large party of skilled trackers—or one of the dogs—had finally stumbled onto their trail, back where it led to the brook. Fanned out on either side, with the dogs casting back and forth in between, they were bearing down on the spot where he and Joe had emerged. There the dogs were certain to cross their scent. Would they pick it up, or wouldn't they?

Ike's jaw squared. Only one thing was certain. The showdown was here!

10

IKE HAD NOT been idle these past few hours, holed up there in the hollow log. Though his body had been confined, his nimble mind had ranged freely, studying their situation from every angle. At the first warning that their pursuers were close, therefore, he did not panic. He did not even waken Joe. He had decided that this would be the best course to follow, should the need arise—as long as Joe slept quietly.

"No telling what he might do," Ike reflected. "For all I know, he might blab right out when they're close by."

Tense, but determined, with his gun ready, he awaited the Indians. Through his screen of ferns, he commanded a good view toward the north, up the brook. He knew too well the vulnerability of their position to be overly optimistic, but he also knew that their only hope was to stay put there in the log. Alone, he might possibly have considered giving them a run for it. After all, he had outdistanced Bomazine, their swiftest runner, on more than one occasion.

But he was not alone. There was Joe to consider, and Joe was slower than cold molasses when it came to running. No, they could not make a break for it. Their pursuers would run them down in no time.

Here they at least stood this much of a chance: the rain might have washed out their trail—what little they had left after the trip down the brook. The Indians would be lucky to pick it up, and if they passed that one spot and went on down the brook, Ike and Joe were saved, at least for the moment. They would witness it and know where their pursuers were. Darkness would soon close in, and the Indians would undoubtedly halt for the night.

The brook at this point swung eastward. This was in Ike's and Joe's favor. It would give them another full night to travel southward—the direction in which they wanted to go. And the rain would obliterate their trail. By morning, they should have given the Sokokis the slip.

Yes, Ike decided, this would be the showdown, right here by the brook. He and Bomazine were matching wits for the last time, and the savage would be trailing his quarry with all the skill at his command. One telltale sign and the chase was over. Grimly Ike examined his priming, checked the flint. Satisfied that the gun was ready, he was about to resume his lonely vigil when Joe snorted in his sleep and rolled over on his back—and then began snoring!

Even this complication had been anticipated by Ike. He did not hesitate a moment. Clamping a hand over Joe's mouth, he shook him awake. "Don't make a sound," he hissed in Joe's ear. "The Indians are coming down the brook."

Joe's blue eyes bulged with fright, and his freckles stood out like brown paint against his white face; but he didn't let a peep out of him—even when Ike took his hand away.

It was well that he didn't. For at that moment, about a hundred yards up the brook, the bushes parted, and a painted warrior stepped into view. Pausing motionless as a statue, he studied the narrow valley before him through savage eyes that glowed like living coals. There was no mistaking that swarthy countenance. It was Bomazine.

Ike's breathing became labored, his heart pounded faster. Since Joe was so situated that he couldn't see up the brook, Ike warned him. "Here they come," he whispered softly. "If you value your scalp, don't even take a deep breath until I tell you to."

His attention fastened on Bomazine. The Indian was now raising his hand, motioning to those behind him. In a moment the whole party broke into the open, crouched low, moving along the brook at a fast trot. There were five of them; Bomazine, Mugg, Adiwando, Hegans and Wexar.

Ranging back and forth across the brook, up hill and down dale, four dogs investigated first this scent and then that, noses to the ground, picking up a false lead, following it a little way, then discarding it for another one.

Within the log, tension mounted as the tenacious pursuers bore swiftly down the brook. The Indians were now almost abreast of the spot where Ike and Joe had emerged. Had either one of them dislodged a stick or a stone on leaving the water? Had the rain washed away their scent? Hardly able to breathe, Ike gripped his gun and waited.

Bent low, keen eyes scanning the ground, Mugg loped past the key spot without a pause. Adiwando, Hegans and Wexar followed, without a hitch in stride. Only Bomazine

was left, and he was proceeding more slowly, more carefully. Now he was passing the very rock Ike and Joe had stepped out on—no, he was not passing! He had stopped! Ike's heart hammered so loudly he was sure Bomazine must hear it.

Joe stirred slightly behind him, and Ike placed a finger to his lips. He watched tensely as the big Indian youth stooped lower—and scooped up a drink of water! A moment later he straightened and trotted on down the brook after the others. Ike let out his breath slowly, with a prayer of thanks on his lips. They were now almost in the clear. Their chances of escape were growing brighter by the—

Then he saw Wokwesis—the sly one. All the other dogs had forged ahead, at the heels of their masters, but the rangy Wokwesis had been diverted by a false lead and was just now slicing down the hillside at full speed, intent on joining the others. His path took him directly past the hollow log!

Ike froze to the gun barrel. Behind him, Joe sucked in his breath. He too had seen the animal streak by. Ten feet past the log, Wokwesis skidded to a halt on the wet pine needles. Muzzle twitching, he turned about and tested the air. Snuffling, he took a tentative step forward, froze, then took another.

With mounting horror, Ike saw the dog's tail begin to wag. Wokwesis recognized the scent, was moving forward eagerly. In a moment he would see them. He would give voice to a triumphant bark. To Ike and Joe it was a matter of life or death. To Wokwesis it was but a game of hide-and-seek.

Ike's thoughts flashed back to those earlier days at Pigwacket; to Bomazine's sneaky trick of using Wokwesis to search out those who were hiding. Ike recalled the way he had coped with this situation; a sneaky little trick of his own. The thought was translated into action instantaneously. Ike's hand was in the food pouch almost before his mind told him what he must attempt to do. Making sure that Bomazine was still trotting away from them down the brook, Ike dropped the savory chunk of moose meat at the entrance of the log. Behind him he heard Joe gasp.

As Wokwesis lunged forward and gulped the meat down, Ike held the pouch to the dog's nose. "Bomazine!" he whispered hoarsely, motioning down the brook with his hand. "Go find Bomazine!"

Then time stood still. While wolfing down the meat, Wokwesis watched him guardedly. Would the dog remember their little game? Ike wondered. Would he obey instructions *after* receiving his reward? Or would he snuff out their lives in an outburst of barking?

Sweat greased Ike's palms as Wokwesis gulped the last of his prize. "Bomazine!" Ike repeated coaxingly. "Go find Bomazine!"

He could have sworn the dog winked at him. Then Wokwesis whirled abruptly and raced down the hillside, streaking past Bomazine a few moments later, just as the Indian was disappearing from view.

Still holding his breath, Ike waited. Joe stirred impatiently, and Ike held a finger to his lips. For a short time there was the faint rustling of leaves and snapping of dried twigs. Gradually the sounds diminished until they were lost in the depths of the darkening forest. Dusk was finally at hand. The only sound left was the incessant patter of rain; that and Joe's wheezy breathing. Ike felt a surge of elation as darkness crept through the trees. He sighed in relief.

On hearing this, Joe could stand it no longer. "What're

124

we waitin' for?" he grumbled. "The Injuns is gone, and it's almost dark. You plan on takin' root here?"

Cautiously Ike crawled from the log and stood up stiffly, massaging life back into his numbed limbs. "Don't go off at half cock now," he cautioned Joe. "We ain't out of the woods yet, you know."

Granted, they now stood a fair chance of eluding the Sokokis, especially with the increasing rain, but there were other hazards in store for them; hunger, fatigue, a hundred miles of unbroken wilderness—and the constant danger of stumbling into other Indians. They still had a long way to go.

The first flush of dawn found them several precious miles nearer Haverhill, but they were miles that had been dearly won. Both Ike and Joe were soaked to the skin, dead on their feet, and badly scratched from clawing their way through junipers and blowdowns and thorn-tree thickets. Traveling at night with no moon took its toll.

They were staggering from exhaustion when the sky began to lighten in the east. The rain had stopped, and the sky was beginning to clear. Overhead, birds were starting the day's search for food; flitting, darting, chirping. Startled at a nearby brook, a doe eyed them nervously, ears cocked forward. With a flick of her tail, she bounded gracefully into the bushes.

Joe stumbled and fell on the carpet of pine needles. Then he rolled over on his back and just lay there. "Can't —take—another—step," he gasped. "I'm all tuckered out."

" 'Bout time we got out of sight anyway," Ike said. "We'll lay up for this one day, just for good measure. But you'd best make the most of it. From then on, we'll keep going night and day until we get home."

Right close by, they found a good place to hide. A big pine, felled by lightning, had lodged snug to a large boulder. They crawled in under and bedded down on some boughs that had broken off. In no time at all they were both fast asleep.

It was still daylight when they came to, about mid-afternoon by the sun. Joe woke up with his stomach growling. "I got to have somethin' to eat," he complained. "All I've et is a few ground-nuts since we left Pigwacket. That's two nights and two days. I ain't takin' another step till I fill my belly—and don't tell me to take up another notch in my belt!"

Ike himself was thinking of food as Joe continued, "A rabbit would look mighty good, or a pa'tridge, or—"

He broke off suddenly, his eyes riveted to a spot over Ike's right shoulder. Slowly Ike turned, and his eyes picked out the pigeon, roosting on a pine limb not ten feet above them. Taking extra careful aim, Ike brought it down with a rock.

Joe began to drool as he eyed the fat-breasted bird. Immediately he scrambled around gathering tinder. Then he reached for the gun. "Let's have the flintlock, and I'll touch this tinder off. I'm goin' to roast that plump little pigeon right here and now!"

Ike grasped the gun firmly. "Can't build a fire," he said.

"Can't build a fire?" Joe's jaw dropped. "How we goin' to cook without a fire?"

"Ain't," Ike said. "A fire might bring the Indians down on us. We'll have to eat it raw."

So saying, he dismembered the bird and handed Joe a leg. Six months before, they never would have believed that they could eat this way; raw meat, still warm, no seasoning

126

of any kind. But six months before, they had not known what real hunger was. Now they not only ate the meat; they relished it, gaining strength and energy from the feast.

Aided by a full moon that night, they made the best distance yet of their headlong flight. Sunrise found them traveling in a pine plain that led slightly uphill. Here their pace slowed considerably.

"I'm a mite blowed," Joe panted. "When we gonna hang up a spell?"

"Ain't," Ike said emphatically. "I've already told you, from now on we go night and day till we get home."

They still had a lot of ground to cover; endless miles of tangled wilderness. Ike was not forgetting Bomazine for a single moment, either. His red nemesis was not to be written off so lightly. Even if the other braves gave up the chase, Ike felt sure that Bomazine would press on as long as he could put one foot in front of the other. Sooner or later, a hunter of his ability and persistence might very well track them down.

"We've got a good lead, and we've got to hold it," Ike thought. "The minute we slack off, he'll gain on us, if he's still on our trail."

Nor were the Sokokis the only enemies to be considered. There were other Indians lurking about. Ike and Joe discovered this abruptly on the sixth day of their flight.

Joe was really dragging by then. "I'm just plumb tuckered out," he announced, sagging to a log. "I got to have more food and rest."

Compassion welled up in Ike. Except for brief snatches of sleep, they had been running and walking continuously since that second day, when they holed up. They hadn't eaten enough to keep a cat alive; that raw pigeon and a raw turtle, a few roots and ground-nuts. Their clothes were in tatters, their feet raw and bleeding. Their moccasins had long since been discarded. Such footwear would stand up to this kind of punishment only if repaired at the end of each day's journey. There had been no time for that.

"Yessir, I'm just plumb tuckered out," Joe repeated. "You want to plough through that spruce swamp, then you can plough it alone." He jerked a thumb. "But if you want to be sensible and take that trail, then I might tag along."

Ike studied the path Joe indicated. This was a wider trail, skirting the swamp and crossing the deer path they had been following; a trail plainly made by human feet. But whose feet? Those of red men—or white? That was the critical question. They had been traveling so long Ike was in a daze. Fatigue had dulled his sense of distance and direction. Was it possible that they had reached the settlements? Could this inviting trail lead at last to food and shelter among friends?

The sun was setting. Darkness would soon be upon them. The trail ran in the right direction, and it offered good footing on a night that threatened to be moonless. Another glance at Joe's bloody feet prompted Ike to make his first foolhardy decision. "All right, let's go," he agreed.

They hadn't covered half a mile when they abruptly emerged from the woods into an open meadow. In the gathering dusk, they saw smoke rising from an encampment. Tears streaming down his grimy cheeks, delirious with joy, Joe broke into a run.

"Were back at the settlements, Ike," he crowed. "Let's give'em a holler so they'll know we're—"

He got no further. Ike leaped like a panther and covered Joe's mouth with one hand, while snatching him back under cover with the other. "If you holler," he hissed in Joe's ear, "it'll be the last time you do!"

"What's ailin' you anyway?" Joe whispered when they were safely shielded by the thick foliage. He massaged his neck ruefully. "You nigh lifted my head off."

"That's better'n an Indian lifting your scalp, ain't it?" Ike said softly.

"Them look like log cabins to me," Joe grumbled. "What makes you think it's Injuns?"

Ike pointed to the path they had just vacated. Where it led through some moist clay, several footprints still showed clearly in the fading light.

Joe sniffed. "So what? Don't settlers wear moccasins?" he demanded.

"You better take another look," Ike said.

Joe stiffened on closer inspection. In his haste, he had overlooked one detail Ike had spotted. On the frontier, even a child could tell the toe-in of an Indian from the wider step of a white man.

Without exception, these footsteps toed in.

That was the last time they followed a trail. Ike and Joe made tracks out of there just as fast as their tired legs would carry them. Soon Ike plunged them into a dense forest of hemlock and pine. Sunrise the next morning found them a good piece farther south, on the bank of a swollen stream. It also found Joe completely spent.

"Ain't no sense in goin' on," Joe gasped, sprawling on the brown carpet of pine needles. "My legs is washed right out from under me, and my lungs is about to bust. And if you ask me, I think we're just goin' around in circles anyhow. I been thinkin' for some time now you was lost."

Ike leaned heavily against a pine, studying the turbulent stream dully. His legs, too, were just about ready to buckle under him. His tortured lungs felt as if they might burst, and he himself wasn't so sure they weren't going around in circles. But he would not admit, even to himself, that Joe might be right. If he should lie down beside Joe, they were licked then and there.

They had to keep going somehow, and they still had to watch their step, too. At any time, they could stumble upon the enemy, or roving Indians might stumble upon them. There was also the possibility that Bomazine might run them down.

"One thing's for sure," Ike mused aloud. "A man never gets where he's going by standing still." The voice was his, but the words were those of his pa, spoken long ago. It was when they temporarily got lost once in some thick country, portaging between lakes. Abandoning their canoe by a tiny brook, Ike was ready to dash pell-mell through the woods in search of the lake when his pa restrained him.

"Now let's start little, boy," he suggested. "Don't ever be so all-fired impatient to get where you're going that you start too big. Doesn't matter whether it's learning your ciphers or finding a lake, you've got to start little and work up to the big things."

Then he shouldered the canoe and proceeded to follow the tiny brook down a ways. This soon led into a larger brook, and a short time later this emptied into a stream. Before long the stream led into a sizeable river, and within the hour the river tumbled into the lake they were heading for.

"You not only have to start little, boy, you have to keep on moving even when it doesn't seem you're making any progress. One thing's for sure; a man never gets where he's going by standing still."

It was a lesson Ike recalled many times thereafter, but it had slipped from his mind during these trying months. He now grasped at it desperately, as a dying man grasps at a straw.

"Just leave me be," Joe protested weakly. He lay with his cheek pressed to the earth, his eyes closed. "I ain't goin' to budge from this spot—not ever."

His cheeks were flushed, and Ike sensed that Joe had a fever. Exposure, hunger, fatigue; these had taken their toll on poor Joe. But if he didn't struggle back to his feet somehow, he might never rise again. And Joe had to do it himself. "I'm just too plumb wore out to tote him a step," Ike reflected.

Picking up a stout alder whip, he turned on Joe. "Oh yes, you are," he said grimly. "And you're going to budge right now!"

Biting his lip, he put the whip to Joe without mercy, lashing him to his feet. The Indians back at Pigwacket had done this to both of them sometimes, when he and Joe were fatigued or rebellious, but Ike had never dreamed he would ever have to use such desperate measures.

"You're a bloody heathen!" Joe screamed at him. "You're worse'n the Injuns ever thought of bein'!"

"Keep on bellowing and you'll be right back with 'em," Ike said. "I'll bet they can hear you clear back to Pigwacket."

"Th-that suits me just fine," Joe sobbed. "They couldn't be near as bad as you!"

Ike ignored his rantings after that. He just drove Joe on ahead of him, following the stream. That was their only hope. If they kept moving downstream, they were bound to reach the settlements by and by.

All that seventh day and through the night they staggered on, but Ike could see that Joe was fading fast. His clothes were in shreds, his body was lacerated, his feet were raw and swollen.

On the eighth morning, Joe collapsed; pitched forward into the leaves. And there was nothing Ike could do to rouse him. Kneeling, he put his hand to Joe's forehead. He was burning up with fever.

"Guess he's gone about as far as he's going under his own power," Ike thought. "Wonder if I can tote him."

He couldn't. He was so far gone himself, he couldn't even hoist Joe's inert form onto his back, let alone carry him. In desperation, he dug roots and fed them to his delirious companion, hoping desperately that they might perk him up. He slaked Joe's thirst with ice-cold water from the nearby stream, but it was no use. Joe revived just long enough to crawl onto a soft bed of moss beside the stream, where he curled up like a hibernating cub bear.

"Say—say good-by to Ma and Pa for me," he moaned. "Tell them I tried hard to git back home, but I—I just couldn't make it." In a matter of minutes he was unconscious.

As he stood there looking down on Joe, Ike resisted the impulse to lie right down beside him. But if he went to sleep now, he knew he wouldn't come to for twenty-four hours, and it was imperative that somehow he keep on going. Joe had to have help. He was in desperate need of food and shelter. He needed poultices and herbs and proper care. If he didn't get them—and soon—he would die.

"A man never gets where he's going by standing still," Ike reminded himself, and he staggered on downstream.

The small stream soon led to a larger one. This, in turn, emptied into a river. Ike's hopes rose, his lagging steps quickened. It seemed to him this must be the Saco River. If it was, he might soon strike the home of some hardy pioneer.

It was the Saco. Before noon, Ike emerged from the forest into a small, sunlit clearing beside the swift-flowing river. Within the clearing lay a newly raised log cabin.

Ike sank to his knees when he saw it and gave solemn thanks for deliverance. Then he searched the cabin and surroundings for the inhabitants. There was no one there.

"Might be hunting or trapping," Ike thought. "Or maybe some man just raised it, and now he's gone to fetch his woman."

He didn't waste much time thinking about it. Joe was lying alone out in the open, burning up with fever, exposed to wind, rain and wild animals. Here, at least, was a snug, dry shelter for him until help could be reached. Discovery of the dwelling gave Ike new strength. He retraced his steps in half the time it had taken him before. By early afternoon he reached his companion.

Joe lay where he had left him, tossing and turning fitfully. His forehead was even hotter to Ike's touch. "We've reached the settlements, Joe," he said gently, briskly massaging Joe's hands and feet. "It's not very far. You think you can make it?"

He had to repeat the news several times before he penetrated Joe's delirium. Briefly Joe's rolling eyes focused on Ike as understanding sank in. There was a flare of hope, a summoning of his remaining strength. He got to his feet, with Ike's help, but his legs were too weak to support him for any distance. Ike led him by the hand at first, then supported him with an arm about his waist. In this manner

133

they struggled on until Joe slipped from Ike's grasp, sagging to his knees. He had passed out again.

Somehow Ike crouched down under and got Joe across his back, one arm through his legs, the other hand gripping Joe's arm. From some deep reservoir he summoned enough strength to move on, carrying his limp burden like a sack of ground Indian corn.

Ike lost all track of time as he staggered on. It became strictly a matter of endurance. His heart hammered noisily under the strain, his breath came in hoarse gasps. Every inch was a challenge, each step a hard-won victory. Sometime in the late afternoon he reached the cabin beside the Saco River.

"I—I've got to get some rest," he muttered aloud, as he deposited Joe inside the building. "Got to get some sleep before I keel over."

Yet he realized, after searching the premises again, that such a course was impossible. There was no food, no medicine. Joe's fever was rising steadily and he was unconscious most of the time. A fever like that would burn him out in a few more hours, unless it was checked.

Ike faced the painful fact: sleep would just have to wait. They couldn't be too far from help. One final dash, just a little while longer—

Once again Ike shouldered Joe and pushed on. Daylight was fading when he first heard the distant roar of a falls. As he drew closer the roar intensified, reverberating through the forest. And then he emerged abruptly from the woods.

Before him rose the gray walls of a massive stone fort, bristling with palisades and flankers. Above it flew the British flag, streaming proudly in the breeze.

Ike's heart sang with joy. This must be Saco Fort, built

in 1693 by Captain Convers and his rangers. He had heard tell of it many times.

So it proved to be. A tall ranger, garbed in the traditional hunting shirt of forest green, hailed Ike a moment later, then rushed forward to lend a hand when he saw the shape Ike was in.

"Where in thunderation did you come from?" he said, easing Joe to the ground.

"P—Pigwacket," was all Ike could manage. Then he collapsed beside Joe.

Everything was a blur in Ike's mind for a while after that. Alternately awake and asleep, he was dimly aware that Joe was being ministered to by the soldiers. He was fed and given a comfortable bed himself—a bed he refused to remain in, except for a few brief hours. That very night he decided to push on. He could not rest easy until he reached Haverhill. Joe's parents should know about Joe. They would want to come up here and nurse him back to health. It would be a long time before Joe could travel.

And Ike wanted to reach home. He was not forgetting what had kept him going all these months. He was not forgetting his backlog. Nothing could stop him for long until he walked back into Haverhill, a free man.

Not even the soldiers could dissuade him. He was bound and determined to go on that night. He pocketed the johnnycake and cheese the soldiers gave him and took a final, lingering look at Joe's flushed face.

"Please watch out for him, Lord," he said solemnly. Then he took up a notch in his belt. He noticed that he had reached the last hole.

He would soon be home—sleeping in a comfortable, dry bed, eating bean porridge and hominy and tart strawberry pie. Best of all, he would soon see his loved ones.

These thoughts sustained Ike as he tottered on through the nights and days that followed. Sometimes he stumbled and fell, but each time he drew himself up by a sapling or rock. The way became easier now, as he traveled between settlements. Help and encouragement met him at every turn.

Then came that long-awaited final morning as he entered country he recognized. He ran into a cedar swamp that was as familiar to him as the back of his hand. If he followed that around he would come into Haverhill, quite close to his house.

He had been traveling hard nearly all night and was fading fast when daylight came. Abruptly the swamp ended. He entered a clearing, found a cowpath. *The* cowpath. There was the garrison house, bathed in sunlight. A hard lump formed in his throat as he gazed at it. It was the prettiest sight he had ever seen.

There was the stump-dotted north lot, too. There was the very spot where he and Joe had been jumped by the Indians, six months before. Six months? More like six years, it seemed to him now.

And there, not ten rods off, was a man notching a big pine. There was no mistaking that powerful, distinctive swing. Only one man could handle an ax like that. It was his pa!

They spotted each other simultaneously, and his pa moved with blinding speed. No settler was ever far from his gun. Before Ike could so much as raise a hand in greeting, a flintlock was leveled in his direction.

"Don't take another step, redskin," his pa called out. "If you do, so help me I'll blow your head off. I've got a mighty big score to settle with you heathens!"

Ike looked down at his torn clothes. He was dressed

in the buckskin shirt and leggings of an Indian, tattered and torn though they were. His black hair glistened with bear grease, which the Indians used as protection against the rain. Wind, sun and wigwam smoke had stained him as dark as any Sokoki warrior. Surely he must look for all the world like an Indian. No wonder his pa didn't know him.

"It's me—Isaac," Ike shouted.

Still holding the gun on him, his pa shook his head. "You ain't my Isaac. He was two inches shorter, and twenty pounds heavier. You're a redskin, if I've ever seen one!"

Ike reached up and ripped his shirt open down the whole front, exposing the white skin underneath. "It's me all right, Pa. Joe and me, we finally escaped from Pigwacket, and Joe's awful sick. I left him with the rangers at Saco Fort. His folks will want to go to him right away."

His pa inched closer, peering, then dropped his gun and rushed forward to embrace Ike. For several moments neither of them spoke.

"It's been a long time, boy," his pa finally said. There was a catch in his voice.

Ike swallowed hard. He was bursting with happiness. "It sure has, Pa," he agreed.

His pa held him out at arm's length. "Pigwacket?" He was astounded. "That's a heap of wilderness to travel through. How in the world did you ever make it?"

"It was easy," Ike said. "We just kept on going, even when it didn't seem we were making any progress."

He grinned. "Of course we did have to take up a notch in our belts now and then."

AUTHOR'S NOTE

THE STORY of Isaac Bradley and Joseph Whittaker is based on fact.* They were "captivated" by the Indians at Haverhill, Massachusetts, in the fall of 1695. They escaped in the spring of the following year, making their way back home against incredible odds.

Isaac's capture was but the beginning of constant harassment by the Indians. His mother, Hannah, was twice made captive by them. When they attempted to take her during a third raid, she resolved to fight to the death rather than endure captivity again. Fighting side by side with her husband, she shot one of the lead Indians herself, thus putting the others to flight. In all, thirteen members of Isaac's family were killed in Indian raids.

In spite of this, Ike had a dream of peace with the Indians that was not to be realized for a lifetime. Haverhill and the other frontier settlements were under recurring attack until the British finally and decisively defeated the French on the Plains of Abraham at Quebec on September 13, 1759.

Ike, however, was destined to serve his people as an Indian scout. Drawing on the knowledge gained during his captivity, he led the famous Indian fighters, Colonel Hilton and Captain Chesley, on their scouting expeditions into the region of the Ossipee and Winnipesaukee lakes during the early 1700's.

* Chase, George Wingate. *History of Haverhill, Massachusetts from Its First Settlement in 1640 to the year 1860.* Haverhill, 1861.